PENGUIN BOOKS

MEMORIES II

Sir Julian Huxley w[...]
ley and grandson [...]
1887, he was a sch[...]
Oxford, where after [...]
and a year of resear[...]
1910. After four year[...] [...]ment
at the newly founded [...]itute, Houston, Texas, and
a period on G.H.Q. staff in Italy, he was a Fellow of New
College, Oxford, from 1919 to 1925, and helped to organize the university expedition to Spitsbergen in 1921.
He then became Professor of Zoology at King's College,
London, Fullerian Professor of Physiology in the Royal
Institution, for seven years Secretary of the Zoological
Society of London, and Director-General of UNESCO
from 1946 to 1948.

Julian Huxley became known to a wide public as a
member of the *Brains Trust* on radio, and often appeared
on television, besides writing and lecturing in many places.
He wrote some forty books, including not only scientific
works, but books on travel, such as *Africa View* and
From an Antique Land, on religion, such as *Religion
without Revelation*, on science and politics, such as *Soviet
Genetics and World Science*, on popular science, such as
Evolution in Action, on natural history, such as *Bird
Watching and Bird Behaviour*, on regional planning, such
as *TVA, an Adventure in Planning*, and a volume of
poems, *The Captive Shrew*. Among his later publications
were *Biological Aspects of Cancer* (1957), *New Bottles for
New Wine* (1957), *Charles Darwin and his World* (with
Dr H. B. Kettlewell; 1965), and *Essays of a Humanist*
(1964).

Sir Julian died in February 1975.

MEMORIES II

JULIAN HUXLEY

PENGUIN BOOKS

Penguin Books Ltd, Harmondsworth, Middlesex, England
Penguin Books, 625 Madison Avenue, New York, New York 10022, U.S.A.
Penguin Books Australia Ltd, Ringwood, Victoria, Australia
Penguin Books Canada Ltd, 2801 John Street, Markham, Ontario, Canada L3R 1B4
Penguin Books (N.Z.) Ltd, 182–190 Wairau Road, Auckland 10, New Zealand

—

First published by George Allen & Unwin Ltd, 1973
Published in Penguin Books 1978

—

—

Made and printed in Great Britain
by Richard Clay (The Chaucer Press) Ltd,
Bungay, Suffolk
Set in Linotype Times

Contents

Preface

IN the Preface to the first volume of these *Memories*, I spoke of being 'possessed by a demon, driving me into all sorts of activity', and added that this diversity of interests prepared me for my work at UNESCO.

This volume begins by dealing with that work. I was not self-driven into the post of Director-General, but pushed into it by circumstances, quite unexpectedly.

At UNESCO, I was almost overwhelmed by the complexity and novelty of what I had to cope with, including many travels. It was for me a time of intense activity, a time which called for flexibility of mind and initiative. It was also a time of great expectations and enthusiasm for new projects, in which my Executive Board (in most cases) and my staff were of tremendous help.

As this second volume was progressing, I realized that it had become almost a personal Baedeker. I have always loved travelling, and still do. New aspects of the world's amazing diversity have never failed to give me a sense of profound gratitude and a desire to widen my knowledge of it, to absorb as much as I could of its bounty. My memories of so many journeys live with me, and indeed are part of me. I could not therefore dismiss them from this account of my life. Sometimes because I had to, as D.G. of UNESCO, or when asked to report on African affairs, sometimes to lecture or attend conferences, or in Britain on friendly visits and as a member of the National Parks Commission, I travelled always with pleasure.

But this is not just a travel book, for I have also journeyed in thought through an equal variety of fields, from scientific research to sociology, from population to planning, from human and animal behaviour to ecological pollution, from conservation to the promotion of international co-operation.

Looking back, at the age of 84, I am astonished – not, like Clive, by my moderation, but by my immoderation – in undertaking so many diverse projects, so many journeys, so many activities. A Swiss mathematician, Professor Gagnebin, once wrote: 'La seule morale est de vivre avec ferveur.' I have tried to do so, not as a self-imposed discipline, but because that is how I am made.

One of my chief characteristics has been the ability, when fit, to throw myself wholeheartedly into a multiplicity of activities; striving also after transcendent experience (that ultimate freedom of the human spirit), as well as enjoying good company, books and humour.

I am lucky in keeping my health, and in my contact with a variety of people, not only other biologists, but planners and artists, critics and atheists, Jesuits and jokers; meanwhile keeping strong ties with my relatives, especially (until he died) Aldous, my sons and their families, including our first great-grandchild, son of Anthony's eldest daughter, and to my pleasure given the name Julian: and above all my great-hearted wife, whom I thank for her invaluable help and advice in the writing of both these volumes of my *Memories*.

CHAPTER 1

Early Days at Unesco

In November 1944, I attended a meeting of the old League of Nations' Institute of Intellectual Co-operation, of which Sir Alfred Zimmern was Secretary. This followed another meeting when representatives of forty-four nations took up the challenge from Senator Fulbright, following the creation of the United Nations, to discuss the constitution of a specialized UN Agency concerned with Education and Culture – like the original Institute, but on a much larger scale. This had been recommended by the Conference of Allied Ministers of Education, meeting in London in 1942.

I was not a member of the British Delegation to the Institute's meeting in 1944, but found myself more and more involved in its proceedings. R. A. Butler was then Minister of Education and received a small group, led by Joseph Needham and myself, to plead that Science, too, should be included in the new Agency. This was approved, and so UNECO became UNESCO (the United Nations Educational, Scientific and Cultural Organization), and came into being – on paper.[1]

A Preparatory Commission was accordingly assembled in London at the turn of the year, with Sir Alfred Zimmern as Secretary, to draw up the Charter and outline the scope of the new Organization. Léon Blum represented France, Archibald Macleish spoke for the United States, Gilbert Murray for Britain, Jean Piaget represented the International Bureau of Education, Jaime Torres-Bodet represented Mexico, Concha Romero James the Pan-American Union – as well as others I have forgotten. I was so deeply interested in the idea of this new international agency that I attended most of its public sessions.

1. For the full story of UNESCO's foundation, and of its activities up to 1954, see *Unesco, Purpose, Progress and Prospects*, by Walter Laves and Charles Thomson, both intimately concerned with UNESCO's affairs and its activities (Indiana University Press, Bloomington, 1957). Also the pamphlet *Looking at Unesco* (UNESCO, 1971), which gives an account of its work after 1954.

After my return from Russia in the spring of 1945, I went to a meeting of the Commission at Lancaster House and was descending the steps with Sir John Maud, who, as permanent Head of the Education Office, had to deal with UNESCO affairs. He greeted me with a rather broad joke in Latin (he is one of the few men capable of such esoteric humour!), and then casually asked whether I would like to become full-time Secretary of the Commission, with the probability, or at least the possibility, of becoming Director-General of the Organization once it had been formally set up. For Zimmern had just undergone a severe operation, and would not be fit for several weeks or even months, and Mrs Brunauer, his American assistant, was left in sole charge. The British Government wanted another Englishman to take Zimmern's place, and everyone else who might have been eligible was in a full-time job.

I was flabbergasted. Apart from the generalities I had heard at the public meetings, I knew nothing about the organizational aspects of such a body, and felt I would be at sea in such a post, but promised to think it over.

John Maud did not let the grass grow under his feet: he got Ellen Wilkinson, who had just become his Minister (or Ministress?), to invite me and himself to dinner at the House of Commons that same evening. After a long discussion, interrupted now and again by an elderly waitress who persisted in calling the Minister 'dearie', I was finally persuaded to accept. We adjourned to Ellen Wilkinson's house, to which the majority of the Preparatory Commission had been summoned by phone, and I was introduced to them in turn.

Though I felt like one of those early Christians who were kidnapped and compelled to become bishops, I announced my agreement, was welcomed by the Commission's members – and went home to report to Juliette. She was shocked – worried about my ability to stand up to the strain (not to mention hers, to cope with the social duties she would obviously have to undertake). We both felt that the momentous decision had been virtually forced upon us; but I had given my consent and it was up to me to carry on.

The offices of the Commission were in Carlos Place. The first time I entered its portals in my new capacity, I was very nervous, as if I were both a Headmaster and a boy entering school for the first time. However, Mrs Brunauer knew the ropes and I soon found my feet in this strange job.

Once I had settled down, I felt that I should try to clarify my own ideas about the role of the Organization. So I took a fortnight off and went once more to stay with Ronald Lockley (with whom I had made the film *The Private Life of the Gannet* on an island off the Pembrokeshire coast, see Vol. I, Chap. XV); he was now occupying a farm on Dinas Head, also in Pembrokeshire. There, in the intervals of walks and talks, exploring the promontory and basking with my host in sheltered nooks overlooking the bird-haunted sandstone cliffs, I wrote a sixty-page pamphlet entitled *Unesco, Its Purpose and Its Philosophy*.

In this, besides stressing its obvious duties in promoting cultural exchanges and giving help to the educational systems of backward (or, as we say now, 'underdeveloped') countries, I maintained that it could not rely on religious doctrine – there was strife between different religions and sects – or on any of the conflicting academic systems of philosophy. UNESCO, I wrote, must work in the context of what I called *Scientific Humanism*, based on the established facts of biological adaptation and advance, brought about by means of Darwinian selection, continued into the human sphere by psycho-social pressures, and leading to some kind of advance, even progress, with increased human control and conservation of the environment and of natural forces. So far as UNESCO was concerned, the process should be guided by humanistic ideals of mutual aid, the spread of scientific ideas, and by cultural interchange.

This was presented to the Commission and was ordered to be printed as an official document. But one Saturday, when I was about to go to Oxford to look for possible staff, I heard that Sir Ernest Barker, the historian, who had been appointed to the Commission in view of his work on the Committee of the League's Institute of Intellectual Co-operation, was to be present at the meeting which was to discuss UNESCO's role in philosophy. He and I had previously quarrelled over my attitude to established religion when I was Professor of Zoology at King's College, London, of which he was Principal, and I

11

scented trouble, rightly suspecting that he would attack my pamphlet.

As an ardent churchman, he argued forcibly against UNESCO's adopting what he called an atheist attitude disguised as humanism, and got the members to agree to state, when circulating my document, that it expressed merely my personal views, not those of the official Commission.[1]

Looking back, I think he was right. Though UNESCO has in fact pursued humanistic aims, it would have been unfortunate to lay down any doctrine as basis for its work. Further, a purely humanist tone would have antagonized the world's major religious groups, including the Russians with their pseudo-religion of dialectical materialism.

The British Government then made what still seems to me a stupid and ham-fisted decision. As soon as Zimmern had recovered from his operation, they sent him back to the Commission as my 'Adviser' ... It was an impossible situation. I was abominably busy and had little time for consultation with him; furthermore, his approach was often opposed to my own – over-stressing the value of classical and traditional cultural studies as against my own views, especially as regards aid for scientific research and the dissemination of its results.

Lady Zimmern felt bitterly that her husband had been unfairly ousted from his post and prospects. In revenge, she accused me of being a communist, presumably on the grounds of the liberal and anti-dogmatic ideas I had expressed in my writings and public lectures. This made my relationship with Zimmern even more difficult, but we just managed to rub along together in the office.

Meanwhile, there was the difficult business of recruiting staff: this I had to begin, whether or not I was eventually appointed Director-General. Some I appointed directly, like Joseph Needham, the eminent Cambridge biochemist, who was also interested in Chinese culture and in the history of science; and John Bowers, who was recommended to me by a war-time colleague for his first-hand experience of an under-

1. John Maud, however, wrote to me saying, 'I find it to my untutored taste very good.'

developed country's basic needs – he had served as a District Officer in the Anglo-Egyptian Sudan.

One virtually appointed himself – with excellent results. I had to find someone to take charge of the Libraries section. Desmond Bernal had recommended an English woman librarian, but I was not sure of her competence, and asked Edward Carter, my Hampstead neighbour (and Librarian of the Royal Institute of British Architects), for advice. His response was simple – 'Why not me?' I had foolishly thought that the UNESCO job would have been a come-down from the position he held – but of course it was not: both the salary and the opportunities for interesting work were greater at UNESCO, and Edward was excellent, especially in getting UNESCO to set up good modern libraries in underdeveloped countries. Later, I was to see the one in southern Nigeria, and be delighted to find that it was not only housed in a fine building (as was to be expected from a man interested in architecture), but also well-stocked, and with many readers in its spacious rooms.

Others were recommended to me by friends. Thus Sir Kenneth Clark recommended the young Australian, Peter Bellew, as head of the Fine Arts section – he had heard of the courageous way in which Bellow had backed modern art in face of Australian philistinism.

Still others were wished on me by their Governments. While the Preparatory Commission was still in London, Julien Cain, the charming and learned head of the Bibliothèque Nationale in Paris, came over with a young man called Jean Thomas, who was officially recommended by the French authorities as my Deputy. It was understood that, in return for waiving the right to nominate the top man, France should be the home of the Organization and one of its two deputy Director-Generals should be a Frenchman. Thomas and I got on excellently throughout my term of office, while Julien Cain became an influential member of the Executive Board. He and his gifted wife (she had once acted as Paul Valéry's secretary) became close friends of Juliette and myself.

Professor Pierre Auger was also recommended by the

French, for a post in the Science Department. He was an excellent physicist, balancing the biologically competent Needham, and eventually succeeded him as Head of the Department.

Alva, sociologist wife of the celebrated Swedish economist Gunnar Myrdal, took charge of the Social Sciences Division, and I myself asked John Grierson, the pioneer of documentary films, to look after the Cinema section of the Arts Department. Flora McGlade (always known as Mac) was already in my office, having been Zimmern's assistant on the Preparatory Commission. She stayed as one of my secretaries all through my time at UNESCO. I also kept Friedl Rothschild, who had worked for me at PEP, but soon had to add others to my personal staff: Mrs Paulette Matthews, as a second secretary to deal with the flood of official correspondence; and Claude Berkeley, cousin of the composer of the same name, as my personal assistant, constantly called on to deal with complaints, and to prepare for the visits and travels I had to undertake.

Alfred Métraux took charge of most of the work in Anthropology and Sociology, while Guy, his younger brother, after working in various sections, later became the very efficient Secretary of the Commission dealing with UNESCO's *History of Mankind* (p. 64).

Emilio Arenales, nominated by Guatemala, was very useful in dealing with Latin American countries in general; with Manolo Jimenez for Mexican affairs and for dealing with internal procedure.

Then there was Dr Irina Zhukova, Russian by birth, who worked in the Physiological section of the Science Department, with special responsibility for liaison with WHO, the World Health Organization. The Russians had declared her *persona non grata*, but as they were not yet members of UNESCO, I disregarded their protest. She did excellent work.

So I could run on. I secured another Frenchman, Michel Montagnier, to deal with arrangements for Conferences, which he did with great efficiency; a Swiss, André de Blonay, to cope with the affairs of national delegates, especially during General Conferences; while a Chinese Professor, Dr Kuo, was made Head of the Division of Education.

Later in the year an American, Walter Laves, was nominated by the USA to deal with questions of internal administration. These, unfortunately, often caused trouble – there were jealousies between different Divisions – and once, I remember, I had to intervene between one Division and the staff responsible for preparing UNESCO's budget. The Division Head thought that the Budget men should come to his office, while they expected that everyone, even Deputy Director-Generals, should come to them at their request. I cut the Gordian knot by inviting both parties to meet in my own office.

But much more taxing than such squabbles was establishing the programme for the coming year. This, together with an estimate of its cost, had to be laid before the next General Conference, which could in theory (and sometimes did in practice) cut out some item, refuse to grant necessary finance, or even press for new items to be included.

This task was made more difficult by an anomaly in the relations between the Executive Board and the Director-General. Under the original constitution, the Board was given a hand in framing the programme, in consultation, of course, with the D.G. This led to so many disagreements, and such waste of time, that in 1948 the arrangement was altered: from then on, the D.G. had sole responsibility for preparing the programme, while the Board could only offer comment or criticism.

This is merely one example of the way in which everything had to be improvised, and arrangements made to patch up the differences of interest between various Divisions, the D.G., and the Board. These were perhaps inevitable in a new organization – indeed a new *kind* of organization, for its scope was very much wider than that of the original League's Institute of Intellectual Co-operation. At any rate, they gave me plenty of headaches during my term of office (and virtually forced some of my successors into resignation).

Headaches, yes, but also interest, and indeed excitement – the excitement of being in charge of a vast new international experiment, a stimulus which kept me going through the gruelling two and a half years of my tenure of office.

Once I started work at UNESCO's headquarters in Paris, I

had to deal with the Executive Board over all major problems. In 1947, the Board numbered only eighteen members. These were chosen from the delegates of member-states, always one from the UK, France and the USA (and a Russian when the USSR joined UNESCO early in 1949), one from the country where the next conference was to be held, and representatives of other countries to make up its number.

In 1947, it included some very distinguished men – John Maud (later Lord Redcliffe-Maud) from Britain, Archie Macleish from the USA, Pierre Auger (soon to become head of UNESCO's Natural Sciences Division), Dr Photiades, an entertaining man from Greece, Professor Carneiro (later to become Chairman of the UNESCO Commission on the Cultural and Scientific History of Mankind, p. 64), Sir Sarvepelli Radhakrishnan, statesman and philosopher from India, Ronald Walker from Australia, etc. Today, I gather, there are thirty-four members of the Board – how they transact business I cannot imagine.

The original principle was that Board members should be men distinguished in education, the sciences and the arts, from different regions, but voting as individuals, not as representing their own country. It was a fine idea, but it did not work out. Board members *were* almost always distinguished, but they usually voted in favour of measures approved by their Governments. So eventually they became representatives of their own countries, as well as specialists in some field of UNESCO's work.

Another difficulty arose over UNESCO's budget. The Board was originally empowered to propose a budget sufficient to carry out the programme submitted to each General Conference. This led to many squabbles, members of the Board too often making proposals that would benefit mainly their own country or region. They had the duty of consulting the D.G., but frequently the consultation was merely formal.

This system was quite illogical, and during my term of office the Director-General became responsible both for the details of the programme, and for presenting the budget estimate. Of course, he had to consult the Board and take into account any comments or objections they might make, but the unworkable system of divided authority was scrapped.

The monthly Board meetings might extend over two or three days, and were often both contentious and tedious. Sometimes I became bored, fed up with all the squabbles, and took refuge in doodling. Once I caught one of the Secretariat removing all my papers. Why? Because he thought my doodles entertaining and was making a private collection of them.

In 1948, we lodged near the Bois de Boulogne and I could take a walk there before breakfast, partly for the exercise (sitting at a desk all day was not only cramping but bad for my health), and partly to make a census of the various species of birds in the Bois. At meetings of the Board, I sometimes diverted myself by tabulating my results and recording the sex-ratio of the various duck species on the lake. This too was considered peculiar, and again some of my records of these extra-curricular activities were abstracted.

These walks were of value to me as an ornithologist, for in the Bois I first identified the European tree-creeper – not by sight, since in the field it is indistinguishable from the British species, but by its song. For here, as always when two closely related and visually similar species overlap, it is their voices that are distinctive. Think of our chiff-chaff, willow-warbler and wood-warbler, all little greenish birds, first distinguished (by their calls and songs) by Gilbert White in the eighteenth century.

It had been laid down by the London Conference that UNESCO could seek help in technical matters from non-governmental International Agencies concerned with subjects within UNESCO's purview; and, if necessary, aid in the creation of new ones. It was on Needham's advice that ICSU, the International Council of Scientific Unions, became the first of such bodies to be attached to UNESCO. We provided it with rooms in UNESCO's headquarters in Paris, and salaries for its staff: previously, the Cambridge professor who was its secretary – and sole executive – had to dictate all its correspondence in his College rooms!

17

The ICSU gave UNESCO much valuable advice – on the peaceful uses of atomic energy, on regional centres for scientific co-operation and exchange of knowledge, on the calling of international scientific congresses, and on liaison with other International Agencies concerned with science, such as FAO for agricultural science and applied ecology, and WHO for medicine, physiology and social well-being.

Soon after, I had a surprise visit from a wealthy American art-lover, a trustee of the Buffalo Art Gallery, and agreed to recommend that an International Commission on Museums should be attached to the cultural section of UNESCO. Thanks to its advice (and that of other international bodies concerned with the arts), UNESCO has done valuable work since then, both in giving financial aid to galleries and museums, and also in publishing and distributing excellent reproductions of little-known paintings, sculptures and architectural achievements from various countries, especially reproductions which could be used in schools.

In the hot summer of 1947, we also set up an International Theatre Institute (for drama, opera, films and ballet) at the insistence of Jack Priestley, an American called Kuntz and John Grierson. The committee responsible for this comprised many well-known names in dramatic circles, such as the French producer and actor Jean-Louis Barrault, Sir Tyrone Guthrie from England, and Lillian Hellman from the USA. She was a strong liberal, but official US bodies chose to consider her a communist, and protested. However, we stood firm and succeeded in getting the Institute approved as another of UNESCO's international non-governmental bodies.

Trouble arose when it was decided to hold the first meeting of the new Institute in Prague. Priestley was to preside, but could not bring himself to go to a country which had 'murdered' his friend Jan Masaryk. The US authorities also disliked the idea of UNESCO's going to a Russian satellite.

However, Grierson and I overcame Priestley's objections, and Archie Macleish, who by good luck happened to be in Paris, persuaded the Americans not to be frightened by the communist bogey: they sent an excellent delegation.

Even when we reached Prague, our troubles were not over.

Now it was the Czech authorities who disliked the presence of anti-communists, notably the Americans, and 'neglected' to announce that the meeting would be open to the public. Perhaps they were worried about possible pro-West demonstrations. So we found ourselves at a long table facing a vast but almost empty hall! However, we got through some very useful business and established the principle that UNESCO as an organization took no notice of ideological and political differences – unlike some member states, such as Poland (see Chap. 3, p. 56).

To stress the universal character of UNESCO, it was felt that we should have a coloured man on the staff; after some searching, we enlisted a Haitian creole schoolmaster. I fear that he proved not to be of much use – except in inducing UNESCO to send a mission to his native island to help over its educational system.[1] The high rate of illiteracy that we found there, and the pitiful condition, both of the villagers and the city slum-dwellers, led us to modify our campaign for literacy and to re-christen it Fundamental Education. In this project, we not only gave help in class-room education, but financed schemes to teach people better agricultural methods, to fight against erosion, and to inculcate cleanliness and sanitation.

The Commission moved to Paris in late November, 1946, and we and other delegates had our offices in the former Hotel Majestic, where the Peace Conference was held after the First World War. During the Second World War, it was commandeered by the Germans, and my official room had the 'distinction' of having been the office of the notorious Nazi Commandant of Paris. Thus my occupancy visibly symbolized the transition from war and racialism to peace and cultural co-operation.

The full Executive Board was now in daily session, discussing not only UNESCO's terms of reference and its immediate activities, but also whom to nominate as Director-General.

Archibald Macleish, the distinguished American writer and

1. Needless to say, with the newly won independence of so many colonies, coloured staff are now a numerous and valuable element in UNESCO.

poet, who was also Librarian of Congress, had written a brilliant preamble to UNESCO's Constitution, in which he had stressed UNESCO's role in promoting Peace – 'Peace through Education, Peace through Science, Peace through Culture, Peace everywhere in the hearts of men' – a starry-eyed hope rather than a guide to practical action.[1]

The USA wanted him as D.G., but he declined, saying he could not spare the time from his real work in literature. The British delegate, Sir John Maud, put forward my name, and there were one or two other candidates.

While these discussions were dragging on, I was told by one of my staff that Sir Alfred Zimmern (perhaps inspired by his wife) was going round the Embassies of countries represented on the Board, urging that I should not be appointed because of my 'communist' (!) leanings. I am not often angry, but this made me so furious that I demanded a hearing from the Board and presented an ultimatum – either Sir Alfred must go, or I would withdraw my candidature and leave Paris. The Board saw my point and dispatched Zimmern on some educational mission.

Eventually John Maud came to tell me that I had been duly elected, but for two years only, in place of the constitutional five: apparently some of Zimmern's mud had stuck, or perhaps some members of the Executive Board mistrusted my humanistic attitude.

Looking back today, I am grateful for having been appointed, but also grateful that I did not have to serve for five years: it would have been too great a strain (indeed one later Director-General found the job too much for him and had to resign in the middle of his term).

*

1. In his Boyle Lecture, *Science and International Relations* (Blackwell's, Oxford, 1948), Joseph Needham gives a full account of the complexity of UNESCO's structure, the dispute between those who thought that UNESCO's main effort should be concerned with preserving and fostering peace, and others who felt that this must be left to the UN Security Council, and that UNESCO helped the cause of peace indirectly by encouraging international co-operation in all fields of culture, science, and learning.

He also writes in detail of UNESCO's work for science – in reconstruction, popularization, and international co-operation.

Chilly it certainly was. The winter of 1946–7 was one of the coldest of recent years, worse even than that of 1917–18. What was more, Paris was still under restrictions of all kinds, with food coupons and severe rationing of all sources of heat. The Hotel Majestic was steam-heated, indeed over-heated, but most private apartments had to fight the cold with pathetic little stoves burning wood or oil, both of which were obtainable only on the black market. We had secured a flat on the Avenue Alphand and depended entirely on one electric heater and an open log-fire – whenever we managed to get any logs ... The maid's room was a frozen attic which no human being could be asked to occupy. There being no one to cook for us, we had to go out for all our meals, except breakfast, and wrap up to the eyes every time we went into the glacial passage to telephone. It was ironical that we should have had to put up with this real hardship while I was enjoying a salary far larger than anything I had ever earned previously – or since! It must be remembered, however, that there was no pension attached to the Directorship, and that, in spite of my entertainment allowance, our costs were high. Paris was expensive as well as cold.

Now my work began in earnest: confirming my earlier staff in permanent positions, finding new staff – and pruning out unsatisfactory members. This last I found one of my most unpleasant duties: luckily there was only one man I had to dismiss.

I had to make my first public speech in French – a trying occasion – at a Government banquet presided over by the Prime Minister, Georges Bidault. He looked rather like a sulky, overgrown boy, and there was no sympathy between us. However, I have to give him full marks for his leadership of the French Resistance during the German occupation.

Soon, I had to fly to New York to explain UNESCO's aims to the United Nations' Assembly, where I was well received. I naturally met Trygve Lie, the then Secretary-General, with whom I discussed the relations of UNESCO to the UN. Then to Washington, where I saw not only Archibald Macleish, but also Mr Justice Frankfurter, a brilliant and liberal-minded member of the US Supreme Court, and, of course, President Truman, who impressed me with his shrewdness.

Back in Paris, I spoke at the Académie des Sciences at the Sorbonne, and was given an Honorary degree. One of my chores was to make official calls on the French President and on the Ambassadors of the various countries represented on the Board of UNESCO, and to receive their calls in return. My meeting with the Brazilian representative, the physiologist Paulo Carneiro, forged the first link which eventually led to his whole-hearted support of my project for a Universal History, stressing its cultural aspects, to be undertaken by UNESCO (p. 64). He was a real friend, as well as a capable administrator and a many-sided scholar.

Russia was the one major power that had refused to join UNESCO, considering it a 'capitalist and a colonialist' set-up; and mainland China was not even recognized by the UN.[1] This left a large gap in our pretended universality.

At the Cains' official residence in the Bibliothèque Nationale, we met interesting people like the writer André Malraux, Aragon the left-wing poet, the actor Jean-Louis Barrault and his wife Madeleine Renaud, and many others. And we soon became friendly with our Ambassador, Duff Cooper, and his beautiful wife, Lady Diana.

I also saw a good deal of Léon Blum, ex-President of France, and an original member of UNESCO's Executive Board. Once when calling on him, I retailed the malicious story of André Gide, who, on being asked who was the greatest French poet, is reputed to have said, 'Victor Hugo – hélas!' Blum smiled, but then barked out 'Pourquoi "hélas"?' in an offended tone of voice. Though Blum may have lacked a sense of humour on this matter, he was not only a charming person but a true liberal, and supported me in almost all my projects.

Then there was Henri Laugier, who also served his time on the Executive Board, and whose friend, Madame Cutolli, knew Picasso and had a wonderful collection of his works (and those of other avant-garde artists) in her apartment; Professor Rivet, the ethnologist; and the brilliant social anthro-

1. Today (1972), China has become one of the most important members of the UN, and of its Security Council.

pologist Lévi-Strauss (who later gave valuable advice to our son Francis when he went on his anthropological expeditions to the Upper Amazon). What a galaxy of talent there was then in Paris!

But perhaps the most interesting acquaintance I made was that of the Jesuit, Père Teilhard de Chardin, to whom I was introduced in the lobby of UNESCO by the geologist Edmond Blanc. Blanc thought that I, as the author of *Religion without Revelation*, ought to know Teilhard, who had written a number of essentially humanist works with an evolutionary as well as a religious background. He had had geological training, and became especially interested in human evolution when, as a young seminarist in a Sussex college, he witnessed the excavations which yielded (besides some interesting Pleistocene remains) the notorious Piltdown skull, claimed by the excavator, Dr Dawson, to be that of the oldest known human being. It later turned out to be an elaborate fake, put there for unknown reasons by Dawson himself, consisting of a modern man's cranium fitted with an ape's lower jaw. But it kindled Teilhard's imagination.

He then became a lecturer in a Catholic college in Paris, but his evolutionary views scandalized the Jesuit authorities, and he was 'exiled' to China. By an irony of fate, his time there coincided with the discovery of Peking man, by himself and one of his Jesuit colleagues, a discovery which definitely put the origin of man far back in the Pleistocene. After this, he became more than ever interested in evolutionary problems, and studied the fossil remains of animals from many geological periods, as well as examining all the evidence for man's evolution from an ape-like ancestor.

Combining his biological knowledge with his religious and philosophical training, he employed his exile in writing a number of books, in which he expounded his evolutionary views on human origins and beliefs, and his reflections on man's unique position and responsibilities. However, the Jesuits forbade publication, so that he was reduced to circulating his writings in mimeographed form; he was also denied the right to air his views in public. This was a serious curtailment of intellectual liberty, but he had taken the vows of complete

23

obedience to his Order, whatever the demands put upon him, and in this he never failed. He suffered greatly, but in silence and with dignity.

When he died, he left all his manuscripts to his niece, who knew the value of his ideas and thoughts. She was not hampered by any vows; and one by one, his books were published, to an enthusiastic reception. I wrote a preface to the English translation of his first and best book, *Le Phénomène humain*, anglicized as *The Phenomenon of Man* – and was bitterly attacked by some of my rationalist friends for supporting a religious (and not fully scientific) work!

In spite of the Jesuits' unyielding opposition, Teilhard has posthumously become a prophet, indeed almost a saint, in France, as well as in many other countries. His writings became a symbol of the reconciliation between scientific humanism and Catholic orthodoxy, which the younger generation of religiously-minded people, including many Catholics, ardently desired.[1]

I was much taken by him, on the too few occasions when we met. He was handsome, with a long, refined face and intelligent and humorous eyes. We discussed our joint problems, we exchanged letters and papers, and found ourselves in almost general agreement over the essential facts of cultural and organic evolution, though he never gave full credit to the basic evolutionary mechanism of natural selection. However, we never touched on the core of his religious beliefs, where we both recognized an ineradicable divergence of approach; this we were able to tolerate because of our scientific agreement. In 1955, the news of his death in New York (where he was supported by the Wenner-Gren Anthropological Foundation, when driven into further exile by the Jesuits) came to me as a deep shock.

An interesting outcome of what one might call the Teilhard de Chardin legend involved us in 1955, when I was Visiting Professor at McGill University, the English Protestant (or rather non-denominational) university in central Montreal. I

1. As I write this, Pope Paul's utterances, especially his Encyclical on birth-control, have set back hopes for such a reconciliation in the near future.

was invited by a biological colleague to attend a special meeting at the French Catholic University, over the fine hill from which the city takes its name. It was announced as an 'unbiased inquiry' into the theological and scientific aspects of Chardin's works, but my friend expected that they would be formally pronounced heretical.

Juliette and I found ourselves sitting in the Magna Aula of the university among a packed audience, comprising a large proportion of students, young seminarists and nuns, as well as the general public. The rostrum was occupied by a long table at which were sitting five lay professors and several clerical theologians, including a grim and majestic Dominican Abbé in beautiful white robes, looking as if he were Pierre Cauchon determined to find Joan of Arc guilty of witchcraft.

One by one, the theologians and the professors got up and said their piece. Was Père Teilhard a good scientist? No, he was not. Was he a competent philosopher? No, he was not. Was he a sound methodologist? No, he was not. People call him a geologist, but he was only an amateur. People call him a theologian – but was he? Finally, the Dominican rose to sum up. He spoke in beautiful French and went through all the arguments. The audience sat spellbound. The Abbé in his sculptural white robes studied all the faces turned towards him, awaiting his verdict. He raised his hand from the ample folds of his cassock: Père Teilhard, he said, was a poet. 'Ses paroles somptueuses sont un piège. Prenez garde de ne pas y tomber.' He sad down in profound silence. Teilhard and all his works had been condemned.

The lay vice-chancellor of the university, who was also chairman of the inquiry – or should I say inquisition? – suggested that, as I had known Père Teilhard personally, I might wish to speak. I accepted, and walked up to the rostrum. Turning to face the audience, I explained that, from my personal knowledge, Père Teilhard was a completely sincere man, an excellent palaeontologist, and that although I did not agree with him on all points, I considered that his reconciliation of scientific fact and religious belief along evolutionary lines was enlightened and helpful. There was a burst of spontaneous applause from the audience, as of a great tension released.

The clapping continued for several minutes, while the panel of assessors looked glum. As I went out of the hall, happy to have done something to vindicate my old friend, I was besieged by eager young questioners.

Père Teilhard had a sense of humour too. At an earlier meeting, on the relations between Science and Religion, in New York State, up the Hudson river, I was sitting next to him when Gilson, the very orthodox and indeed reactionary French philosopher, indulged in a tirade against all attempts to reconcile scientific and evolutionary thought with Catholic doctrine. Teilhard leant over and whispered in my ear: 'Pauvre Gilson: Il croit que nous vivons toujours au treizième siècle ...'

Another good friend we made in Paris was Joe Davidson, the politically left-wing sculptor, who had a studio in the city and an enchanting country house on the river Indre near Tours, called Le Bécheron. He wanted to do a head of me and we had sittings at Bécheron, while he talked of the ups and downs of his curious life. Joe had the amazing gift of seizing a likeness in clay in the minimum time – he managed a remarkable portrait of de Gaulle in two hours – and in his Paris gallery were represented many of his famous contemporaries – Rockefeller and Roosevelt, Gide, James Joyce, Gertrude Stein, Helen Keller, Weizmann, Gandhi, Shaw and many others – a superb collection.

My bust, cast in bronze, was later acquired by UNESCO, and now sits in the new building, together with that of Gilbert Murray, as Chairman of UNESCO's forerunner, the League's Institute of Intellectual Co-operation. During my time, it stood in the entry hall of the Hotel Majestic and I was told that the typists used to tweak 'my' prominent bronze eyebrows as they came in to work – for luck. A nice piece of superstition in an organization dedicated to enlightenment!

Week-ends at Bécheron were a wonderful rest from our hectic life in Paris. We would go down to the river in the afternoon, have a swim and bask on the grassy bank while Joe fished – usually without success. Or I would scramble about on the look-out for interesting birds. Once I traced a grass-hopper-warbler, in spite of his ventriloquial powers of projecting his song away from his meagre hide-out – a vocal camouflage.

I also made the trivial but curious discovery that the rhythm of the wood-pigeon's cooing, which is usually syllabized in English as 'Take two coos, Taffy' repeated several times, is really *Two coos, Taffy take* – the repetition ending with a final *take*. When I got home I found that another English bird-watcher, Philip Brown, had made the same 'discovery', and we published a brief joint note in *British Birds*.

Exploring the country by bicycle, we went to the romantic château of Azay-le-Rideau down the valley, a magnificent turreted castle in a lovely setting, impregnated with historical memories. I also remember a whole field of sunflowers in their golden glory, all turning their yellow faces to the sun; grown for the oil of their seeds, but contributing beauty as a bonus. I had never seen such a sight in England – the areas I knew were too cool and damp – though they can be grown as a crop in parts of East Anglia.

In the evenings we played childish games like Antelope Halma. Joe was a passionate player and used to mutter grimly into his beard when losing; but it was all good fun. Dear Bécheron! We spent some of our happiest times in that rambling, comfortable house.

In Paris, we made the acquaintance of Princess Marie Bonaparte, a remarkable woman who had known Sigmund Freud and translated his works into French. We were asked to dine one day, and her husband, Prince George of Greece, showed us some Napoleonic relics, mostly marble busts of members of Napoleon's family. Taking us into his library, he flung open the door and exclaimed: 'J'ai tué tout cela!' Almost the whole wall-space was taken up with trophies of the chase – fine heads of red deer, antelopes, elk, wolves and so forth, leaving very little room for books ...

Of course, we had to give official dinner parties of sixteen to eighteen people, which we did mostly in the old dining-room of the Hotel Majestic, nicknamed by us 'Salle Louis *ix*' – as it combined the worst elements of Louis XIV, XV and later styles, up to the Restoration. On one occasion, we placed our guests in accordance with their cultural and intellectual interests, instead of in strict order of precedence. The experiment was not a success – some were deeply offended and there were complaints from several embassies! After this we duly consulted the *chef de protocol* on UNESCO's staff, and harmony was restored, even if conversation sometimes suffered. But I doubt if we were ever forgiven for this breach of diplomatic ritual, this infringement of the pecking-order of human figure-heads. We had to admit, in the end, that protocol was a wise arrangement wherever prestige was involved.

We invited the Bonapartes to one of these dinners, the Princess, of course, in the place of honour on my right. This time the atmosphere became explosive. She began talking of her travels in Egypt, where she had been studying the psychological effects of the horrible operation of 'female circumcision' (cliteridectomy) on Muslim women. The trivial chatter among the other guests died down and all heads were turned to listen to the Princess's rare observations. I am not sure whether the party was a success, but at any rate it was unusual ...

The high-brow Duchesse de la Rochefoucauld invited us to her *salons*. Juliette went to congratulate the veteran poet-playwright Paul Claudel on his becoming, at long last, a *Membre de l'Institut*, and found him enthroned, wearing his palm-embroidered uniform, with Princess Marthe Bibesco at his feet. We also spent lovely musical week-ends at Royaumont, where the rich industrialist Henri Gouin had created a centre for music-lovers.

Juliette, herself an amateur sculptress, made friends with the Rumanian sculptor Brancusi, and visited him in his draughty studio. During the bitter winter of 1946-7, he had lain at death's door, but he recovered – and told Juliette the strange story of his cure. There was a block of chestnut-wood in his yard waiting to be carved. In early spring, the sick man asked to be taken out of doors for what he thought might be his last look at the outside world – and saw, to his amazement, that the chestnut block was sprouting vigorous twigs ending in thick, sticky buds. He decided there and then that if the chestnut could recover, though rootless and mutilated, he, Brancusi, could do so too. Actually, he survived for another six years. His output was never abundant, but what he created was magical – an essence of pure form.

But I anticipate. To celebrate the formal inauguration of UNESCO, which took place on 4 November 1946, the French authorities had arranged for a series of lectures, concerts and plays to be given in Paris, and I got my poet friend, Stephen Spender, to come over from England to help. Bernal gave a brilliant talk about the Origin of Life, Shakespeare's *King Lear* was performed by the Old Vic Company from London, and lectures were given by various eminent Frenchmen.

The Abbé Breuil, a world authority on prehistoric man, gave a fascinating talk on his subject, including slides made from his own drawings, showing the wonderful prehistoric cave-paintings and sculptures from Lascaux, Altamira, and Saharan Africa. Those from Europe depicted hunting scenes of wild horses, bison and deer, from about 12000 B.C., while the African paintings were more recent, depicting antelopes, giraffe and other grassland fauna, showing that the climate was not then so arid. Breuil's talk stimulated me to make an expedition to Lascaux, in order to obtain colour photographs for a work on prehistoric art to be published by UNESCO.

Immediately after the lecture, I had to attend another celebration, so it was left to Spender to thank the Abbé and see him off. As they left the hall, Breuil stopped and said: 'Est-ce qu'il n'y a pas une petite enveloppe?' Spender was surprised – he had not realized that French custom was to pay on the spot.

Meanwhile, I was busy recruiting more staff. I cannot mention all of them, even if they numbered only 74 at the beginning, as against 3,287 today (1,387 in the field). Then, only 40 nations had joined UNESCO; now there are over 120, all with representatives in Paris, many from newly independent ex-colonies. The task of the present D.G. in reconciling diverse national interests is far harder than mine ever was.

One fact struck me in those early days. Vital young people came to me to ask: 'What can we do for UNESCO?' Indeed, the staff as a whole was imbued with enthusiasm for this new international venture. Alas, this fine pioneer spirit lasted only a few years, and was later too often superseded by the question: 'What can UNESCO do for me?'

This was a natural phase in the evolution of such a new instrument of hoped-for progress. Since then, however, a new level has been reached. Led by the present Director-General, René Maheu, particular projects hitherto unfulfilled by any other agency, such as the preservation of man's cultural heritage, have been promoted; regional studies of diverse subjects have been widely extended, and all-round research such as the study of oceans has been fostered. The latest exciting project is that of a General History of Africa. (See also p. 73.)

In the programme submitted to the General Conference at the end of 1946, what I aimed at was to achieve better education for the underprivileged; a greater understanding of the role of science, especially biology and psychology, by all nations; exchange of students and teachers between countries with differing ideologies or at different levels of cultural development; conservation of natural beauty and sites of historical interest; a greater understanding of evolution and its workings, both in nature and in human society; the extirpation of ideological and nationalist interference in matters of art, literature and science; measures against over-population (though here I had to share responsibility with WHO and the economists). Above all, a consciousness of the unity of mankind and the need to co-ordinate efforts towards cultural and social progress on a world-wide scale.

The achievement of peace, as I have mentioned, was one of the aims laid down in UNESCO's constitution. However, I felt the 'impossibility of UNESCO's producing the rabbit of political peace out of a cultural and scientific hat', as I urged at a session of the Executive Board. Indeed, the issues of peace and war could only be safeguarded by the UN. UNESCO's contribution to peace, I said, must be indirect, through cultural and personal exchanges, through greater understanding between people of different creeds and social systems, and through the reduction of tensions due to over-population and to damage to man's environment. The key concept behind all our activities, I felt sure, should be *fulfilment* – fuller realization of capacities by

30

individuals, cities, nations, and humanity as a whole. I set out to lay the foundations for such a programme, ably supported by my staff.

Only in the matter of birth-control was I unable to obtain official sanction from the Board. Fortunately, various Foundations, notably the Ford, stepped into the breach, and with their aid useful projects were set up in India and some African countries.

The chief obstacles were Roman Catholic hostility; the mistaken idea of some underdeveloped nations that birth-control would actually diminish their numbers and therefore – another false conclusion – their power; the conservatism which regarded large families as an insurance against the parents' old age; and a general mistrust of innovation.

However, the menace of over-population is now generally recognized, and I hope that my successors at UNESCO will be able to play an important part in a world-wide programme of population-control, now actively supported by the UN, and endorsed by the World Bank and WHO.

This is one answer to people who ask me about UNESCO's future role. For the rest, I hope it will continue along its present lines, though with more emphasis on higher education and facilities for artistic creation as illiteracy gradually diminishes; and less political jockeying for national advantage among the official delegates on the Board, and within the Organization itself. Today, UNESCO's personnel has become almost too numerous and too disparate for efficient (and economical) administration: might it not be better now to have regional rather than national representatives?

In the summer of 1947, Juliette and I flew out to Haiti with a couple of assistants to take a more detailed look at their educational facilities. As I have already mentioned, they were deplorable, and the general misery of the people was profoundly depressing. We came back resolved that UNESCO should do all it could to solve Haiti's educational and social problems, but in the light of later trends our efforts accomplished very little. The deeply rooted Voodoo beliefs dominated every action; fear, superstition and over-population remained major obstacles to improvement; while a harsh and corrupt dictator-ship has since made matters even worse.

Back in Paris, to a perpetual rush – and a heat-wave. The amiable American, Wilson, the first US representative at UNESCO (whose command of the French language, according to a malicious colleague, was fully extended at 'Oui, oui' and 'Non, non'), was replaced as Assistant D.G. by Walter Laves from New York, an experienced administrator who helped a good deal in straightening out internal confusion, though I sometimes felt that he set too exacting a standard of organiza-tional perfection. It was no doubt necessary in our new or-ganization.

In spite of the heat, meetings continued; we got the Inter-national Copyright Convention ratified by a majority of our member-states; and we accepted Mexico's request that we should hold our next General Conference in Mexico City in November.

CHAPTER 2

Latin America and the Mexico Conference

In preparation for the Mexico Conference I was sent to visit as many South American countries as possible, to make contact with their Education Ministers and other important personages, and to whip up enthusiasm for the Conference and for UNESCO's ideas in general.

In New York, I again paid my respects to Trygve Lie at UN Headquarters. There had been considerable friction in the United Nations, and he was badly overstrained. I shall never forget his muttering, 'Dr Huxley, I have had a terrible time, yes, a *terrible* time', as tears began to run down his contorted face. I inwardly thanked my stars that I was concerned with cultural and educational matters, while he had to cope with the violence of power politics.

Thence I went to my friend Dr Weaver at the Rockefeller Foundation, who again helped me – this time by sending John Marshall to represent the Foundation at UNESCO. Marshall was extremely helpful, with his liberal views and international vision, and later supported our project for an International Scientific and Cultural History of Mankind.

I then left for my journey through Latin America, accompanied by two Spanish-speaking assistants, Emilio Arenales from Guatemala, and Manolo Jimenez from Mexico. We had a bare month for fifteen nations, but our lightning tour was successful. The Latin American countries attended the Conference in force, and UNESCO had its first opportunity of hearing the views and wishes of this major region of the world. To me, it was an eye-opener, but I must confine myself to recording only a few of my many impressions.

Looking through my diary, I am appalled by the number of engagements I had to fulfil. In all the countries, I had to pay a courtesy visit to the President and to see the Ministers of Foreign Affairs and Education, the former to deal with the formal aspects of the country's membership of UNESCO, the latter to persuade him to send a delegation to the Conference, composed of prominent people genuinely interested in education, science and culture, and in international co-operation. I was also in duty bound to meet the vice-chancellor or head of the country's university, besides visiting national museums, and seeing people eminent in the arts and sciences. Usually I had to give a lecture – sometimes in French – and in every country there was a press conference, at which I had to answer a multitude of questions, and correct various misunderstandings.

The section in UNESCO responsible for spreading information about the Organization and its aims seemed to have been rather inefficient, for in almost every Latin American country there were complaints that very few documents about UNESCO had been received. As a result, many Ministers believed that UNESCO was interested only in the affairs of Britain, the USA and France. Jimenez, Arenales and I had to work hard to explain that UNESCO was truly international.

In this task we were much helped by Torres-Bodet, then Mexican Minister of Education. He not only arranged a meeting of the Ambassadors of all Latin American countries in his office, but sent letters explaining the importance of UNESCO in general, and of the Mexico City Conference in particular, to all their Ministers of Education.

As a result of this, and of our own efforts, all the Latin American countries sent delegations – and good delegations – to the Conference; and those who were not yet officially Members of UNESCO set about ratifying their adhesion.

Of course, there were ceremonial banquets, where I generally had to speak, and often special trips to places or institutes the authorities wanted me to see – and several universities gave me an honorary degree (one in medicine!). It was a whirl of travel and multifarious encounters – new faces, new minds, new places and new social attitudes. Luckily I was still full of energy at 59, and survived the hectic round, in spite of several spells of overtiredness.

The two UNESCO projects that interested most of the Latin American Governments were the equal validity of academic degrees in all countries – of immediate importance in planning

34

their systems of higher education; and our so-called Fundamental Education programme – valuable to those nations with a high proportion of illiterates and of people ignorant of the importance of cleanliness, both their own and that of their surroundings.

The slums around most of the big cities in the region were terrible – hovels to live in, garbage and filth in the streets (Santiago was an exception: indeed, in many ways Chile seemed the most progressive of the countries we visited). Most Latin American nations had plans for better housing of the 'lower' classes; yet, apart from a few modern blocks of flats – whose rent was usually more than slum-dwellers could pay – little was actually being done.

Most of the Governments seemed unaware that the slums (and the high rate of unemployment) were the result of over-population, coupled with the large-scale movements of peasants to the cities – because so many of them could no longer make a living on the land. But I became ever more conscious of this, and of the fact that over-population was aggravated by the opposition of the Roman Catholic Church to what they called 'unnatural' (i.e. deliberate) birth-control, using 'artificial' methods.

The other general fact that struck me in Latin America was the way in which the mass of the people (with a few exceptions) not only accepted the Catholic religion in place of their original beliefs, but enjoyed it, because of the elaborate ritual and the almost garish decoration of the churches, and also because of the numerous Saints' Days. Besides being holidays from work, these were gay, with elaborate processions. In many cases, Church feast-days were actually fixed on the dates of ancient rituals.

Thus on St John the Baptist's day I saw an enormous procession in the streets of Lima (doubtless replacing the pre-Conquest celebration of the summer solstice). Life-size painted effigies of St John and the Virgin were carried by smiling Indians, the crowd were shouting for joy and deliriously throwing fire-crackers into the path of the procession, even igniting full-scale models of cattle and sheep (presumably replacing similar models of llamas), which were stuffed with rockets – noisy and rather dangerous, but what fun!

As a biologist and conservationist, I naturally took advantage of the little spare time at my disposal to see (or learn) as much as I could of the continent's natural history and varied scenery.

The natural history was especially interesting, because South America was cut off from the North some thirty million years back, and its animal and plant types started to evolve along their own lines, producing strange creatures, some of which, such as armadillos and opossums, have found their way to southern USA in the million years, more or less, since the 'Panama' isthmus bridged the gap. I was especially glad to see llamas, distant relatives of camels. These were the only beasts of burden in the continent, yet even so, capable of carrying only light loads, not the weight of a man.

Other products of South America's separate evolution were the monkeys with prehensile tails acting as a fifth limb (surprising that old-world monkeys never produced this admirable adaptation to tree life). I heard the fantastic howlers' chorus in the Colombian jungle, and saw rheas, exactly like small ostriches, but in fact quite unrelated – a nice example of parallel adaptation, in both cases to fast running on dry, open plains, the power of flight being lost in the process.

South American amphibians, too, are extraordinary. In Rio I visited the Research Establishment run by Bertha Lutz. Her father had discovered that malaria could be transmitted by a species of mosquito whose larvae lived in the miniature water-reservoirs provided by the leafy cups of Bromeliad plants, and that many larvae were eaten by frog tadpoles living in the same curious tanks. What is more, in one species, tadpoles developed into frogs adapted to this micro-habitat, with flat and spiky heads shielding them from attack. When I went out into the forest with Bertha, I kept on asking the names of the birds I heard; but in almost every case they were not birds at all, but amphibians – green tree-frogs, musical tree-toads, croaking marsh-toads and the deep bass of bull-frogs.

Rheas reminded me of Darwin, who saw them, as described in *The Voyage of the Beagle*, and realized that they were only pseudo-ostriches. Darwin also came to my mind in Quito, the capital of Ecuador, for Ecuador owns the Galapagos Islands, and it was during his visit to this archipelago that he first became fully convinced that evolution was a fact – birds and tortoises had changed into different species when isolated on separate islands, and one species of giant iguana lizard had become aquatic.

My recollection of this crucial moment in Darwin's career was one of the factors that led me to propose the creation of IUCN, the International Union for the Conservation of Nature (p. 56), and this in turn persuaded Ecuador to make the archipelago a National Park – a Park which is also a natural biological laboratory, supported by the International Galapagos Foundation, where important studies on evolution and adaptation are now in progress.

I also remembered that when Darwin landed at Rio, he was not only struck dumb (like all visitors) by the fantastic mountain scenery, but overwhelmed by the majesty of the tropical forest round Botofogo Bay. Today, however, to my surprise and grief, little was left – it had been cut down to make way for the villas bordering Brazil's Riviera, the crowded bathing beaches of Copo Cabana.

It was during this trip to South America that I started to improve my technique of taking colour photographs, though it was not until my journeys to the Middle East that they became good enough for reproduction.[1] It became a serious hobby which gave me many hours of deep enjoyment.

On my way south, it was a great delight in Panama to see so many unfamiliar creatures, especially birds, in the Barros Colorado Reserve, established by the US Government; and in Colombia, to visit the naturalist William Beebe, inventor of the bathysoapho, but at the time studying the beautiful and often mimetic butterflies of the hill jungle, where he had his laboratory.

In Peru, after my official calls and a visit to the museum, I was given a piece of pottery which stood on my desk at UNESCO for months – until Juliette discovered that it was extremely indecent. This coastal tribe enjoyed ribald sexy fun in their work. The pot was immediately banished to a high shelf.

The Peruvian visit included a trip to Cuzco, the ancient capi-

1. The photographs were included in a book about the Middle East, illustrated by Sir Julian Huxley, entitled *From an Antique Land*.

tal of the Incas, well over 11,000 feet up, on the so-called *altiplano*. My first surprise was that it lay close to the source of the Amazon, which started between the two main ranges of the Andes, a bare 100 miles from the Pacific, to wind its immense course through the jungle to the Atlantic. The second was the extent of the Inca empire, as set forth by our guide – an empire almost half the size of ancient Rome's, and like Rome's, traversed by a splendid network of roads. Finally, the quality of the Incas' building technique, achieved without any iron tools.

One day was spared for an excursion to the guano islands to the north, where the sea's fertility is transferred to the land. This meant a sixty-mile journey along the desert road – and what a desert! The narrow strip between the Pacific shore and the towering barrier of the Andes was as waterless as the Sahara, with moving sand-dunes driving their crescent shapes across the plain.

But if the desert was barren, its off-shore waters were rich. This is due to the cold Humboldt current, which runs north along the coast, bringing abundant plankton from the subantarctic region to feed the local fish – and to settle on the stony shores. In turn, the fish provide a rich source of food for the sea-birds nesting on the rocky islands and promontories, and their droppings provide vast quantities of guano, which man employs as a penultimate link in the food-chain, to fertilize his fields. Before human beings began to exploit the deposits by modern methods, there were veritable cliffs of guano, up to 150 feet high – the semi-fossilized droppings of thousands of bird-generations ...

We headed out for the main island in a government launch. As we drew near, we saw the richness of the fauna: the rocks were covered with a brilliant patchwork of sea-creatures – rosy sea-anemones, scarlet star-fish, and enormous chitons (armoured sea-slugs), which here grow over eight inches long; not to mention incrustations of barnacles, blue and green sea-squirts, yellow sponges and well-camouflaged bristle-worms crawling over the mass; while the open water was full of jellyfish trailing purple tentacles.

We clambered to the flat top. The giant cliffs of guano had gone, but there was a rich deposit several inches deep, stinking to high heaven, almost ready for collection. The place was crammed with birds. Besides the regiments of boobies, a tropical species of gannet (which reminded me of the great gannetry Lockley and I had filmed in Wales), I was much struck by the beautiful Inca terns, with dark-russet heads striped with white, blue-grey backs and scarlet bills; and the vast and noisy population of cormorants, which provided the bulk of the guano. Luckily, we had been provided with sea-boots, so were spared having our trousers and shoes fouled with dung; but the smell lingered in our clothes for days.

The guano islands were not only an extraordinary spectacle, but also very pleasing to the conservationist: for wherever guano yields profit, sea-birds are rigorously protected.

I have space for only a few other incidents. Earlier, in Bogotá, the capital of Colombia, I found that Corbusier, the noted French Swiss architect, had been called in to plan the city's expansion. As I entered the room, Corbusier, bent over a map, said, 'Gentlemen, before we proceed, will you please tell me why Bogotá is *here*?' A justified question, for it is sited on a high plateau, approachable only by crossing the double range of the Andes from the western seaboard, or from the north by a 500-mile boat-trip up the Magdalena River; in both cases with a steep climb to the plateau. I did not hear the Colombians' answer, but suppose that the site had been chosen because of the safety provided by this very isolation.

Bogotá also surprised me in another way. The intellectuals I met were little interested in UNESCO, but deeply in French cultural life, and kept asking me about modern Parisian writers and painters. I still wonder why this Francophilia – or rather Parisophilia – should have taken such a strong hold on this isolated Hispano–American country.

Leaving Peru for a brief two days in Chile, I enjoyed seeing the best-kept city in Latin America, with scarcely any slums. I then flew over an appalling desolation of ice and snowy mountains to the broad, sunny Argentine, where I was amazed by the vast herds of 'wild' horses on the pampas; the more so since I knew that the horse, though it had evolved in North America, had died out long before Europeans reached the New World. No one knows why the horse became extinct in the double continent, but an old African acquaintance of mine, now in charge of the Tsetse Research Institute at Bristol, tells me that the same trypanosomes that kill European horses and other domestic stock in East Africa have been found in parts of South America.

For me, as head of a United Nations Organization devoted to cultural freedom, Argentina posed political problems. I had to pay my courtesy call on President Perón, though I knew that he had become a ruthless dictator, banishing liberals and forcing teachers to introduce propaganda for his regime into their schools, as well as establishing strict censorship on newspapers and books. Vittoria Ocampo, a friend of Aldous and publisher of the liberal magazine *Sur*, told me that her offices in Buenos Aires had been wrecked, while she herself felt so vulnerable that she moved out of the capital to a remote *estancia*.

Luckily, my hotel apartment had two doors. I arranged with Jimenez, who had been getting the political feel of things, that officials and government supporters should use one entry, and known anti-Perónists the other.

It was clear that Perón's tyranny, coupled with the ostentatious extravagance of his wife Eva, was making him unpopular; and some few years later, he was forced into exile.[1]

Meanwhile, on my return to Paris, I reported Perón's tyrannical measures to my Executive Board, and they courageously protested against these actions, as being contrary to the aims and indeed the general spirit of UNESCO, to which Argentina was already affiliated.

Brazil was the last country I visited. I have already spoken of my visit to Bertha Lutz and Botofogo Bay; I had also paid official calls on the President and the Minister of Education, meanwhile seeing something of Rio's centre and its gay crowds, of Portuguese, other Europeans, Japanese, Negro ex-slaves, a few Indians, and plenty of cross-breeds (there seemed to be no colour prejudice in Brazil, though the Negroes and Indians tended to get lower-paid jobs).

I had a day to spare, so got Carneiro, back in his home town

1. As I write, Perón has just returned to Argentina and we wonder what will happen.

as representative of Brazil at UNESCO, to borrow Bertha's little car, in addition to the grand official vehicle put at my disposal, and we all set off, hoping to reach the spectacular city of Petropolis by lunch-time and enjoy the panoramic view of the bay, the city and the magnificent jungle-clad mountains opposite. But we failed. Carneiro, driving up the winding mountain road, with me at his side, was just about to overtake a large lorry when it turned without warning into a field, and despite vigorous efforts, Carneiro could not avoid colliding with its rear. All I remember was the moment of crash, though actually the car turned over and landed upside-down.

The party in the second car thought we must all be dead, but when they pulled us out, there was no damage except a slight cut on Carneiro's face and me with mild concussion (which, as is usual, robbed me of all memory of the events immediately after the collision), and two fractured ribs.

I was taken back to my hotel on the sea-front, my chest bandaged and my arm in a sling. Apart from a mild ache in my chest, aggravated by the heat of the plaster bandage, and the annoying fact of having to stay in bed instead of exploring the splendid country and the baroque churches of the metropolis, I was perfectly well. One incident did something to relieve my boredom: a pure white tropic-bird, with huge wing-spread and elongated tail, floated past my window ...

After a few tedious days, I was fit enough to travel back. The first stage was a flight over the great Amazonian jungle. This gave me the same feeling of fear that Juliette and I had experienced over the Russian taiga or pine-forest a quarter-century earlier, but here intensified by the vastness of the region: over tens of thousands of square miles there was virtually no landing-place.

However, we safely crossed this arboreal ocean and landed at Belém, the Portuguese fortified town south of the main Amazon river; then to fly on over the huge delta, and see the brown flood discolouring the sea as far as the eye could reach – and, of course, removing vast quantities of fertile soil from the land. We witnessed a similar waste of soil where the Orinoco discharges its muddy flow on the north coast.

After a stop-over in Georgetown in British Guiana, just long enough to call on the Governor (and get a glimpse of the poverty and wretched housing of the blacks on the water-front), we flew on to Trinidad. Here again there was plenty of misery among the descendants of Negro slaves in the slums.

I was pleased with my success in persuading so many Latin American governments to send strong delegations to the UNESCO Conference, but shocked by the widespread ignorance and misery of the Amerindians and Negroes, and determined that UNESCO should help in all projects of family planning, education and medical aid for the peoples of this enormous region.

Still encased in my plaster cast, I returned to Paris in the height of summer, my energy sapped by excess of travel. There was still much to do in preparing for the Mexico Conference, and we had to endure the shimmering hot days cooped up at our desks at the Hotel Majestic. However, we escaped at weekends to places like Château Gaillard on the Seine, to Fontainebleau, where we wandered in the forest among enormous rocks, and to friendly Bécheron. Without these brief respites, I doubt if I could have survived the combination of torrid heat and exacting work.

However, the heat abated, the outlines of our programme for the next year were ready in late November, and I set off again for Mexico, this time accompanied by the Executive Board, a large contingent of UNESCO staff, and, of course, Juliette.

As we flew in towards Mexico City, we saw one of the famous sacrificial pyramids below us, and I heard the air-hostess informing the passengers that it was as large as the Great Pyramid in Egypt, and as ancient ... Neither of these assertions was true, but it was good propaganda.

We were put in a pleasant modern hotel and I got down to business – meetings of the Board and of its committees – on finance, on all aspects of the programme and on procedure during the Conference. In addition, I or my Deputy had to make official calls on various Ministers. Unfortunately, Torres-Bodet had become Head of the Foreign Office and the new Minister of Education seemed unable to understand our projects.

There were receptions, of course, by the Government and various foreign Embassies, where one always seemed to be meeting the same people, chattering away in a deafening babel of many tongues. Although Soviet Russia was not yet a member of UNESCO, their Embassy gave the most sumptuous of all the parties: they had a special plane flown from Moscow, laden with masses of caviar, vodka and other Russian delicacies. I do not know if this increased their political prestige, but it resulted in a prodigious amount of guzzling.

Mexico proved to be as poverty-stricken as most of the South American countries. Though the upper classes, including many mestizos, lived reasonably well, and though the towns and cities boasted splendid churches and cathedrals, mostly in the exaggeratedly florid baroque styled called churriguresque, the bulk of the ex-Aztecs and other Amerindians, in spite of their bright *serupes*, were extremely poor and lived in city slums or country shacks. But their condition was much better than that of the lower classes in Haiti – or in India, as we were to see later.

In Prescott's *Conquest of Mexico*, I had read of the astonishment of Cortés and his little band of followers at their first sight of the island city across its defensive, brackish lake, larger than any town in Spain and glittering with handsome buildings and strange pyramids, confirming all they had heard about the country's wealth.

But if they were impressed, they were also shocked. The temples were dripping with human blood, and so were the priests' hands and hair. For the Aztecs believed that only by constant human sacrifice could they ensure that the sun would rise after his nightly journey into the dark realms beneath the earth. This, to them, was the unquestioned basis of their theology. Pre-Conquest art, therefore, represented many scenes of horror. It must be in memory of those times when violent death was so close at hand that now, on All Souls' Day, little sugar skulls are offered for sale, often with the name of the recipient in coloured sugar on the forehead.

The UNESCO delegation was given every opportunity to see the sights. In Mexico City itself there were the remains of

Montezuma's great aqueducts. Though the city now, of course, had a piped water-supply, it was unsafe to drink unboiled water or eat raw vegetables.

Here too, as in Peru and other Latin American countries, the Indians had perpetuated their ancient practices under the cloak of nominal Christianity. They enjoyed religious processions as much as in their indigenous past, with the additional pleasure derived from the white man's fireworks; they went on pilgrimage to the same places, though now in honour of the Virgin instead of the cruel gods of the Aztecs; and they still drank pulque, the traditional liquor brewed from a kind of agave. I tried it once, and found it very potent; but I disliked the customary *bonne-bouche* with it – fried grubs extracted from the agave leaves before their distillation. I ate one, just to try. When asked what it tasted like, I had to admit that it made me think of a dead shrimp from a graveyard.

We visited the two great revolutionary painters, Diego Rivera and Orozco. Diego, a violent anti-colonialist, had painted a huge mural in Cortés' old palace at Cuernavaca, showing Cortés' retreat among the crowds of hostile Indians: it must have contained as many figures as Michelangelo's *Last Judgement* in the Sistine Chapel. The tall, rather gaunt-looking man was very affable and showed us his remarkable collection of pre-Columbian art in Mexico, which he later left to the nation.

Orozco's huge frescoes adorned the Palace of Justice. But, true to his revolutionary principles, most of the scenes were of Injustice – by the Spanish Conquistadors as well as by modern white or mestizo landlords. Like Rivera (and the Russians), he believed that art must be an instrument of 'social realism', which here included anti-colonialist and especially anti-USA feelings. To what degree of violence this could lead him was shown later, when we visited him and his wife at an exhibition of his work: horrific pictures of cannibal Aztec warriors carrying the severed limbs and decapitated heads of Spanish soldiers. Yet he himself was a gentle creature, full of charm: he reserved his inner core of hatred for his work.

We failed to see Siqueiros, who had been cruelly jailed for 'deviation' from socialist principles, but we saw a good deal of his powerful painting, expressing itself with the aid of incrustations of stones and shiny grit, to achieve stunning effects.

At Chichen Itza, down in Yucatan, we saw a splendid temple founded by Mayas. Its forecourt, the Hall of a Thousand Pillars, was set with ranges of slender columns; among these lay a reclining figure known as a Chacmol, a life-size carving of a man resting on his elbows, with drawn-up knees, holding on his stomach a round dish on which were offered the still-smoking hearts of sacrificial victims. Unlike the over-elaboration of much Aztec and Toltec art, the Mayan Chacmols were carved with stark simplicity. Indeed, Henry Moore was struck by Chacmol figures and created some of his finest sculpture under their inspiration.

Uxmal, further west, also of Mayan origin, gave a completely different impression. It appears not to have been used for human sacrifice; it reminded one more of an Oxford college, exhaling the same feeling of peace and security. There was a square for the ball-game, but it was adorned with peaceful images, unlike those at Chichen Itza, which depicted the actual killing of the losers. Most interesting were the numerous calendrical inscriptions, reckoned in sixty-year cycles, indicating the Mayas' intense preoccupation with their historic past and possible future. (The Mayan calendar was the most accurate invented before our own times, an astonishing achievement for a neolithic civilization.)

This whole area was once swarming with people, from the dry northern coast to the jungles of Guatemala to the south. Why did Mayan civilization die out and the Mayan population dwindle, leaving only a handful of peasant farmers, unaware of their ancestral glories? My feeling is that the cultivation of maize promoted its rise and also its eventual downfall. the burning of the jungle gave a short spurt of fertility to the moist soil, and when it dried out the peasants moved to a fresh patch, leaving their old fields to the quick matting of weeds under a merciless sun. Their agricultural tools of stone were as primitive as their calendar was advanced – they could not cope with the clearing of weed-infested land which had lost its fertile moisture; they had no artificial fertilizers (nor natural guano, as in Peru), and the process became self-defeating.

*

The Mexico Conference of 1947 formally adopted our programme of Fundamental Education which, as I have said, included help in raising the standard of living, teaching hygiene and better methods of cultivation, as well as mere literacy. It endorsed a project for promoting 'peace and goodwill' by sending young people to help backward countries (euphemistically rechristened 'underdeveloped' or even 'developing') in teaching posts and public works: this was the embryo that grew into the UN Foreign Aid programme and sprouted projects like the American Peace Corps and our own Voluntary Service Overseas, both operating on a large scale.

It ratified the International Museums Convention, which has since proved so valuable in the world of art, and one on the Conservation of Nature, for whose inclusion I had to fight hard. Delegates asked what seemed to me silly questions: Why should UNESCO try to protect rhinoceroses or rare flowers? Was not the safeguarding of grand, unspoilt scenery outside its purview? etc., etc. However, with the aid of a few nature-lovers, I persuaded the Conference that the enjoyment of nature was part of culture, and that the preservation of rare and interesting animals and plants was a scientific duty (see p. 56).

We were given a final picnic-feast on the floating gardens of Xochimilco, which must have looked much the same in Aztec times – lovely flowers and copious vegetables on patches of soil floating in a bay of the ancient lake. This, by the way, later prompted UNESCO to support a similar scheme for artificial islands on rafts, in north-east India, which Juliette and I saw during a visit to Manipur. It was wonderful to see the crops raised on these man-made fields and the inhabitants emerging from their snug little huts to fish (p. 153).

As soon as the Conference was over, we took advantage of an invitation from Emilio Arenales, the delegate from Guatemala, who had been with me on part of my tour of Latin America, to stay with his family.[1]

It was indeed a perfect holiday, with no strings attached.

1. Sad to relate, he died prematurely in 1969, in his mid-40s, when he had risen in the UN to become President of the General Assembly – a great loss, for he was a liberal-minded and successful conciliator.

Emilio and his charming wife Lucy took us all over the country in the family Cadillac.

Our most wonderful excursion was to the highlands. After traversing a broad belt of tropical forest, we emerged into open bush upland and halted at a little town with the mouth-filling name of Chichicastenango. Here, pre-Conquest and Christian religious rites co-existed in apparent peace.

Then to Atitlan, an exquisite, deep-blue crater-lake with an extinct volcano in full view across it, lined with hedges of scarlet poinsettias and purple Bougainvillaeas, while trails of heavenly-blue Ipomeas blazed everywhere.

The people were decked in all their finery, the men with feather head-dresses like glowing aureoles, the women lovely in hand-woven white robes, with coral ornaments in their black locks and gold necklaces hanging on their bosoms. Over their dresses they wore embroidered aprons in rich reds and ochres, beautiful under the brilliant sun. The Indians here, as indeed in all Guatemala, seemed happy and contented.

Sadly we left this continent of bright patterns and strange ceremonies, to return once more to Paris, early in 1948.

CHAPTER 3

Another Round at Unesco

MY time at UNESCO seemed to be swallowed up by every sort of job. Looking back now at the list of daily chores which somehow had to be got through, I realize that their very variety gave an impetus to their accomplishment. It was interesting to go from the Estimates Committee to a study of our Programme, to confer with heads of sections on their special needs, to look into staff grievances, to give a lecture here and there; not to mention an occasional trip to WHO Headquarters in Geneva, to deal with the problem of who does what in UN's Technical Projects in medicine, health and education. It was stimulating to be stretched to the utmost – though often exhausting.

I have sometimes been attacked for the multiplicity of my interests. As a fellow-worker put it: 'There was no province of education, science or culture, in which he was not at home. Ideas excited him, and he communicated that excitement to his colleagues. Almost all ideas excited him with equal intensity; whatever idea was before him was for the moment of transcendent importance.' I do not deny this, but I did always try to relate each new project to some central philosophy, some overall system of ideas and aims. This inborn capacity for wide-ranging interest was of great help in my work at UNESCO, and indeed for my career in general.

This was recognized by my Assistant Director, Walter Laves. In his account of UNESCO he wrote: 'Probably no one person more directly influenced the content and direction of UNESCO's programme than did Dr Huxley. Indeed he was largely responsible for charting the broad course to which the organization became committed during its early years.'

My official travels to member countries were, I am sure, of value to UNESCO, in familiarizing the authorities with UNESCO's aims, and with the idea of co-operative cultural and educational development. They were also of value to me. They provided the opportunity of witnessing ancient cultures being 'modernized', sometimes with unfortunate results; of seeing on the spot the effects of illiteracy and over-population, wild life and splendid scenery endangered by short-sighted commercial development, and – all too rarely – the benefits of imaginative large-scale planning.

Ever since my early years, I have enjoyed travel and sight-seeing, in spite of occasional discomfort and fatigue; new knowledge, of places and people, of plants and animals, has always fascinated me. Indeed, I have rarely refused an invitation to travel, even if it involved heavy lecturing duties. For travel strips off one's insularity, opening one up to a natural world of infinite strangeness and variety, and the equally curious and varied world of man's thought and culture. Perhaps most important of all, it enabled me to see with my own eyes the cultural differences between nations, and to grasp the importance of history and environment in affecting the lives of individual people. It was this that led me to advocate so strongly the suggestion, first made by Joseph Needham, that UNESCO should undertake a History of Mankind, stressing scientific and cultural progress rather than purely military and political events.

All too soon the process began again of whipping-up member nations for the next General Conference, to be held at Beirut late in 1948 at the invitation of the Lebanese Government. This meant my visiting all the countries of the Near and Middle East, a region even more interesting than the Americas; for here our own species achieved civilization, with cities, codes of law and alphabetic writing; here man first domesticated plants and animals and improved food-yielding capacities; here the earliest large buildings were erected; here history was first permanently recorded; and here there evolved three of the great religions of the world.

As companions on this pre-Conference trip I had Dr Raadi of Persia, Manolo Jimenez and Claude Berkeley. Since I have recorded most of our experiences, together with a good deal of historical background, in my book *From an Antique Land*, I will give only an outline here.

Constantinople and Ankara lay on our outward route, so we

stopped for a few days in Turkey for talks with the Ministers, and for some interesting visits – to the new National University, with girl students mixing with men and an up-to-date curriculum, to the very practical Technical College for boys, and to the fine Hittite Museum and Archaeological Institute. Our last visit was to Hasanoglu, remote on the bare steppe, where there was a training college for rural teachers, pledged to teach in rural areas for five years after graduation. This was an excellent proviso, and a necessary one if rural illiteracy was to be wiped out. I made a point of commending such schemes at the Beirut Conference.

After flying south over the snow-capped Taurus, with a view of the marvellous, sheltered coast below, we reached Beirut. As usual, between discussions with the Lebanese authorities and anxious inspections of the site for the Conference Hall – where building had barely begun! – I did a little exploring. The region opened up for me a new world of historical and cultural interest as well as of wild natural beauty. My trips before and after the Conference enabled me to make various new recommendations concerning UNESCO's programmes for education and, more particularly, for conservation.

Beirut itself was an amalgam of cultures: merchants descended from the ancient Phoenicians, rich Arabian oil-sheiks, Syrian traders, Jewish brokers and Lebanese bankers; while French, British and American Colleges competed in providing higher education. One important result of the Conference was to be the creation of a single National University, with the foreign Colleges affiliated to it.

Our next stop was Amman in Jordan, where my first appointment was with King Abdullah. As an absolute (but beneficent) monarch, he naturally had to be called on before any of his Ministers. His guard, like that of many autocrats, was composed of foreigners – fine-looking Circassian Christians who had fled from Soviet Russia to avoid persecution.

The King's handsome face gave the impression of intelligence and power, yet with it went a certain naiveté, as though he were caught between the advancing world of technology and the ancient traditions of his kingdom. He greeted me through his interpreter with the disarming remark that 'Conversation between learned men is the highest pleasure'. He was much more interested in UNESCO as a repository of science and learning than in any possible material or cultural advantage that might accrue to his country through joining it, or in sending a deputation to the Conference.

When the question of women in public life came up, the King thumped the table, and delivered himself of a violent remark in Arabic. The French-speaking interpreter explained: 'Sa Majesté dit que les femmes sont un mal nécessaire' – which was probably true in *sa Majesté*'s case; for, as I discreetly ascertained, he had a large harem, drawn from many races ...

It was a great tragedy that he was later assassinated in Jerusalem; he might have done much to mitigate the bitterness between Israelis and Arabs. Like the Emperor Frederick II seven centuries earlier, he wanted to make Jerusalem an open city, open to members of all nations and creeds; and he opposed the idea of fighting Israel.

For the visitor to Jordan there are two *musts* – Jerash and Petra. In Jerash, with its unique oval forum, its temples and pillar-lined streets, I first realized to the full the extent of Rome's power, and her astonishing capacity to impose her ideas on diverse and remote peoples. But Petra crowned all. Its remoteness had prevented Rome from stamping her image too firmly on it, and one's main impression was of the Nabataeans' alien and ancient culture, safely planted in a mountainous wilderness.

To get there, we flew to Ma'an, passing over the enormous Crusader castle of Kerak. I wondered at the enterprise of those medieval adventurers, who managed to provision this outpost all the way from the coast, across what is now Israel, over the Jordan in the great rift valley (whose southern end I had seen in East Africa), and up its high eastern scarp.

From Ma'an, we rode down a rocky track to the great natural rampart of red-purple sandstone, guarding Petra far better than any man-made wall. The approach to the ancient Nabataean capital lies through the Siq, a mile-long gorge, just broad enough to take an ancient chariot (or a small car today), with cliffy sides rising to 300 feet, sometimes actually overhanging. The Nabataeans had carved troughs along its wall to convey

51

the precious water of the Wadi Musa – Moses' river – into the desert stronghold.

Petra made a profound impression on me. Here, there had once existed a great city, with its own king and priesthood, thronged with merchants from far lands and rich with the tolls levied on the caravans, boasting a theatre for entertainment (built after the Romans had conquered it), and containing irrigated fields within its desert barrier of parti-coloured cliffs, then clothed in trees. It had lapsed into obscurity for close on 2,000 years, and now, empty of all life, its only houses are those of the dead, its only population a few wandering Bedouin, plus the guides and the camera-toting bands of tourists. It should, I felt, become a National Park preserved for all time against the depredations of goats and human vandals.[1]

We arrived back in Amman, exhausted but exultant, and next morning flew across the interminable desert of sand and black pebbles, and over the harsh Zagros mountains, to Teheran.

The city itself, like so many others in the East (and in Latin America), was a startling mixture of luxury and poverty. Its modern architecture combined flashiness with bogus antiquity and included government offices meant to commemorate the glories of ancient Persia. I asked about one of these, in neo-Achemenian style, and was told in French, 'C'est la Police'; to which I retorted: 'C'est plutôt la Persepolis.' This bad but effective pun, I was told, had quite a success in the Embassies.

After innumerable official conferences and inspections of institutions, my last visit was to the Royal Palace. I was escorted through the glittering Hall of Mirrors, a succession of rooms encrusted with looking-glass mosaics, to the Hall of Reunion, where I was introduced to the young Shah, with his beautiful bride, and heard from his own lips the efforts he was making to break the grip of the big landowners. Then I was taken through heavy, padlocked doors into a room-size safe, to see the fabulous Crown Jewels. Here I enjoyed the improbable experience of dabbling my fingers in bowls of emeralds and dishes of diamonds, while admiring the fantastic Peacock Throne, over-ornamented with gems and gold-embroidered cushions.

From Teheran, on the return leg of my travels, I went to

1. See p. 178, and the report of Guy Mountfort's Jordan Expedition.

Baghdad, preceded by official documents, saw the appropriate Ministers, and discharged my duties. As a result, Iraq too promised their support for the Conference.

There was time for a quick trip to Ctesiphon, now only a lonely, ruined arch in the desert. Rollers were flying about, which pleased me enormously. Isaiah prophesied that owls would nest in the ruins of Babylon; he doubtless was right, but these daylight inhabitants of the great vault were much more brilliant, and lived up to their name with their aerial acrobatics. They were also a welcome addition to my world bird-list. So were the bee-eaters, perched on telegraph wires or hawking for insects – most elegantly-tailored of creatures, with brilliant colours and long, pointed tails.

After Baghdad came Cairo, where I had an entertaining experience. Russell Pasha, the head of Narcotic Drugs Control, was also a keen ornithologist. I was talking to him about Egyptian birds when an attendant brought me a card from a young son of a prominent family of another Middle Eastern country, who, I happened to know, was engaged in extensive drug-smuggling. I was amused to see how his face fell when I introduced him to the redoubtable Pasha.

Next morning I got up before breakfast to explore the city. From the main street, lined with expensive shops and with splendid mosques near by, I turned into a stinking side-alley. Never had I seen such terrible slums (Calcutta, worst of all, was still in store). I had my camera with me, but had not used it in this wretched place, when a man came up to me, and after making some rude noises in Arabic, fetched a policeman, who hauled me off to the nearest police station. There I was told I had broken a law forbidding photography in Cairo. I eventually got permission to telephone to the Under-Secretary for Education, Egypt's representative on UNESCO's Executive Board. He seemed amused by my disagreeable predicament, but told me there were no regulations against photography, and got me released in time for a late breakfast.

Just outside Cairo, I was taken to see a remarkable experiment by Habib Georgi, Chief Inspector of Art in the Ministry of Education. At his special school, village children were encouraged to develop their own artistic talents with a minimum of formal teaching: I was much struck by the freshness and originality of their productions. As I had already seen in Haiti, and was later to find in East Africa (and, indeed, in my own country), there is a vast, untapped reservoir of artistic – and intellectual – talent among 'primitive' and poverty-stricken communities, only waiting for an opportunity to manifest itself.

In spite of the Government's many valuable social and educational projects, the spectre of over-population threatened Egypt and the living standards of its people. What the country needed above all else was a comprehensive campaign for birth-control. Today, two decades later, it needs it even more urgently. The population has already caught up with the new resources made available by the Aswan Dam, and in spite of Nasser's reforms (and also because of the costly war with Israel), the Egyptian future looks grim.[1]

A more cheerful visit was to the great Nile Barrage, which provides irrigation for the fertile Delta. In the well-kept grounds, with their beautiful, blue-flowered jacarandas, a mass of white blossom crowning a group of trees suddenly revealed itself as animal, not vegetable – a flock of pure white egrets resting in the branches. Rarely have I seen anything so miraculous as this flowering of snowy birds among the greenery, under the bluest of blue skies.

My last port of call before the Conference was Tunisia. There, after my formal visits, I was taken to see the Great Mosque of Kairouan, the oldest university in the world, older than El Azhem in Cairo or the teaching mosques of Morocco, and for many centuries the main teaching centre of Islamic law, literature and mathematics. But now it had degenerated into a simple Koranic school: I saw a teacher sitting against one of the pillars of the splendid mosque 'teaching' a group of Berber children to recite the Koran by rote. However, there were some attempts at improvement: classrooms round the great Court had been provided with blackboards and chalk. I realized what an immense step forward the addition of visual to oral methods had meant.

1. Today, 1971, it remains to be seen how President Sadat, Nasser's successor, will succeed in his proposed reforms, and if he will avoid a renewal of war with Israel.

Since then, with UNESCO's aid, considerable further progress has been made in the country's educational system, culminating in a modern university.

No sooner had I got back from that hasty visit than I was sent, accompanied by Juliette and Jacques Havet, the brilliant young head of UNESCO's Philosophy section, on a hurried tour through central and eastern Europe.

We began with Czechoslovakia, and in Prague I met Jan Belehradek, who had worked with me at King's College, London. Though now Rector of Charles University, he was under suspicion because of his espousal of freedom of speech – and his Western connections. He accompanied me in the 'official' car, containing two members of the secret police, anxious to overhear all we said. We kept off controversial subjects, but not long afterwards he was deprived of his position and forced into exile. I was fortunately able to find him a post first in UNESCO, later in the research section of a London hospital.

From Prague, we made a delightful trip to Brno (Brunn), where the Abbé Mendel had made his famous experiments in crossing pea varieties, which laid the foundations of modern genetics.

Next on our list was Hungary, where the highlight of our visit was an excursion to Lake Balaton, ostensibly to see its hydrobiological research station, but also as an occasion for an official lunch, at which I met eminent writers and musicians, including Kodály. Among our hosts were the charming Education Minister, Molnar, the (to me) unpleasant character Rakosi, and other members of the government. Rakosi was short and stocky, with a bald head on a very short neck, beady eyes and thick lips. He had spent twelve years in solitary confinement and suffered horrible cruelties. He made light enough of them that day in the sun, but they were never forgotten; when he became powerful, he visited unbelievable tortures on his victims, and only just escaped with his life during the counter-revolution.

Our third country was Yugoslavia, where we found many changes since our visit in the 1930s. All the squabbling provinces had been united, at least nominally, into a single

Republic under Tito My old zoologist friend Stampar was now Minister of Education, and the country was peaceful, anxious to escape from subjection to the USSR through contacts with the West. The terrible destruction of the Second World War, and of the civil war within it, was being vigorously dealt with by squads of young people of both sexes; libraries and laboratories were being restocked, and some 'free enterprise' was being encouraged. The authorities welcomed the Conference as a possible bridge between communist and capitalist ideas, and nominated Stampar as chief delegate.

Finally, we made a quick stop in Vienna, where I secured the adherence of the new Austrian Republic to UNESCO, and a promise that it would send a delegate to the Beirut Conference.

We got back to Paris just in time for a Conference on Nature Conservation at Fontainebleau, which followed up the decision of principle, that UNESCO should concern itself with nature conservation policy, by establishing IUCN, the International Union for the Conservation of Nature, as an agency affiliated to the organization. IUCN has since done a great deal for nature conservation in many parts of the world – setting up new national parks in Latin America, aiding those in Africa and helping ecological research on wild life, as well as co-operating with conservation bodies in the USA, Germany, and elsewhere.

In late August of 1948 came a strange visit to Poland. I had been invited by Boresza, a smooth-tongued Polish politician, to attend a conference 'Des Intellectuels pour la Paix'. Writers, scientists and artists from all over the world were to meet at Wroclaw (new name for Breslau) and were, he assured us, to debate in freedom and friendship the possibilities of cultural rapprochement between the two sides of the Iron Curtain. After our recent experiences in eastern Europe, I was well aware of the necessity for this, and still simple-minded enough to believe that the two sides had only to get together to achieve worthwhile results. The Executive Board reluctantly granted me permission, though only as a private person, not as representing UNESCO.

Juliette and I set out from Paris in an ancient war-plane, together with a number of left-wing sympathizers, including Ivor

Montagu, the physicist Desmond Bernal, the historian A. J. P. Taylor, J. G. Crowther, Edward Carter, head of UNESCO's section on libraries, Kingsley Martin of the *New Statesman*, Lord Boyd-Orr, late Director-General of the UN Food and Agriculture Organization, Dr Hewlett Johnson, the 'Red Dean', Joseph Needham (from UNESCO's staff), Hyman Levy, a mathematician from Britain; Joe Davidson, Martha Gellhorn, and a few other US citizens; some Latin Americans; and a large French group, including Fernand Léger, the painter, the great Picasso, the Joliot-Curies, so eminent in atomic physics, and the poet Eluard.

Wroclaw was a picturesque old city, and the Conference was held in the Magna Aula of its ancient University. The place was full to the brim; three-quarters of the benches were occupied by primed representatives of Russia and her satellites, the remaining section by the non-communist delegates. We 'westerners' attended the first session in hopeful anticipation. However, the communist bloc speedily displayed its real intentions, which were simply to denigrate Western culture. Fadeyev's opening speech set the tone: 'If hyenas could type, and jackals use fountain-pens, they would write such things as the so-called poetry of T. S. Eliot and Auden.' This and other similar utterances were wildly applauded by the communist crowd.

Bernal, though an ardent communist, was surprised at the turn of events, but tried to restore our spirits by assuring us that this was a harmless letting-off of fireworks, and that we would soon really discuss Peace. In the afternoon, A. J. P. Taylor made a spirited and refreshing reply to the morning's attacks, but his speech was drowned with boos from the opposing bloc.

Ilya Ehrenburg, in spite of his friendly reception by French intellectuals during his exile from the USSR, made another vitriolic attack on Western culture, and refused to leave the rostrum when I pointed out, as Chairman of the session, that he had exceeded the twenty minutes allowed for speeches. He simply turned to the audience and asked what he should do: of course they roared 'Go on!' I wish now that I had stepped down from the chair, and had not lacked the courage to do so. I shall always think of Kingsley Martin with gratitude; egged on by Juliette, he was the only person who supported me.

The Congress gave a frightening display of the power of doctrinaire opinion in a cultural confrontation. Stampar told me privately that he was there 'by order' of the Kremlin, to toe the Party Line. He was as disgusted as we at the turn of events, but knew that it was both useless and dangerous to protest.

Juliette asked Léger, a non-political artist, why he had joined the communists. He replied that he had wanted to give Soviet painters and sculptors a chance to come to Paris and share in the modern movement in painting and sculpture. Yet he must have known that the USSR only permitted 'socialist realism' in the arts as well as in literature.

Picasso was braver. As a member of the Party, he had been 'ordered' to paint in the way the Soviet authorities wanted. He just replied 'Merde!', and went on as before. He actually presented a collection of his lovely ceramic plates to the Prague Museum, and such was his prestige that they were accepted, though far from embodying 'socialist realism'.

I did not sign the final manifesto presented to the Congress. It omitted all references to the many causes of, or predispositions to war, and placed the blame for the present state of tension almost entirely on 'a handful of self-interested men in America and Western Europe, who have inherited fascist ideas of racial superiority and the denial of progress, and adopted fascist methods of solving all problems by force of arms.' Boresza was furious with me – his international prize had escaped his trap.

We left, profoundly discouraged by the intransigent attitude of the communist intelligentsia. As I wrote on my return to Paris in a statement to the Press:

The Congress, from the start, took a political turn; there was no real discussion, and the great majority of the speeches were either strictly Marxist analyses of current trends, or else polemical attacks on American and Western European policy and culture.

Purely political, or politico-economic matters, such as the Marshall Plan, the Atlantic Union, and imperial and colonial policy, were frequently brought in. No or negligible references were made to the United Nations or to the possibility of cultural, scientific and technical collaboration through the specialized UN Agencies, such as UNESCO, FAO and WHO.

This gathering of scientists and artists from many countries could have provided an opportunity for reconciling, in the intellectual and cultural sphere, what may be broadly called the Eastern and Western points of view. I can only express my regret that the opportunity was not taken.

Nevertheless, when the USSR at last adhered to UNESCO, and (very properly) obtained a seat on the Executive Board, we continued to try for more cultural exchanges, more freedom for tourists from tiresome restrictions, and did our best to meet the objections to certain parts of UNESCO's History of Mankind made by the very pleasant Russian historian on the History's steering Committee – of course at the behest of the official Soviet Academy of Sciences, which included Historical Science in its purview.

From Wroclaw we made an excursion to Cracow, in charge of a spy-guide. Cracow's old castle had been well restored (the restoration of ancient monuments is, curiously enough, one of the activities most zealously pursued in communist countries). The sunny banks dominating the Vistula were studded with groups of chess-players, who had set up their boards on convenient outcrops of rock. Chess seemed to be the one activity without ideological connotations. (I was right – the communist countries regularly take part in international chess tournaments, and their teams are often among the most successful.)

I wanted to see the Pianiny Nature Reserve, further down the river, where a few of the scarce European bison had survived (the same species as that depicted in the cave paintings of prehistoric man at Altamira and Lascaux), together with porcupines and other interesting animals.

We embarked in an extraordinary craft – two canoes lashed together by boards, like a catamaran. We needed all its extra stability, for we soon found ourselves hurtling down a series of rapids. In the smooth water beyond, we were surprised to see children up to their waists in the river, holding arches of flower-embellished greenery for us to glide through. Our guide told us this was a ritual to bring luck to newly-married couples embarked on the troubled waters of matrimony – and also to greet distinguished visitors. We appreciated the honour, but were

59

sorry for the children, blue with cold, and threw them all our small change.

We saw very few wild animals; but today, IUCN reports that a considerable herd of bison survives here, and that Nature Conservation flourishes in Poland.

CHAPTER 4

The Beirut Conference – and Farewells

AT last, in early November, we were on our way to Beirut, via Constantinople, where the Executive Board was meeting to make final decisions on the agenda for the Conference.

It was snowing – a rare event in this temperate area. A group of us, including Beebe, the amusing Education Minister and UNESCO delegate from New Zealand, were staying at a hotel overlooking the Bosphorus. But apart from a couple of quick dashes into the snow-covered streets, we were reduced to lying on our backs on sofas in the hotel lounge, looking up at the double row of convex skylights in the roof. Beebe said it felt like being inside a gigantic sow.

For want of anything better to do, I began making up limericks. The following was composed ('in dejection', according to my note) on 11 November 1948:

THE RESTIVE AND
GROANING BOARD

On the beautiful shores of the Bosphorus,
Our Board's being rather prepospherous:
   It is wasting its time
   By the Porte called Sublime –
In fact on the whole it's a loss for us.

It has got to elect a new boss for us,
If Unesco's to be really prospherous –
   A man with a spark
   Who will shine in the dark,
With a glow like the purest of phosphorus.

It was indeed the Board's duty to propose to the Conference someone to succeed me as Director-General. My limerick, though ingenious, was not very good; but it correctly foreshadowed trouble to come. When the matter arose at Beirut, I heard a rumour that the Board intended to put forward one of its own members (however, I have since learnt that the Americans and other important nations had withdrawn their support from this candidate). Meanwhile, I and others pleaded that Dr Jaime Torres-Bodet from Mexico should be invited. The Board had not officially dealt with him at the Mexico Conference, for he had been promoted from Minister of Education to Head of the Foreign Office. Those who had met him formed a very high opinion of his qualities, and the Board eventually cabled him. He arrived and was rightly elected as UNESCO's second D.G.

On later visits to Paris, I found that he was doing well, though perhaps too shy to be popular with the staff. The counterpart of his personal shyness was his pride in UNESCO, and his self-assurance in the rightness of his views. He twice put forward budgetary demands so large that the Board had to reject them, and both times threatened to resign if his requests for increased expenditure, especially on education, were not met. The second time the Board took him at his word and accepted his resignation. Since then, of course, with UNESCO's increased staff and activities, the Budget has inevitably soared upwards.

It was a pity that after four successful years Torres-Bodet had to go; for he was a highly cultivated man, a poet in his own right, and keen on helping the under-dog all over the world. He can never have heard of the Duke of Wellington's famous advice to a British official: 'Never apologize, and never resign.'

On retirement from UNESCO, he was made Mexican Ambassador to France. Later, I took the opportunity of calling on him. As I expected, he found more pleasure in his diplomatic work than in the hurly-burly of UNESCO – and was able to give more time to his own writing.

I happened to be in Paris when the Board was electing his successor. To my surprise it chose Luther Evans, one of its own members. Like Archie Macleish, he had been Librarian of Congress in Washington, but in contrast to Macleish, a sensitive and cultured man, he was a stentorian and practical-minded Texan character. He was, however, intelligent, willing to take advice and followed a sensible policy as D.G.

I am glad to say that the original ban on French candidates for the top post has now been abrogated and that the present

Director-General, René Maheu, is a brilliant and indefatigable Frenchman, deeply interested in every aspect of UNESCO's many-sided programme. His indefatigability has just been demonstrated by his accepting a second five-year term of office.

To revert to 1948, at the Beirut Conference there was a curious side-effect of having all documents printed in the language of the host country as well as in English and French. The symbol of the organization was a temple, whose six pillars were represented by the elongated letters UNESCO, with a simple pediment above. In the Arabic equivalent, however, the letters had curious, crooked shapes, so that the pillars were all cockeyed, and the symbolic edifice looked as if it were collapsing. The real UNESCO was, of course, in no danger of collapsing; but the official use of Arabic, and the presence of delegates from so many Arab countries, foreshadowed difficulties in this troubled region.

Sure enough, at the opening session the Arab delegates protested against the presence of a couple of Israelis in the hall. Only after the President of the Conference, backed by myself, had pointed out that UNESCO was by definition an international organization, and that Israel, despite Arab hostility, was *de facto* a nation, was order restored and the Israelis allowed to remain – but only as observers, not full delegates entitled to vote.

This minor incident was a foretaste of major disaster in the Middle East, with Arab hostility confronting Israeli defiance and culminating in two wars. As I write, the future of the region hangs in the balance. Though I sympathize with most of Israel's claims, especially its insistence on recognition as a nation-state, I also feel deeply for the plight of the Muslim Palestinian refugees. In common with many others, I deeply wish for a stable peace, and proper conditions of co-existence.

At the Conference, we had a gruelling agenda. I only managed to survive by taking advantage of the midday break to go swimming on the lovely beach of the Baie des Pigeons, lunching on fresh-caught crabs and fish at a little restaurant below the cliffs, and then dozing in the sun with the wild rock-doves flying overhead.

My most difficult task was to persuade the Conference to implement the proposals for a History of Mankind (see p. 49), to be undertaken by UNESCO itself, laying stress on the cultural achievements of the human race, and dealing with war and politics only in so far as they influenced cultural and scientific progress.

Eventually it was decided to set up a Commission of experts to supervise the task, with my old friend and colleague Carneiro, a physiologist by profession, as Chairman, with a secretariat and budget of its own, paid from UNESCO funds, and to appoint author-editors for each volume. It also had the power to appoint corresponding members almost *ad libitum*, who could provide specialized information on obscure subjects, and help in adjudicating on the disputes over facts (and still more over their interpretation) which were bound to arise between partisans of different ideological systems. The USSR were now full members of UNESCO, and rightly claimed representation on the Commission.

I might add that the enterprise has been on the whole very successful. The difficulty over objections has been obviated by printing an abstract of them in each chapter; though some, especially from the Russian Academy of Historical Sciences, have been of inordinate length, the objectors have agreed to cut them down to manageable proportions.

Although the work was hampered by the premature death of two of its author-editors, Dr Frankfurter and Professor Turner, the Commission has published in English all the six volumes agreed upon, abundantly illustrated with maps, pictures and photographs; and I have just received the sumptuously prepared French version. Work is in progress on editions in other languages, including Spanish, Russian, Serbo-Croat, Hebrew, Arabic, Dutch and Japanese.

I served on the Commission as Vice-President from the outset, and can testify to the hard work put in by its members, especially by Carneiro, who as Chairman had the difficult task not only of keeping order when disagreements occurred, but of screwing money year by year out of UNESCO's Budgetary Commission; and also by Professor Ralph Turner of Yale, rightly recommended by the US as Editor-in-Chief, who was largely responsible for the general tone and universalist approach of the Commission – this in spite of (or perhaps because of!) occasional bursts of temper when his ideas were opposed. He was unfortunately cut off in his prime.

At the weekends the Lebanese arranged excursions for us. These escapes from the heavy routine of the Conference were both a refreshment and a catalyst for members of the staff and also for our hosts. They promoted not only relaxation but also better understanding between Unescans and Lebanese, giving the visitors fascinating insights into the ancient history of the region and its contemporary life.

Thus there was a delightful trip to Baalbek, where we had plenty of time to explore the ruins; also an unforgettable sight of the source of the Orontes, and Homs with its ancient *norias*, extraordinary, huge water-wheels filling the air with their creakings and splashings.

After the Conference, a friendly Lebanese lawyer took us to Tripoli to see dancing dervishes, for this was one of the few places where the famous sect had survived. After chanted prayers the dancers began to twirl to the sound of flutes and drumbeats. Throwing off their abbas to reveal white robes below, they started turning, pivoting on the left foot as they stepped round with the right. Their rotation became faster and the white skirts flared out in a whirling cone. The men had a rapt expression on their faces; sometimes they varied their performance by making a graceful dip at each turn or throwing out their arms in striking gestures.

The twirling went on for over an hour, with an occasional rest for some of the dancers, yet somehow the ceremony never became boring, and we remained fascinated by their reiterated and stylized movements and the hypnotically recurrent pulse of the music. I was reminded of the ritualized displays of non-human creatures, of birds cementing the pair-bond or affirming territorial rights; here they seemed to unite a group in shared ceremonial.

It was an eye-opener to see how these strange rituals could help in providing ordinary men with an escape from their humdrum, everyday life into a state of mystic exaltation. What will emerge in the modern world to take their place is hard to see. Some take refuge in the heady wine of nationalism; but this, as the Arab–Israeli wars have demonstrated, can lead to mass confrontation and horrible results. Others find their escape in hallucinogens, like heroin and lysergic acid; but these can result in mental discomfort, physical damage and spiritual disaster.

The majority of human beings, of course, are concerned with the stark business of keeping alive; many are absorbed in acquiring material riches. This was often so in the highly commercialized society of Beirut. We came across one example at a luxurious lunch given by a prominent businessman. The conversation turned to race-horses, and Juliette asked her host if he kept a stud. 'Not I,' replied the portly gentleman. 'I prefer carpets' – pointing to a splendid one on the wall. 'They don't eat anything, and every year their value goes up a nice little bit ...'

An official visit was paid to Damascus, where the Executive Board were received by the Syrian President himself. Juliette alleges that I behaved in a very unprotocolaire – or should it be unprotocolic? – manner. It was extremely hot, so, ignoring the row of photographers and officials lined up to receive us, I calmly took off my jacket and waistcoat, just as the President was stepping forward to shake my hand. However, neither he nor anybody else appeared to mind – and I certainly was much more comfortable.

On another occasion, Kemal Jumblatt, a cultivated young Druze chief, already prominent in Lebanese politics (he now occupies some important official position), invited us to his castle at Mukhtara, high up in the mountains. The Druzes practise an esoteric semi-Islamic religion, based on the notion that God had revealed Himself to man in a series of seventy incarnations, the latest in the eleventh century.

The fortress stood impressively on a high rocky bastion. We were ushered through a formidable portcullised gateway into a gallery cut in the solid rock, and lined with armed Druzes. They burst into song as we passed through their ranks, while in the hall above a group of buglers announced us with medieval fanfares.

In the courtyard was a great assembly of Druzes, who linked

arms to perform in our honour one of their slow traditional dances, chanting their greetings. Then I was introduced to a group of Druze sages. There are grades of these, and one had reached the highest pinnacle of Druze wisdom – he knew all the seven Sacred Books by heart. In lieu of a tiara, he wore an enormous white turban crowning his dignified and saintly face.

He engaged me in philosophical discussion. 'Do you in England venerate Aflatoun and Aristo as we do here?' he asked. Luckily I knew that Aflatoun was the Arabic transliteration of Plato; and Aristo clearly meant Aristotle. Of course, I said, we all knew their works, but I, as a scientist, preferred Aristo. 'No, honoured Sir, you are wrong', he replied. 'Aristo merely copied from Aflatoun, while Aflatoun knew everything that was to be known, and set it all down in seventy tomes.' I was fascinated to find how legends grow.

We were interrupted by Jumblatt, who announced that, as climax to my welcome, I was to be 'chaired' round the courtyard, standing on the shoulders of Druze warriors. This was extremely precarious. I found it very difficult to maintain a dignified posture with my feet bridging the gap between a pair of moving shoulders, even with the aid of a couple of sword-hilts thrust into my hands by two other soldiers. It was a great relief when I dismounted without crashing on to the stone pavement.

Then it was Jumblatt's turn. Although he must have been used to this alarming ordeal, I was not sorry to see that he wobbled even more than I.

We left, feeling that we had been vouchsafed a glimpse into the traditional customs of an ancient tribal sect just entering the portals of modernity.

Our most extraordinary expedition from Beirut took place immediately after the Conference. This was when the Lebanese chartered a couple of aircraft to take the whole UNESCO staff to the ruins of Palmyra, half-way to the Euphrates across the great desert.

A vast spread of apricot-coloured stone pillars and arches marked the site of the ancient city, showing how important it must have been as a point of interchange for the caravans crossing the desert in every direction – a fabulous place, beautiful even in decay.

As I rambled through the ruins, I was startled by a flock of sandgrouse – my first sight of these remarkable desert birds, who supply their fledglings with water by wetting their breasts in the rare springs where they drink, and letting the young suck the water off their feathers on their return.

I got so interested in watching them that a search party had to be sent out to find me. Our planes were strictly forbidden to fly after dusk, but I had lingered so long that only one plane was able to take off; the other plane-load had to spend the night at Palmyra. I was told afterwards that the ruins in the moonlight were indescribably beautiful, and no one regretted their enforced stay.

On the last day of the Conference, Juliette and I were invited to dine by the British Delegation, headed by David Harland. He complimented me on my work for UNESCO, making me feel that I had done something worthwhile in launching that cumbersome organization on a reasonably successful career. Finally, Sir John Maud launched forth on one of his inimitable imitations, this time of an egregious Latin-American delegate, reciting the Preamble to UNESCO's constitution, with 'porpoise' replacing 'purpose', and with a physiological substitute for 'peace', which made the party extremely hilarious. He turned what might have been a sad farewell into an uproarious and memorable evening. Dear John! His combination of deep seriousness with farcical humour was – and still is – irresistible.

My formal duties were now over, and we had ten days to ourselves before moving to Cairo, on a tour offered to the Board and chief delegates. So I hired a car, and we indulged in the care-free pleasure of exploring Syria.

We pushed on as far as Aleppo – a rightly famous city. It contains a fortress of Hittite date perched on a rocky acropolis, built long before Abraham pastured his flocks on the flanks of this very hill. The fortress had been repaired many times; the latest alteration was made during the Crusades, when Saladin added a formidable glacis and a multiple gateway. The approach was up a steep ramp, the main gate hugely massive, its stone doors reinforced with iron clamps.

Here I had an ornithological surprise. A wall-creeper, a bird which I thought was confined to high mountains (I had seen one in the Alps years before), was jerking its way up the face of the huge outer wall, probing the crevices for tiny insects, at each upward step flicking its wings to reveal a patch of deep crimson on their mouse-brown surface — an unexpected flash of living beauty on a grim building.

Our guide, a young Armenian who had learnt excellent English and French in the local American College, took us to see the museum. This had a fine collection of strange clay figures, representing bird-faced female deities. But the most impressive objects were a couple of Hittite statues from about 1200 B.C., an over-size god and goddess hewn out of black basalt, with gleaming white shell-fragments for eyes, crude-featured and staring. The effect was of harsh, dark powers, malevolently brooding — visible embodiments of the cruel Hittite religion, which demanded human victims in its sacrificial rituals, just as Baal did in Phoenicia and its outposts.

Most religions, I reflected, are strangely ambivalent. Some gods and goddesses protect their worshippers from danger, others persecute the violators of taboos and sacred laws. Some religions deify human sexuality, male and female, while others worship the mother's fertility. Christianity had to bring in an ancient mother-goddess, in the shape of the Virgin Mary, and the Confessional as an escape from the Furies of conscience or the guilt of breaking religiously-backed taboos. Some cults deify animals and trees, even springs and volcanoes, and all demand some form of sacrifice, even if this has come to be symbolic, as in the burning of incense, or in the denial of pleasure; and all claim to be in sole possession of *The Truth* ...

'What is Truth?' said Jesting Pilate — and so did I, as I looked at these baleful effigies (and later at the self-torture of Indian fakirs). Even the Buddhist idea of the gradual approach of the soul through reincarnations to Nirvana, spiritual bliss free from all human cares, puts the *nothingness* of total detachment as its main goal.

I personally can see no escape from the diversity of conflicting creeds and inner moral and emotional claims — except in some form of humanism, which dismisses all rigid dogma; all ethical and intellectual absolutes, bombinating in their perfectionist vacua; all narcissistic self-deification, of individuals or nations; all personified divinities; and puts in their place the ever-receding goal of improvement of the human lot, and the greater fulfilment of individual human beings, through thought and art.

We flew to Egypt with some relief. The Board had a final meeting in Cairo; but I was now free from the cares of office. The first day we spent in Cairo Museum, where the party was shown round by the brilliant Frenchman Abbé Drioton, then head of Egypt's Department of Archaeology. He warned us that he would show us nothing but the very best, and therefore managed, in less than two hours, to show us a series of incredible treasures, perfect specimens of their kind. Even the well-known and rather decadent grave-furniture of Tutankhamun's tomb revealed new qualities under his expertise.

In the many reliefs and frescoes found in royal tombs, there were often scenes of the chase, the sport which the Pharaohs expected to pursue in the after-world. As an ornithologist, I was able to identify most of the birds, notably pintail ducks, and even a solitary red-breasted goose. These beautiful birds, patterned in russet and black, with strange designs outlined in white on neck and wings, breed only on the Siberian tundras in northern Russia, though they migrate south to Persia and the Hungarian lowlands. (I had secured a few from Peter Scott when I was at the Zoo, and had established a small breeding colony at Whipsnade – they still flourish today.) But what were they doing in Egypt? Perhaps it was an offering from one of Egypt's tributary kings in northern Syria or Persia – who knows?

This ancient and ingrown civilization, the Abbé told us, had many strange customs besides mummifying their pet (but divine) cats, their hawks and baboons, their sacred bulls and ibises. His most bizarre piece of information was that they prepared *pâté de foie gras* from hyenas' livers, slaves being entrusted with the unpleasant task of stuffing the unfortunate creatures, their legs bound, with the livers of geese and ducks ...

After a few days back in Beirut, winding up my affairs with UNESCO, we left in early January for home. We went via Athens, to stay with our old friends, Sir Clifford Norton, the British Ambassador, and his energetic wife Peter, a great lover of art, both classical and contemporary. It was a wonderful experience, enriched with unforgettable expeditions, some of which I described in *From an Antique Land*.

From there, we went on to see Reinhardt Dohrn at the Naples Aquarium. We had hoped to bask in sunshine, but it was an exceptional winter and we shivered in our hotel rooms. Tired by UNESCO and much travel – and mostly by the re adaptation required in my life – I began to feel depressed. We revisited several places in Italy, but the heart had gone out of our travels, and all we wanted was to get home. We left for Paris and a last week of farewells; and also for the presentation, by my old staff at UNESCO, of a lovely little gouache by Braque, which hangs today in our dining-room, a happy reminder of my friendly and zealous colleagues.

This marked the end of a strenuous two and a half years of being, in the words of Lord Reith, 'fully stretched out'. I had had to call on capacities I hardly knew I possessed – powers of co-ordination and conciliation, essential in a community of such diverse interests; quick understanding and resilience; initiative, even against opposition; and above all, faith that what I was aiming at was right, or at least in the right direction.

I was tired, but much cheered by various praiseful letters. Thus John Maud wrote that the Government representatives on the British Commission for UNESCO wished to put on re cord that I 'had done a tremendous job, against appalling odds', since I first came to preside over UNESCO, three years before. Milton Eisenhower, brother of the American President, and Chairman of the US National Commission for UNESCO, wrote:

Speaking for myself and my colleagues, I wish to express profound gratitude for the inspiring leadership you brought to UNESCO ... I hope and trust that UNESCO has not entirely lost the use of your remarkable talents, and that I may have the pleasure of working with you in the future on UNESCO matters. I want particularly to express my gratitude for your Report on the activities of the Organization in 1948. Your 'general survey' aroused great enthusiasm in the American delegation – it was a remarkably stimulating and challenging statement.

And from the Board's Vice-Chairman, Dr Sarvepelli Radhakrishnan, philosopher-statesman (who later became President of India): 'The Board will shortly take an appropriate opportunity to express to you in public the deep appreciation of your great service to UNESCO. Meanwhile I would like to assure you how deeply grateful to you all Members of the Board feel.'

I was particularly touched to receive a letter at Christmas 1970, more than twenty years after I had left, from a charming woman staff-member, in which she wrote: 'I shall never forget the first exciting and happy years of UNESCO under your leadership.'

That I had helped to guide UNESCO in the right direction was proved, I think, by its subsequent activities. These have included: a much intensified programme of technical aid, especially in education and the arts, to so-called underdeveloped countries; UNESCO's initiative in helping to preserve Egyptian antiquities, notably those threatened by the rising waters behind the Aswan Dam; its efforts to save Venice from rotting into the sea, rising steadily as the city's foundations sink and the ice-caps melt; the translation of great literary works into other languages; UNESCO's share in the International Biological Programme and in UN's World Conservation Year; and the proposal at a recent Conference (1970) of a long-term programme on Man and the Biosphere – in other words, conservation. This, like other previously mentioned projects, sprang from the International Union for the Conservation of Nature (p. 56). In addition, there have been the special reports, carried out with the aid of other UN Agencies, on Man against Disease (written by Lord Ritchie-Calder); on Man and the Desert, a study on how to prevent the world's deserts from spreading, and how to utilize their agricultural and mineral potential; on Man in the Humid Tropics, where life is a constant struggle against the expanding jungle; and, as I have already mentioned, an ever-increasing commitment, again in conjunction with other

UN bodies, to the problem of over-population and how to deal with it.

There was also, of course, UNESCO's *History of the Scientific and Cultural Development of Mankind*, and the journal, *World History*, which supplements the *History* itself. Nor must I forget UNESCO's other publications, especially the *Courier*, which each month explains and comments on some important UNESCO project.

The record is cheering. UNESCO is not just talking; it is continuing to do things that need doing, to create new organizations that need to be created. This is largely due to the energy of René Maheu, who rose from a minor position in 'my' UNESCO, to become its first French Director-General. He has infused new life into its cumbersome machine.

CHAPTER 5

Home: New Tasks and Old Friends

BACK in London in the spring of 1949, after UNESCO's multifarious bustle, I wondered at first how I should fill my days. However, I soon found that there was almost as much to do at home. I was at once made a member of the British Commission on UNESCO, which decided what projects the British would support at later Conferences, and discussed and commented on UNESCO's activities and plans.

I had also been appointed Vice-President of the Commision dealing with UNESCO's Cultural History of Mankind, whose frequent meetings in Paris I now began to attend. I secured Leonard Woolley and Jacquetta Hawkes as co-authors of the work's first volume, on pre-history and the dawn of civilization. Knowing them personally, I was sure that they would produce a fine work which would set the standard for further volumes, and my faith was justified.

Meanwhile, I did my best to catch up with my biological interests, by attending meeting of various scientific societies – the Royal, the Genetical, the Zoological, the Eugenic, and that for Experimental Biology (which I had helped to found nearly thirty years earlier), not to mention those concerned with Ecology and Ornithology.

With the support of scientific naturalists like Peter Scott and Charles Elton, I helped to put Ecology on the biological map by founding an Ecological Society, which would lay the scientific basis for conservation in Britain. I also attended meetings of the Nature Conservancy, ably headed by my friend Cyril Diver, who was later succeeded by another friend, Max Nicholson. And with Thorpe and Hinde at Cambridge, I played a part in founding a society for the Study of Animal Behaviour (or Ethology, as it is technically called). It was a triumph for this branch of scientific natural history when, some fifteen years later, the Royal Society asked me to organize an International Symposium on Ritualization in Animals and Man (p. 217). It was also a personal joy for me, as I had been the first to use the term *ritualization* in analysing the display behaviour of the great-crested grebe, half a century earlier.

Besides this, there were meetings of the editorial board of Collins' *New Naturalist* publications, with ever new subjects to consider. We have now issued fifty general volumes, and twenty monographs on single species; recently, we brought out a timely volume on pollution, and we are anxiously awaiting the completion of one on Pollination of Flowering Plants – a subject which interested Darwin so deeply, and where so many strange adaptations have been discovered.

I also became editorial consultant for another publishing firm, Adprints, to advise on a remarkable illustrated encyclopaedia, not alphabetically arranged, like most encyclopaedias, but dealing with a different major subject in each successive volume. The three other consultants were all old friends – James Fisher for birds and field natural history,[1] Bronowski for physics and chemistry, and Gerald Barry, knowledgeable in arts and crafts and museum techniques. In spite of long hours of proof-reading, I enjoyed having my nose poked into subjects other than biology and learnt a great deal from our discussions and the resulting volumes.

I often went down to Oxford, to enlist men like Ronald Syme, the historian, as a further member of the advisory panel for UNESCO's Cultural History of Mankind; to see the brilliant talker and writer David Cecil, now Professor of English literature; and to look up old friends like Alec Smith, now Warden of New College (who had restored the Library and secured some fine medieval figures, removed from the University Church of St Mary's for safety's sake, to adorn the College's beautiful cloisters). There were also, of course, old pupils to see, like Hardy, Ford, Baker and Elton, as well as new members of the zoological staff, notably Niko Tinbergen, Professor of Animal Behaviour, which in my time at Oxford was left to amateurs, and Bernard Kettlewell, who was busy proving that the normal mottled camouflage of the pepper moth, *Biston betularia*, was being replaced in industrial areas by a black

1. In December 1970, the sad news was reported of the death of this fine all-round naturalist in a car crash.

melanic mutant, which gave better concealment on smoke-darkened tree-trunks. (I once helped him to collect pepper moths in a London square; as expected, we found a high proportion of melanics.)

On one of these visits, Alister Hardy approached me to discuss the scope of a memorial volume of essays by various of my old pupils and colleagues, and persuaded me to write a general introduction. It was to be presented on my 65th birthday, with the title *Evolution and Ethics*. I much appreciated the compliment, and what is more, the volume itself was a valuable contribution to evolutionary biology, from a number of different angles.

It was not long before I was off on another journey. In mid-June 1949, accompanied by James Fisher, we went to Iceland at the Government's invitation, with the agreeable duty of touring the island, to see what they were doing about conservation, and with the sole obligation of giving a lecture on the subject in Reykjavik.

Reykjavik may be small and remote, but it was and still is highly civilized. It had more book-shops in relation to its size than any other capital city (perhaps because of the long winter nights), and excellent theatres – indeed, there were two different performances of *Hamlet* during our visit.

There was little to remind one of its original Viking conquerors, only the medieval Danish of the language and the old custom, lost everywhere else in Europe, of having no enduring surnames, but only patronymics, changing each generation. How they managed to keep official records and to construct directories, I do not know; but they did. Reykjavik's other remarkable feature was its water-supply: not Company's water but, as Fisher and I nicknamed it, Devil's water, brought from a geyser ten miles off to fill our steaming baths. The island's volcanic heat was used in further ways. When we flew in, I had been puzzled by what looked like greenhouses dotting the barren lava desert. They really *were* greenhouses, heated by hot volcanic springs, and growing tomatoes and carnations – even peaches and bananas.

The university hall where I gave my lecture adjoined the

modern *Thing*, the old Norse name for the gathering of warrior-nobles who originally ran the island, which is retained for the highly modern and democratic Parliament of today.

The original *Thing* was held on the lake-shore in a cliff-bordered valley, a splendid site for a barbarian gathering. It reminded me of the African Rift, and Gudmunsson, our biologist host, told me that it was indeed a true rift valley, continuing the submarine rift in the Atlantic Ridge, which is steadily widening the distance between Europe and North America. The rifted ridge traverses the whole island, to submerge itself once more in a deep fjord leading to the Arctic Ocean.

Iceland aroused our ornithological interest. For one thing, it is the only spot where North American and North Eurasian birds (mostly water and marsh species) overlap. Further, as in other islands with no or few mammalian predators, the birds were almost all ground-nesters, and exceedingly tame. In Spitsbergen, I had had to push a red-throated diver off its nest with my foot. The same was true here for the eiders and other ducks, and the little red-necked phalaropes let us approach till we could have reached down and touched them, as they twirled in the shallows to stir up their tiny prey. In Spitsbergen, the small ground-nesters had to cope with foxes, which they did by luring them away from their nests, pretending to be wounded. Here, there were no indigenous predators, and the birds were even tamer.

Unfortunately, against Gudmunsson's advice, the Government had permitted the importation of mink, to be farmed for their pelts. As Gudmunsson prophesied, a few escaped – and naturally multiplied, taking advantage of the eiders' tameness to kill them on their nests, thus damaging the Icelanders' valuable trade in eiderdown, as well as preying on many species of lake-duck, whose eggs and flesh formed an important part of the local diet. I remembered Fiji and the mongooses; but here the financial (and biological) damage was even greater.

In the north, I heard a song which I could not identify. It was like a meadow pipit's, but with some melodious notes like those of its close relative, the tree-pipit; and the bird's song-flight began from a tree, not from the ground.

Actually, the birds *were* all meadow-pipits, taking advantage

77

of the tree-pipits' absence (they need a warmer climate) to adopt the safer perching habits of the tree-pipit. There was also no need for a sharply distinctive song to warn off rivals from a closely related species, so the Iceland meadow-pipit had reverted to a general pipit-type song, more varied than our meadow-pipit's, but without the tree-pipit's distinctive richness.

The climate, too, has had its effects on Iceland's life, both human and avian. When the Norsemen first colonized the island, in the seventh or eighth century, it was temperate enough to grow barley and oats. Then came the so-called Little Ice-age of late medieval times (when our own Thames froze solid and fairs were held on the ice), and the Icelanders had to live on mutton, fish and ducks, supplemented later by potatoes, brought originally from the Americas, via Ireland or perhaps Scotland.

However, since about 1900, the climate has become milder. As a result, a number of bird species have been added (or rather restored) to the island's fauna – tufted duck, three kinds of gull, starlings, coots and others; while old-established species of bird and plant are spreading northwards, and the only truly arctic bird, the little auk, has left its northern breeding grounds, as its fishy prey has moved further north, towards Greenland and Spitsbergen.

But perhaps the most startling evidence of warmer climate (apart from our own experience of heat right up to the Arctic Circle) was the sight of a painted-lady butterfly in northern Iceland, 1,500 miles north of its nearest breeding-place.

In the course of our tour, we reached the large duck-haunted lake called Myvatn. As we approached, Gudmunsson said, 'Look at the smokes' – grey columns rising all round the lake's margin. We wondered at this multiplicity of fires, but he was pulling our leg, for *Myvatn* means 'Midge-water' and the 'smokes' were columns of midges (luckily not biters) in their mating dance. There were clouds of them over the lake itself, and its surface was strewn with fallen midges. We witnessed the extraordinary spectacle of ducks, and even fish-eaters like grebes, forsaking their usual diet for this insect manna, while waders picked up the stranded corpses on the shore. Fisher and

I estimated that the midge population of Myvatn was several times greater than that of all mankind.

Here I had my first and only sight of the well-named harlequin duck, with its clown's pattern of bluish-black, russet and white stripes and crescents. Gudmunsson told us it was also called the torrent duck, and we soon saw why: though it nested on Myvatn's shores, it sought its food – I suppose mainly caddis-fly grubs – in the rushing waters of the stream that cascaded out of the lake. Myvatn enchanted us with its ducks and whooper swans, its Slavonian grebes and great northern divers, its herons and many waders; it had the most varied and abundant bird population that I have ever seen on a single sheet of water except perhaps on Lake Edward in Africa.

Birds can fly to Iceland; but how do plants reach it, plants like the sea-rocket, with its handsome lilac-blue flowers? It differs slightly from the north-European sub-species, but is identical with that found in north-east America and, strangely enough, in the Azores – perhaps the Gulf Stream has something to do with its distribution.

Later, in the Vestmann Islands off the south coast, Gudmunsson told us a curious piece of history. Pointing to the caves in the basalt cliffs above the little fishing town, he said it was there that the indigenous islanders took refuge from the Barbary pirates in search of slaves, while their Danish masters got safely away by ship. Strange to think of North African corsairs raiding the sub-arctic ...

Back on the mainland, we drove to Reykjavik through a hellish lava landscape. There was one final job to do – to count the gannets on the cliffs, for Fisher's world census of the species, interesting in itself, but also valuable in estimating fishery prospects.

At about this time, I had begun work on my book on the Middle East. It was based on my personal experiences when travelling for UNESCO, reinforced with much reading, and illustrated by my own photographs. It eventually appeared in 1954 with the title *From an Antique Land*, taken from Shelley's sonnet on Ozymandias. It seems to have supplied a need, for it is

79

still selling and a new edition is just being prepared. I wrote it with pleasure, hard work though it certainly was.

Among the public bodies with which I had been concerned was the Preparatory Committee on National Parks (as mentioned in Vol. I, p. 287).[1] This arose out of a report in 1945 by John Dower, whose widow later became a Member of the Commission. Now in 1949, it held its final meeting in Hobhouse's country house, and submitted its recommendations, which were accepted by the Government in April the following year. National Parks and Nature Reserves were originally the responsibility of the Ministry of Town and Country Planning, but they were later taken over by the Countryside Commission, dealing with all aspects of rural amenity and ecology. Today this is under the aegis of the newly-created Ministry for the Environment.

I was, of course, still going to Paris for meetings of the Commission for UNESCO's Cultural History of Mankind. This gave me an opportunity to meet old friends from UNESCO days, such as Princess Bibesco, 'princesse lointaine', a witty woman and entertaining writer; various members of my old staff; Roger Seydoux, ambitious and very able head of the French Delegation to UNESCO; our old friend George Raut, an expatriate Roumanian, who cooked us superb dinners in his treasure house in the Place Dauphine; and, naturally, the Julien Cains.

A little later, the new UNESCO House was finished, all glass and cement. Henry Moore's splendid marble figure reclined in front of it. There was also an eye-catching mosaic by Miro, gay-coloured; a mobile by Calder; and a curious sculpture by Arp. Near the boundary stood an extraordinary equestrian figure which Juliette naughtily said looked like me impersonating Don Quixote, tilting at international windmills. Inside the building was an enormous fresco by Picasso. We had all hoped he would produce something splendid, but this work I (and many others) felt was monstrous – over-large, grotesque, indecent, and without any relevance to UNESCO.

In spite of my profound admiration for Picasso's achieve-

1. All page references to Volume I refer to the hardback edition, published by George Allen & Unwin Ltd.

ments, I eventually plucked up courage to attack the work in a long letter to the *Manchester Guardian*, expressing my disillusionment. Of course, I was rapped over the knuckles by the 'faithful', but I was, and still am, unrepentant.

Family and friends – for us the two are virtually one – have always been a source of great delight. When George Trevelyan, the historian (married to my cousin Janet Ward), was Master of Trinity College, Cambridge, we much enjoyed staying there. After he retired in 1951, we were able to continue our visits, for he was succeeded by another friend, Professor Adrian (soon to become Lord Adrian O.M.).

Adrian was a truly extraordinary man, managing to combine the duties of the Mastership (which involved a good deal of entertaining as well as administration) with the Presidency of the Royal Society in London and later the Vice-Chancellorship of Cambridge – meanwhile bicycling to the Physiological Laboratory to continue his brilliant work on the nervous system, which had earned him a Nobel Prize nearly twenty years earlier.

Hester, his wife, was equally remarkable. They had both been keen mountaineers, until one day, with Adrian leading on a steep pitch, a piece of rock came off in his hand, and they both fell. One of Hester's legs was badly broken, and had to be amputated. Fitted with an artificial limb, she managed to keep up all her activities, including the strenuous one of extending hospitality to their many visitors, as well as acting as a J.P.

We recall with gratitude our many week-ends in the Master's Lodgings, sleeping in the great bed reserved for the Judge when he came on Assizes, and deeply enjoying the atmosphere of this happy house, with its many academic memories and its interesting guests. Incidentally, it was thanks to Adrian that I went to India as Kalinga Prizeman; but more of that later.

We often talked of having a cottage in the country, but never took the plunge; apart from the complications of a dual household, we were always being invited to stay with friends. I recall many such happy visits to Dartington, for instance, with our old friends Leonard and Dorothy Elmhirst. We were there in February one year, when the heights of Dartmoor were more beautiful than ever, glistening with snow under a pale blue sky. Yet the lovely gardens round the Hall were already tremulous with the first breath of spring, touching the majestic Turkey oak, the row of ancient Spanish chestnuts, and the congregation of rare deciduous trees, reassuring in their budding green mantle.

From that Devonshire retreat, we sometimes went on to Par, in Cornwall, to stay with the Charles Singers. In summer there was bathing in the rocky coves, while winter enhanced the wild beauty of the place, with great rollers dashing against the cliffs. One year, the cold forced even goldcrests to come to the bird-table, a rare adventure for these tiny, shy creatures.

Singer was engaged in the tremendous task of editing (and largely writing) a huge History of Technology. When its two volumes appeared in 1956, we were deeply impressed. He began this task in old age, after a serious illness, yet was able to give it the creative energy of a young man. Both he and his wife Dorothea were great scholars, delving among the myriad books carefully arranged in their vast library.

A few years later, much of the Cornish coast was proclaimed a National Park, following the Hobhouse Committee's establishment of a coastal National Park in Pembrokeshire. This was a welcome help in preserving Britain's coastline, a project which has since been furthered by the National Trust's 'Operation Neptune'.

What a coast it is! Perhaps the most varied in the world, and one of the longest in relation to the area it encloses. Yet in spite of its indented length, Britain's population was by then so large that, according to my calculations, if every British man, woman and child were to visit the coast on the same day, each human being would have a space of only about one yard. (Since 1950, the population has grown by over eight millions, and my yard has shrunk to about two feet.)

Population-increase: I fear it is my King Charles's head – a head with two faces; over-population is one, conservation the other. Even our National Parks and Reserves are now (1970) becoming what the Americans describe as 'over-visited'. It is true that over-population, and its terrible consequences – pollution and the risk of unplanned building spreading over the open countryside – are today major topics of public and even governmental concern; but the concern is a little late. Had they been attended to twenty years earlier, while at the same time setting aside more unspoilt country to be protected, what grim problems we would have been spared!

Another dear friend whose hospitality we often enjoyed was Leonard Woolley. He then lived at Sedgehill Manor, near Shaftesbury, where, despite increasing deafness, he created for himself a happy old age, after a marriage which brought him little joy. At Sedgehill, there was good talk about the Middle East, where Leonard had supervised so many excavations, and discussions about the section of UNESCO's Cultural History of Mankind which he was writing. In the mornings he would show us his collection of pictures. These were almost all salvaged from obscure sales in country places, where, for a few shillings, he had bought some forgotten drawing or painting and lovingly restored it. Among the junk, he had secured some fine Ruskin water-colours, good Varleys and Cotmans, a small Brueghel, a delightful Angelica Kaufmann, and many others. He took great trouble to have them verified, and in his will left the whole collection to the Ashmolean Museum at Oxford. They declined the gift, however, on the plea that they were already overcrowded. We were glad he never knew this, for it would have grieved him.

Gentle and unassuming, he was a truly remarkable man, his archaeological work of first-class importance, his honesty in acknowledging his few mistakes striking. He was that rare creature – a man at peace with himself

As I mentioned earlier (in Vol. I, p. 71) my father married again in 1912, and had many years of deep happiness with his second wife and their two sons, my half-brothers. These boys were now grown up, married, and engaged in their avocations: David, the elder, read history and became Attorney-General of Bermuda before he went to live in New York, where he practises law for a firm of brokers. Andrew had a deep interest in physiology, speedily became a Fellow of the Royal Society, and at the early age of 46 got a Nobel Prize for his joint work with Hodgkin on the mechanism of conduction and excitation in nerves. I always enjoyed their company and found myself the richer by having two half-brothers much younger than myself, but able to exchange, as time levels its depth, many interesting experiences.

My two sons, Anthony and Francis, only a few years younger than David and Andrew, likewise give me much joy and add their diversity to family life. Anthony was a keen amateur botanist, and though he took his degree in English, he made his hobby a serious study. While editing a horticultural magazine, *Amateur Gardening*, he also managed to publish two excellent books, *Flowers of the Mediterranean* (with Oleg Polunin), illustrated in part with his own colour photographs, and *Mountain Flowers*, a guide to the flora of the Alps. Francis at Oxford abandoned zoology for anthropology, spent two years on the Amazon studying the Urubu Indians and their habits, and then after extensive travel in the USA went to Haiti, where he looked into the extraordinary trances and spells that confer 'divinity' on participants. He wrote two books, *Affable Savages* about his Indians, and *The Invisibles* on his Voodoo experiences in Haiti. They are both delightful and beloved companions, and we are lucky to see much of them.

A particularly precious friend is Dora Clarke (the sculptress, now widow of Admiral Middleton), whom we came to know in 1929, when she allowed me to use a reproduction of her Kikuyu girl bronze as a frontispiece for my book, *Africa View*. She still joins us regularly at the letter game (see Vol. I), while the bronze head itself has been for years one of the valued objects in our house.

Writing as I do now at the advanced age of 84, I realize more than ever the value of friendship, and am grateful to have so many good friends, in so many different ways of life. It would be invidious to make a list of them, and I must forbear.

In March 1950, I took part in a gratifying sequel to some earlier scientific work. This was a Royal Society discussion on the Measurement of Growth and Form, in which my work on relative growth and its mathematical formulation was definitively approved. It followed an article by Reeves and myself in the memorial volume to D'Arcy Thompson five years previously, in which we had tried, with some success, to establish a recognizable terminology for the processes involved – a necessity for international and inter-disciplinary discussion.

In May, I was asked by the British Commission for UNESCO to attend the UNESCO Conference at Florence as a member of the British Delegation. We took the opportunity for an Italian holiday beforehand, and with fresh eyes revisited Perugia and the neighbouring Etruscan cities, which still keep the secret of their origin. From there we went to Siena to see its Palio – a pageant dating from medieval times, starting with a flurry of dancing flags thrown to flutter like awkward birds by young men in Gozzoli costumes. After this came the ferocious horse-race round and round the stone-paved piazza, each quarter of the city putting in its own horse and jockey. The jockeys were free to break every rule, even to whip their human rivals, to the frantic acclamations of the crowd. It sometimes happened that the leading horse had its rider pushed off during the contest; yet it was still recorded as winner, and by tradition occupied a place at the banquet given to the winning team.

Arezzo also had its competitive *fiesta*, its ritual re-discovered when an antiquary was looking for an ancient recipe for sugarplums. The contest here was in tilting: each quarter of the town had its champion, provided with a huge medieval lance, to thrust at the centre of the quintain. Heralds and banners, caparisoned horses and helmeted champions rode in a glittering prelude to this highly skilled contest.

But I must move from these passionate frivolities to the Florence Conference. Torres-Bodet was now Director-General, and made the mistake, referred to above (p. 62), of threatening to resign if the financial support he needed was not forthcoming. Carneiro told the assembly of the auspicious beginnings of the UNESCO Cultural History of Mankind, and the International Union for the Conservation of Nature reported successes in many parts of the world. But the chief achievement of the Conference was the agreement, prompted by the US Delegation, to concentrate the bulk of UNESCO's efforts on a 'decalogue' – ten major tasks, which included fundamental education, free flow of knowledge and ideas, dissemination of scientific knowledge and its applications, worldwide fostering of international understanding, exchange of students and teachers, and fuller co-operation with the UN. This prescribed framework was useful in preventing undue dissipation of UNESCO's resources on a multiplicity of small projects.

I have already spoken (in Vol. I, p. 289) of my chance encounter with Helen Keller. She happened to be in Florence with Joe Davidson, and we had a happy reunion with her at lunch in a typical Florentine restaurant. She was thrilled with Florence, though she confessed to me that the rough walls, with their rusticated embossment, did not give her the *feeling* of the Florence she had read about, with its great piazza, its river, Brunelleschi's domed cathedral and Giotto's superb bell-tower.

After lunch, Joe took her to the Medici Chapel, and later told us that he had learnt something new about sculpture from the manner in which she caressed Michelangelo's great figures. She *felt* form, and could distinguish good from inferior sculpture, through her fingers.

Only a fortnight after this agreeable work-holiday, I was invited to deliver a talk to a Congress of the Swedish Academy of Sciences (I chose my favourite subject, 'Bird Courtship and Display') and to receive an honorary degree from Uppsala university, the oldest seat of higher learning in Scandinavia.

On the way, I spent a few days in Stockholm, where the style of the famous Town Hall, which I had so much admired on my return from Spitsbergen, now seemed out-dated. I also had time to slip across the Norwegian border to Oslo, where I was thrilled by the wonderful reconstruction of a galley which had once belonged to a Viking queen, almost a thousand years ago. What a craft! – with dragon-headed prow, a huge pair of sweeps astern to steer with, gold and silver ornaments for the queen's cabin, and two banks of seats for the rowers.

And so up to Uppsala, Sweden's quondam capital. Here I was confronted by one of those large-scale geographical phenomena which, like the rift valleys, have always fascinated me. The city is built on a gigantic esker more than 100 miles long, rising over 100 feet from the surrounding marshy plains.

What, my readers may ask, is an esker? It is the terminal moraine of a glacier; and here the ice-age glaciers had been so enormous that their eskers became major features of the landscape. What is more, since they run along the ice-excavated valleys, there is always a stream below them, while their summits are dry and firm, and their stony sides form a natural glacis. There are eskers in Britain too – think of Eskdale! – but they are dwarfs compared to these products of the great arctic ice-sheets.

Besides some ancient pillars with runic inscriptions, carefully preserved in the city's centre, there was another moving historical monument: the old Anatomy School, very like that of Padua,[1] except that here the Church's ban on human dissection had been lifted earlier, windows had been put in, and the students on their steeply rising benches no longer had to hold candles to illuminate the dissections.

The Congress (whose badge was a brooch representing *Linnaea borealis*, the delicate, twin-flowered inhabitant of high mountain-forests, called after Linnaeus because it was one of his favourite plants) commemorated the bicentenary of Linnaeus' first publication of his new system of plant (and eventually animal) classification. Instead of writing an elaborate verbal description of each plant, he gave it a Latinized name of two words only, first the 'surname' – of the *genus* or small group of related species to which it was assigned – and then the name allotted to the *species*. Thus *Rosa canina* became the name for the common dog-rose, while the low-growing burnet rose, also in the genus *Rosa*, is called *R. pimpinnellifolia*.

There are still troubles about the naming of hybrids, local forms and graded variations, but the Linnaean system remains the basis of all modern classification, with the genera ranged in Families, the families in Orders, the orders in Classes – all according to their degree of resemblance, and, since Darwin's time, to their presumed evolutionary relationship (see p. 94).

Linnaeus lived on the outskirts of Uppsala, and the Congress was taken to see his home (most of his collections had been bought by the Linnaean Society in London, where they can still be seen). We were astonished by the number of Swedish visitors, both to his house and garden and to his tomb in the cathedral. What a contrast to Britain's interest –

1. See Vol. I, pp. 115–16.

or lack of interest – in Darwin, an even greater man than Linnaeus. I have never heard of pilgrimages to Darwin's tomb in Westminster Abbey, and although his home at Down has been bought by the nation, there are few visitors, even to see the table at which he wrote the epoch-making *Origin of Species* and all his other books, or the garden walks where he elaborated his thoughts and theories.

The memory of Linnaeus also pervaded the degree-giving ceremony. Those who had achieved a doctorate in any subject but science wore top-hats with a special gold buckle on their bands; there were scores of them, including the King himself, and many women, who looked particularly absurd in this masculine headgear.

The ritual for the scientists was much more interesting. As I stood before the Vice-Chancellor in my Oxford D.Sc. robes, he intoned in Latin, *'accipe hoc annulum'*, slipping on my finger a gold ring chased with myrtle leaves (for which, I may add, I had to pay); handed me my Latin diploma, saying *'accipe hoc diploma'*; and finally, with the words *'accipe hac coronam'*, placed on my head a crown of bay myrtle, plucked from an ancient tree planted by Linneaus himself in his own garden.

This was indeed a splendid piece of symbolism, though we foreign doctors felt a little foolish wearing our wreaths at the evening banquet – bogus Roman senators at a Swedish feast. One of my colleagues looked rather like Nero after an orgy, while I tried, without much success, to imagine that I resembled Julius Caesar.

The ring is still on my finger, and the leafy crown, though faded and dry, hangs in our drawing-room as a memento of Linnaeus, alongside the Royal Society's Darwin Medal, a reminder of that even greater scientist.

At the Congress, I met many ornithologists who previously had been mere names, and on the excursions, saw many 'new' bird species, such as the red-spotted bluethroat, a robin-like creature with even more brilliant plumage; nutcrackers like those of north-western America, but with slightly different markings, the same species as I had glimpsed as a boy in Swiss pinewoods; and capercaillies, largest of the grouse tribe, the cock with enormous fan-shaped blue-black and white tail. We heard his *boom*, proclaiming his occupation of a territory, but failed to see his fantastic display.

Just before leaving for the Congress, I was called on by Professor Bernard Rensch, who during the war had written a general book on evolution very similar to my *Evolution, the Modern Synthesis*. Neither of us had known what the other was doing, but the coincidence showed that the time was ripe for a revaluation of this all-embracing subject.

He invited me to lecture to his biological students at the University of Münster, which I did in the following year, 1951. I had hoped to speak in German, but my old fluency had left me, and I had to switch to English. Luckily his students were much better grounded in English than most of ours are in German, and followed me so well that I was asked plenty of pertinent questions.

I had the same feeling of being in enemy country as I had had when passing through Germany on my way back from Spitsbergen, but it was now much slighter – indeed, I got the impression that after their defeat in the Second World War, most Germans, especially the younger generation, felt a revulsion against Hitler and his maniacal policies. Today (1970), I read that there is a slight revival of Hitlerism; but the neo-Nazis seem to be gaining little real support.

Later that summer of 1950, we were back in Switzerland, where we met Roger Godel and his wife Alice. Roger was a heart specialist who ran a large hospital in Ismailia, where his ideas and methods had much impressed Aldous. Aldous saw cases of serious heart disease that had been cured by psychology – by getting the patient to confess his anxiety, and then explaining that reducing the fear would increase his chances of getting better.

Roger was a courageous and dedicated man who saw no limit to the power of the human spirit – even over the most deadly diseases. Alas, he himself died of a failure of his own heart, some time after the take-over of his hospital by the Egyptian authorities. He was a seeker, but very practical; his death robbed us of the important work he was planning on the influence of the mind on the body.

Godel and I corresponded until his death; and lately, his widow very ably translated my *Religion without Revelation* into French.

In July, Aldous paid us another visit – as always a time of intensified activity, social as well as intellectual. In age we were separated by seven crucial years, and in our lives by very different destinies. Yet we were alike in our approach to ideas and problems, in our appetite for knowledge, and its attempted synthesis. Sharing a common approach, we understood each other without need for ponderous disputation, so our discussions were a source of deep delight for us both. Our talk was wide-ranging, for we both tried to keep up with interesting and curious facts and new discoveries. Breakfast might go on to mid-morning before we tore ourselves away from these wonderful exchanges of ideas – how I wish I had had a tape-recorder! – and we would take up the thread, easily and naturally, when we had time to talk again.

From these encounters, I always returned to my work stimulated and refreshed, my mental and spiritual batteries recharged. I cannot remember a single subject, even in my own speciality, on which Aldous was not sufficiently informed to enable us to discuss it competently, enriching my own thinking in the process.

How Aldous managed to absorb (and still more to digest) the colossal amount of facts and ideas which furnished his mind remains a mystery, especially with his grave deficiency of sight. To overcome this, his wife Maria devotedly read aloud to him for hours at a time; and with his one good eye, he managed to skim through learned journals, popular articles and books of every kind. He was apparently able to take them in at a glance, and what is more, to remember their essential content. His intellectual memory was phenomenal, doubtless trained by a tenacious will to surmount the original horror of threatened blindness, and the later discomfort of impaired vision, which had hung over his life ever since he was a schoolboy of sixteen.

I often wondered about his bouts of silence – sometimes embarrassing to the company. They were, I think, partly a protective armour against pity for his predicament; but their basis could have been something deeper still, an unacknowledged desire for spiritual privacy. When our mother was dying, she wrote, in her understanding wisdom, a few words for Aldous at the end of the little book storing memories of his childhood: 'Don't be too critical of other people; love much.' Perhaps his silence was also the silence of peacefulness and love, of the wish to avoid arguments and wrangling.

His powerful intellect seems to have kept his emotions imprisoned, and inflicted on him some sort of resistance to giving or receiving confidences, as well as a need to avoid outspoken emotional involvement. This does not mean that he experienced no emotion: on the contrary, he was a man of deep feeling, but he chose not to expose his inner heart.

Another of Aldous's characteristics was a taste for the oddities of existence, the ludicrous side of human nature, the macabre accidents of life. He would relish such quirks with his favourite exclamation: 'Extraordinary!' said with only a pinpoint of malice, like a connoisseur appraising some new wine or some curious *objet d'art*.

All this, of course, is apparent in his writings, especially the early works, a curious twist of mixed feelings, not always appreciated by his public. Thus in 1918 he wrote to Juliette:

I have done an admirable short story – so cruel and heartless that you will probably scream if you read it. The concentrated venom is quite delicious – while the subtle horror of my modern epic 'Leda' beggars description: you will have to read them to realize to the full the truth of your judgement about me – about one of the ME's: but the other is – what? a sentimentalist? a hero of romance? a bon bourgeois?

Whatever his inner complexity, he was essentially gentle, with a gentleness unchanged throughout the years. Like my father, he hardly ever lost his temper: but he could show his disagreement in no uncertain way, as when Buchmanites tried to involve him in the Moral Re-armament movement (distasteful to us both) by inviting him to a party where Buchman was present. When Buchman began spreading his tentacles in an attempt to catch Aldous, or at least to get his approval, Aldous just shut up and walked out, in silent but conspicuous distaste.

Visits from Aldous were also occasions for inviting interesting people to meet him. I remember a lovely summer day when our garden was full of relatives, with a few special friends we called 'honorary Huxleys'. After they had all left, Aldous murmured: 'And a jolly good bunch they are.'

We once went together to a lecture by General Smuts, and though we found him personally charming, were not impressed by his doctrine of 'holism', which attempted to include everything on earth, human minds and human societies, in a single embracing system. This, like Bergson's *élan vital*, seemed to us both unscientific and pseudo-mystical, failing both in immediate and in evolutionary relevance, and in biological accuracy.

On another occasion, we met Albert Schweitzer, and with him too we were slightly disappointed: there was more proclamation than scientific analysis in his utterances; a hollowness in his main theme – that all life must be equally respected. Indeed, his own course contradicted his theories. He did not respect the microscopic agents of typhus or yellow fever, but attempted, quite rightly, to destroy them and cure the diseases they produced.

On one of these fraternal visits, I took Aldous down to Prior's Field, where there was a meeting of the governors of the school our mother had founded. While we worked, he wandered about the place, recalling his happy childhood. But when, on our way home, he insisted on seeing the grave where both our parents were buried, he was overcome with grief; for besides respecting and admiring our father, he had loved our mother perhaps even more passionately than I had, and certainly, at his tender age when she died, had missed her and her love more deeply. In several of his novels he has recorded, barely disguised, his little boy's overpowering grief at her graveside.

We were both strangely moved to see that wild meadow saxifrages, one of Mother's favourite flowers, had sprung up on the grassy grave, and were in full bloom: they seemed a spontaneous tribute of the nature that both my parents had so much loved.

CHAPTER 6

A Familiar Trouble and a Fresh Honour

I NEVER could refuse a lecturing trip to America, laid out on a plate. It was generally foolish to go, as I was in any case overworked, but I needed the money, no longer having a regular income (and no pension from UNESCO). This year, 1950, I went for a short tour in September, and then again in April 1951.

It was, of course, stimulating and pleasant to meet old friends and colleagues again, such as Ernst Mayr and G. G. Simpson at Harvard, and E. G. Conklin at Princeton.

At Princeton, I saw the extraordinary distorting room set up by Hadly Cantril, with advice from Adalbert Ames. Its walls were asymmetrical in length and tilted in various ways, but all arranged so that, viewed from the front, it *looked* cubical – or rather the brain's visual cortex, accustomed to ordinary rooms, *interpreted* it as cubical. Accordingly, when someone moved across the back wall, one corner of which was actually further away than the other, the onlooker saw him change from a dwarf at the more distant corner to a giant at the other, thus forcibly demonstrating how the human brain rearranges direct visual impressions into an expected shape and dimension, our view of the external world ruled by habitual perspective.

This proof that we 'see' what we are accustomed to, instead of what is really there – or, if you like, that not only beauty, but form itself is in the eye (and brain) of the beholder – made a deep impression on me, and explained how different witnesses often give different accounts of the same happening. Wordsworth wrote: 'We live by adoration, faith and love.' We can say: 'We see by expectation, habit and familiarity.'

I also had the good fortune, at the Princeton Institute of Advanced Studies, of meeting Einstein. What a man! – with his shaggy hair, his violin, and his withdrawn expression; yet with an inner fire of genius. We discussed the social functions of science, and its need to be free from political and ideological pressures. I had the impression of a gentle but sad person – sad for the horrors of the Hitler regime and the gullibility of man – a profound originator of ideas, living more in their world than in that of ordinary human beings.

In New York, I saw Warren Weaver of the Rockefeller Foundation, and secured his blessing (and a little cash) to start a body for studying the principles of biological classification, which had become much more complicated since the time of Linnaeus. This came into being as the Association for the Study of Systematics, with branches in Europe as well as in the USA.

Later, with the help of Mayr, Alfred Emerson and others, I persuaded American biologists to set up a new Society for the Study of Evolution.

As a result of the two Societies' discussions, superimposed on his own unrivalled knowledge of birds and their classification, Mayr later wrote an outstanding book, *Animal Species and Evolution*. He sent me a copy inscribed 'to one whose work has been an invaluable source of stimulation and whose friendship has been an inspiration for more than a quarter of a century'. I was deeply moved, and proud that I had in any way stimulated him to pursue his brilliant studies. The book cleared up most of the difficulties of defining genera, species, subspecies, local varieties and genetic aberrations.

In Bloomington, where I was to lecture, I naturally visited my friend and erstwhile colleague at Rice Institute, Hermann Muller, now a Nobel Prizeman for his work on induced mutation, but much depressed by his wife's poor health. I think my visit cheered him a little; anyhow, he took me to see Indiana's newly established State Park, with splendid stands of tulip-trees and sweet-gum (*Liquidamber*). These State Parks are like our Nature Reserves, but with much more provision for visitors – camping sites and restaurants, guides and marked trails. I reported this to our National Parks Commission, but they, I think rightly, wanted less interference with the landscape, both in Reserves and National Parks.[1]

1. Recently (1970), the British Forestry Commission has set lodges and camping facilities in some of its forests – a welcome move for lovers of nature and solitude.

My lectures at the University of Indiana – six of them – were a heavy assignment. They were later published by the University of Indiana Press, and after revision, by Chatto and Windus in London, under the title *Evolution in Action*; they dealt with the factors influencing the formation of new species and affecting the direction along which larger groups, like Families and Orders, evolved over long periods.

The strain was relieved by visits to Muller's home and his laboratory, where he and his team were continuing the work on mutations in Drosophila. Apart from its scientific value, it alerted the lay world to the dangers of deleterious human mutation implicit in the use of atomic bombs.

I also saw Professor Kinsey's department, where he had collected the world's most complete assortment of material on human sexual habits and aberrations. The only other two such collections are in the British Museum and, interestingly, in the Vatican ...

The whole place was lined with steel cupboards and had a surgical appearance; the middle-aged women assistants even looked like hospital nurses. Their main job was to look up what booksellers call 'curiosa and erotica' in the huge library: but even they were not given free access to a double-locked cupboard in an inner sanctum – which Kinsey unlocked for me. Herbert Read once wrote: 'The basis of all art is a certain measure of sensuality': here indeed was the proof of it, for this collection of drawings and writings on astonishing perversions was mainly the secret work of notable and distinguished people.

When Kinsey published his huge reports on the sexual behaviour of American men and women, the high rate of abnormality they revealed shocked the American public. They still cherished the belief that America's sexual *mores* were of a much higher standard than those of 'decadent' Europe. I was not shocked or surprised, but it interested me to see here proof that sexual morality in animals (of which I knew a good deal) is higher than in man.

During my stay, I walked round the campus every morning before breakfast, finding many bird species new to me; and once I was taken out at dawn by some ardent bird-watchers to see a pileated woodpecker at work – a splendid creature, black, with white-marked face and scarlet crest, the blows of its beak so violent that I wondered how its brain could stand the shock.

I had taken my pocket Dante (interleaved with English translation) and found it a welcome refuge from work, from scientific reading in connection with my lectures, and as antidote to Middle-Western brashness outside the University.

On returning home from my second tour in June 1951, there was, as always, much to do: meetings in Paris of the UNESCO History Commission, examining in zoology at Birmingham University: further, besides the Hobhouse Memorial Lecture (on Conservation), I had agreed to give six talks on evolution for the BBC. They were based on the lectures I had given at Bloomington, but they needed much revision, and the producer was very fussy about details, insisting on many rehearsals and what I felt to be unnecessary alterations.

After the last talk in mid-November, I was exhausted – almost too tired to care. That same evening, Juliette drove me to stay with our charming and original friend, Stephen Tennant, poet and painter, at his home on the Avon near Salisbury. It was nearly midnight, but he had stayed up for us with a delicious champagne supper before the fire. His house is the embodiment of a fanciful dream, with *trompe l'oeil* swags, mirrors, crystals and exotic shells, polar-bear rugs and ornate curtains, like himself full of enchanting surprises.

Was it perhaps part of the fantasy that he took us to dine with Cecil Beaton in his fine house, there to meet the fabulous Greta Garbo? She was looking as beautiful as in her haunting films, dressed merely in black slacks and sweater. Sitting at my feet, she asked me in her deep, husky voice to tell her something interesting about animals. I told her the story of the praying mantis, of how the male advances stealthily behind the female and leaps on her back to mate with her – but, should he land ever so slightly askew, the female swivels round and devours his head. Yet so prophetically is the rest of his nervous system adjusted that he can achieve insemination although his brain is already in the female's gizzard – a wonderful but macabre instance of biological adaptation.

Far from being shocked, Greta delightedly said: 'Tell me more.' So I went on to the courtship of spiders, whose females are as voracious as those of the mantis, but whose males, not resigned to a fate so final, take infinite precautions to avoid untimely death. The web-spinners use a special code when reaching the female's web, vibrating it gently and soothingly, in contrast with the violent disturbances set off by a captured fly. 'May I come into your parlour ...' said the spider to his mate. The message is understood and the mating consummated.

The hunting spiders, on the other hand, execute a prominent display with their coloured fore-limbs ... So my natural history knowledge paid off in an unexpected way: I shall never forget this delightful encounter.

The magic, however, was short-lived. Soon afterwards I plunged into another breakdown, another descent into a mental hell. As I wrote after recovery from an earlier one, in a long poem entitled 'From a Freudian Faustulus':

> Whither to turn? the vesture of my being
> begins to tear – my very being's self
> is rent, with ghastly rendings of live flesh.
> And through the rents, intolerable shapes
> protrude themselves upon me.
> They are not ME – I swear, and yet, oh God,
> they live upon my life, and somehow part
> and parcel of it, though I knew it not.
> What foul and unsuspected intimacy ...
>
> The shapes that share me with myself! The things,
> the crawling things that have a right-of-way
> about my heart's strings!

I seem to be a manic-depressive type, perhaps by inheritance from my grandfather T.H.H., who had several serious depressions during his life. It could be due, like schizophrenia, to a biochemical imbalance, but so far this has not been proved. I have never quite understood what triggers off my nervous breakdowns. After a period of over-optimistic energy, some conjunction of over-work and emotional set-back, the vulnerable nerve-centres collapse and leave one in a state of bodily feebleness, mental depression and confusion. I read in a medical journal how common this state is: in the USA some 25,000 people are affected by it, and many commit suicide; in Britain about 20,000. Various drugs alleviate it, and also electric shock treatment, but it always takes some time to recover one's full capacity.

While I was in a nursing home at Pinner, making my slow way out of this tunnel of misery, Lord Adrian, then President of the Royal Society, rang Juliette up to say that the British Committee set up to make recommendations to UNESCO for candidates for the Kalinga Prize had nominated me for the award, 'for distinguished services in popularizing science and scientific progress'. The prize was £1,000, with the proviso that some of it should be spent on a voyage to India, and that the recipient should lecture on scientific subjects while there.

The capital for this annual prize had been given by a remarkable Indian called Bijayananda Patnaik, a man whose adventures would fill a book. Trained as an aeronautical engineer, he became a brilliant pilot in the Indian National Airways; during the Second World War, he did wonders in rescuing British residents stranded in Burma at a time when the risks were so great that few British pilots ventured to take them. But the danger appealed to his daredevil spirit, his courage and endurance. On one of these missions, his plane crashed in the jungle and only himself and the flight engineer escaped death, the latter suffering a broken leg. Given up for dead, Patnaik carried the man four days to the border, and turned up at home, to the intense surprise and relief of his family.

He was also dedicated to fight for the independence of India, and while carrying out his goodwill missions, dropped pamphlets inciting people to rebellion against the British. His subversive activities attracted the suspicions of the authorities, so much so that, although his heroic flights were invaluable to the British, he was arrested and put in jail, in company with Nehru and other campaigners for Indian independence. Like them, he profited from the enforced leisure, reading voraciously, learning history and Sanskrit, discussing and planning the coming rebellion and new political structure. For there can be no doubt about it, many leaders of the independence movement wanted to throw out their British rulers by every available means, and were prepared to kill as well as die for their country. Patnaik was assigned the future task of building a textile factory with a large secret basement where counterfeit money would be printed to destroy the British economy in India.

After some months of detention, his wife, herself a remarkable woman, knowing her husband's restless nature and fearing a wild attempt to escape, went to Wavell, then Viceroy, and secured Patnaik's release on parole, in Orissa, his native state.

Once relatively free, he began planning his factory. However, Cripps' foresight in pledging an early date for Independence made all preparations for the great rebellion unnecessary. Patnaik was advised to carry on only with his industrial scheme, and as soon as the war was over, he started actually building his factory, training labour and planning a brighter future for Orissa. In this enterprise, and further following ones, he achieved remarkable success, and incidentally became a millionaire. He later entered the political field as well, and is now an active member of Congress.

On a visit to Paris, he had looked into the work of UNESCO, approved it, and set up a fund for this prize (called 'Kalinga' after the dynasty which ruled for centuries over Orissa, his native state, and neighbouring areas). In establishing it, Patnaik wrote:

I am convinced of the necessity of making the great masses aware of the methods and achievements of scientific research, and understand the impact of science on our daily behaviour. One can scarcely envisage raising the standard of living of the world's population without a very broad understanding of scientific progress. This can only be achieved by developing to the largest possible extent the dissemination of scientific information among all people.

When Juliette told me the news, I protested that I was quite unworthy of such an honour and must decline it – a typical reaction from a sufferer of depressive neurosis. However, Adrian, our loyal friend, told Juliette to disregard a sick man's delusions and to send the array of my less technical writings in support of the application.

I duly won the prize, the second to do so (the first recipient was Prince Louis de Broglie, the French physicist).

By late March 1953, I was fit enough to go to Paris to receive my cheque. There was a little ceremony, with a speech from the D.G., and I felt very lucky and no longer unworthy. I was luckier than I knew, for at the airport I managed to lose the precious cheque! However, it was finally found by a porter and restored to me with many 'Oh, la-la's'.

At about this time I began to be interested again in the problem of problems – man's destiny and the role of religion, or some substitute for it, in helping him to fulfil it better and more usefully. Thus, after reading Lance White's *God the Unconscious*, I noted: 'What could be more revealing – it is the "*idea* of God" which alone is real – as I realized thirty years ago in the woods of Hawthorden. It remains to analyse the idea, to find what objective elements are involved in it!' This had set me off to writing *Religion without Revelation* in 1927. Later, I made a note, while travelling on a bus: 'There is dualism with monism, the dualism of man and his world of thought, as a unique and special kind of reality, within the unitary realm of which he forms a part.'

Paul Klee said about his art: 'One leaves the realms of here and now and builds forward into the beyond, where there is still a possibility of a relative YES' – to which I added, there is also a possibility of a relative No. And again I noted: 'Religion is concerned with our relation with our destiny. The next step must be a religion of fulfilment, of world humanism, where man co-operates with his planetary environment to create and realize new possibilities.'

Here were the germs of the ideas I later developed in my *Essays of a Humanist* (1964).

Religion without Revelation was a success; a second edition was called for in 1957, and an abridged version was published by Watts' in their Thinkers' Library series. In it I had touched on the foundations of morality, and the linking of particular moral codes with particular religions (or pseudo-religions, like Marxism), and with man's idea of the sacred.

I continued to be preoccupied with the problem of morality, and with ethics in general. As a result, I published in 1947 a book which I found extremely interesting to produce, *Touch-*

stone for Ethics, which included both the Romanes Lecture delivered by my grandfather at Oxford in 1894, entitled *Evolution and Ethics,* and my own Romanes Lecture on *Evolutionary Ethics,* delivered in the same place – the Sheldonian Theatre at Oxford – fifty years later; together with T.H.H.'s lengthy 'prolognomena' and my own introduction and conclusions.

Further, I was able to do something that my grandfather could not. I could take into account the work of Freud and other modern psychologists, and their demonstration that all ethical systems and moral codes involve a certain degree of mental suppression and even repression; and that this repressed element may burst out of its mental dungeon and lead us to strange and sometimes dreadful actions. In addition, I underlined that some form of ritual was involved in all religions.

Of course, I pointed out the relativity of ethical ideas and practice to tribal or national tradition, to the degree of our knowledge of our own selves, to our response to the opinions to others, and to our religious and magical beliefs.

I also dealt more thoroughly than my grandfather with the difficult problem of conscience, whose origin too usually involves some degree of repression and unconscious guilt.

I quoted three definitions of conscience. One was from Mark Twain's *Huckleberry Finn,* as representing the average untutored human being: 'It don't make no difference whether you do it right or wrong, a person's conscience ain't got no sense and just goes for him anyway ... it takes up more room than all the rest of a person's insides, and ain't no good nohow.'

The second was from a theologian (whom I did not name): 'a special exercise or activity of the faculty of reason; it is the mind of man when it is passing moral or ethical judgment.' This I felt was quite unrealistic in omitting all the irrational and compulsive elements in conscience, and failing to consider its developmental origin during our early years.

The third was the definition of a pessimist and one obsessed with the unpleasant aspects, both physical and mental, of our human nature – Dean Swift: 'Is not conscience a pair of breeches, which though a cover for lewdness as well as nastiness, is easily slipt down for the service of both.' This last provoked a murmur in the audience followed by a stony silence. But I had made my point.

Both of us discussed the origin of moral and ethical systems in relation to changes in society and increases in knowledge, and both quoted various definitions of morality and of the guardian of morality, conscience; but there was a considerable difference between our conclusions. My grandfather's main thesis was that the cosmic or general process of evolution was opposed to man's inventions in agriculture and technology, while ethical systems and their application have enormously reduced the pressure of the struggle for existence in man (minimizing, I felt, the constant recurrence of war and violence), with very little mention of conscience and repressed guilt; while I felt that man was entering the cosmic process by producing more efficient social and moral systems, modifying them as facts changed and new ideas developed for coping with the changed facts.

Late spring of 1953 saw us in Italy, on a tour organized by the *Società di Cultura*, strongly recommended by our friend Stephen Spender. This meant lecturing in Turin, Milan, Genoa and Rome. A pleasant assignment, made particularly memorable by a chance meeting with an Italian, Professor Blanc, who invited us to his archaeological site on Monte Circeo.

Blanc had been searching the local caves, which legend had long endowed with a prehistoric past, but had found nothing – until a neighbour reported a cave behind his shop. A landslide had blocked the entrance, perhaps half a million years ago, thus keeping it inviolate.

Blanc descended the narrow shaft with a flashlight and was confronted with a rough vault, on the floor of which, beside the bones of creatures which had been eaten, he found a ring of stones encircling a human skull. This was an undoubted specimen of Neanderthal Man, with its low brow and occipital bulge; he told us he nearly fainted with joy.

We saw a replica of the skull, with its base smashed, in order, said Blanc, to extract the brain. He surmised that this had been eaten by the group in order to acquire the dead man's wisdom and valour, in some ritual ceremony also involving the ring of stones.

It moved us as profoundly as had our previous visits to Lascaux and Altamira, or to Olduvai in Tanzania, where Leakey had shown us part of a skull of the million-year-old ape-man he chistened *Zinjanthropus* – or to the much later, Neolithic, shafts for flint-mining at Grimes Graves in Suffolk, where in a poor-yielding pit the ancient miners, to propitiate their angry gods, had left offerings, including an exquisite ribbed cup carved in hard clunch chalk.

In June, we watched the Coronation procession of our present Queen, the day after I had written a letter to *The Times* reporting the unusual occurrence of a great crested grebe on the pool at Kenwood; I was happy to have Ornithology as well as Royalty brought to public attention, but it was lost sight of when the news broke that same day that Everest had at last been conquered – by a British team.

CHAPTER 7

To Australia, via the Pacific

STEVENSON once wrote: 'To travel hopefully is a better thing than to arrive, and the true success is to labour.'

Certainly, I travelled hopefully when I took advantage of my Kalinga Prize to visit as many countries as possible on my way to India. I accepted invitations to lecture in the USA and the Pacific Islands, besides helping Sir Charles Darwin on the biological side of his inquiry into the role of science in higher education in Thailand; and after our long stay in India (for Juliette was to join me in Java), we came home by way of Iran, where I was to speak at the millenary celebrations of Avicenna's birth.

Certainly, too, there were many chores involved – paying respects to the authorities and inspecting schools and university laboratories, not to mention social and agricultural projects; and often even fatigue in sight-seeing, however beautiful or interesting the sights.

I do not know how successful I was with my lectures, but both of us brought back imperishable memories. I cannot here resist mentioning some of them.

I was off by late August 1953, first to New York, then California, for a short stay with Aldous and Maria, now settled in a comfortable house in North King's Road, Los Angeles. This made a pleasant interlude, with a visit to the Californian desert, much loved by the Aldouses, where giant yuccas, adorned with exquisite white bells, reared their spiky branches in its wide solitudes, with swarms of wild eschscholtzias blossoming on its fringes.

Thence to Honolulu – garlanded girls to meet visitors, lovely scenery, with all the tropical glories of palm-fringed bathing beaches and fine mountains.

H. J. Muller, my old colleague at Rice, was spending his sabbatical year here with his wife and daughter, and we all went across the mountain shoulder to the marine laboratory on the north. It was well equipped for research and had open-air show-tanks with a wide array of tropical fish and invertebrates – some bizarrely beautiful, like the gay parrot-fish, with powerful teeth for chewing off bits of living coral; others merely grotesque, such as the enormous sea-cucumbers looking like large Bologna sausages filled with water (and with the unique capacity, when roughly handled, of ejecting their digestive system to confuse their enemy, regenerating a new set of intestines later).

I was interested to find a bird-rock, like the sea-bird islands I had visited in Peru, with a fine coating of guano, but so precipitous that the harvest was difficult to exploit. Through my binoculars I saw male man-of-war birds trying to attract females by lying back on their nest-sites, calling loudly and distending their scarlet neck-pouches to the size of a child's balloon – rapt in urgent biological compulsion. They looked less like birds than exotic fruit; but fruit with a raucous voice and flapping wings.

To my surprise, beautiful, white, long-tailed tropic-birds were nesting on the walls of the crater of the active volcano Mauna Loa. There were areas of splendid rain-forest on the lower slopes, but on the uplands, owing to excessive lava flows (and browsing by goats), the forest was now confined to a few isolated patches on the hills rising free of the lava. These forest islands have been isolated from each other for so long that their bird and insect populations have evolved into new sub-species and even species: the situation was like that on the Galapagos, or on the high peaks of East Africa.

In a world racked by racism, it was good to find in this American colony, now a State of the Union, an almost total absence of race prejudice. The nobles of Hawaii and members of its royal family were so handsome and intelligent that American colonists were happy to marry them. In later years, Japanese, Chinese and Negro colonists have been added, yet they, and all their combinations with other races and peoples, live happily together in these enchanted isles. There are no slaves, and no discrimination by colour, as still persists on the US mainland.

*

From Hawaii I flew on to Fiji, with a beautiful sight of the fringing coral reef as we came in to land on Viti Levu, the chief island of the group. Like most Pacific archipelagos, Fiji has become a racial melting-pot. The dominant tribe, which is accorded kingship, is that of the Tongans, from an island just off to the north. But the Fijians, too, are proud people, of extraordinary strength and physique; they play rugger, and I was told that any fifteen male Fijians picked at random would be up to Rugby League standard.

The British Governor, Sir Harry Luke, kindly suggested that I should accompany him on a tour of the interior. Horses were waiting at the foot of a great cliff, and we rode through splendid upland forests, full of lovely tree-ferns, flowering tree-orchids, and great Ficus trees, with shoots hanging down ready to take root as soon as they touched the ground. But there was a sad absence of native birds, owing to the introduction of some kind of stoat or mongoose, which was supposed to keep down the population of rats – also introduced, but accidentally – which were making devastating inroads on the sugar and rice stores. After a few decades, however, mongoose had spread all over the island, and were finding easy prey in the multitude of birds which nested on the ground, as in other islands originally free of mammalian predators.

At greater heights, the forest gave way to open tropical moorland, equally free of birds, but rampant with the obnoxious Lentana plant, ousting the native flora.

Thus Fiji provided me with yet another example of the dangers of upsetting a whole eco-system by alien animals and plants, even when they were supposed to be of some benefit.

Suddenly the rock on which we were sitting began to quiver – an earthquake! The Governor rushed off to see what had happened to the capital, and I was left to continue the journey with a fuzzy-haired black Fijian trooper as escort. I remembered the tales of Fijian cannibalism and glanced suspiciously at my companion: but he seemed completely civilized, and the only barrier between us was that of language. So we rode in silence through bush country to one of the main villages of the interior. Here an elaborate welcome had been prepared for the

Governor, so I had to deputize for him. I rode through an arch of branches and flowers, and on dismounting was led between lines of huge Fijian drummers to the chief's dwelling, a large hut with mud floor and domed roof of wattle and daub, dim-lit by lamps whose wicks were set in saucers of coconut oil.

The traditional kava-drinking ceremony then took place, to honour the distinguished visitor. Kava, I discovered, is a semi-intoxicating liquid, made from the bitter-tasting roots of the pepper-tree. The method of its manufacture is somewhat primi-tive – the village women chew the roots and spit the result into a stone basin; here it is further pounded, water added and the whole left to ferment, when it is transferred to a handsome wooden bowl.

The women brought in the kava bowl and presented it to the local medicine-man. He passed it to the chief, who, after a ritual sip, passed it to me. I did my best to forget the chewing and the spitting and took my swig – after all the white man's honour was at stake! It was very bitter, but stimulating; so much so that after a few rounds I began to feel agreeably muzzy, though not drunk. Kava is sacred because its cere-monial use, along with the monotonous and haunting rhythm of the drums, helps the villagers to forget their troubles and prevents quarrels from breaking out.[1]

On returning to the capital, I found that the earthquake had been quite serious. Many houses were in ruins and there was a great crack across a main road just outside the town. The eruption that had caused the quake must have been submarine; for, as I learnt from the Governor, there had been a so-called tidal wave – the sea had swept up the beach and then retreated beyond low-tide mark, leaving multitudes of fish, squids, crabs and other sea-creatures stranded on the sand. The Indians and many Europeans had fled to the hills; but the tough Fijians, with an eye to the main chance, had pushed through the stream of refugees to collect as much as they could carry of the bounty so generously provided by the catastrophe.

My next hop set me down in Australia, where Sydney pro-

1. The chewing of bitter kola nuts seems to perform the same func-tion in West Africa – joint and friendly euphoria.

vided a sharp contrast to Fiji – a sophisticated city, with art galleries, excellent theatre and ballet, and sky-scrapers rising on both sides of the famous bridge spanning the entrance to the inner harbour. Land values had soared to prodigious heights, and I thought with some regret of the action of my great-grandfather Heathorn, father of the pretty girl who had captivated T. H. Huxley on his visit to her guardians, the Fannings, and whom he eventually married. Heathorn had acquired some land in what is now the centre of Sydney's harbour district, but eventually sold it for a song.

I saw little of the vulgarity and harshness depicted by D. H. Lawrence in his book *Kangaroo*. In all the main Australian cities, there was respect for the arts and literature, though Australian businessmen were tough, and proud of their humble origins; indeed, in some circles it had become a status symbol to be descended from a convict.

In the same sort of way, bandits like Ned Kelly had become national heroes, their ingenuity and ruthlessness commemorated by fine painters like Nolan and Drysdale, praised in doggerel verse, and described in books written about their adventures. I felt that the Australians' sympathy for the outlaw was enhanced by the fact that many of their own ancestors had been outlawed – transported for life under the harsh penal code of the eighteenth and early nineteenth centuries.

One of my lectures was at Canberra, capital city of the whole continent, deliberately sited, like Washington and Brasilia, away from the main centres of wealth and power, to reduce political and commercial pressures. How long it will be able to preserve this political isolation I do not know. But if Washington is any guide, it will soon be full of lobbyists for every conceivable project and interest. Not built to a well-thought-out plan, it was just an agglomeration of buildings set up almost haphazard round a central lake. Since then, Lord Holford has been called in to draw up a coherent scheme for this fine site, and I am sure that a beautiful and convenient city will eventually emerge.

I stayed with my old pupil Francis Ratcliffe, who was in charge of the Wild Life section of the Council for Scientific and Industrial Research and Development. He took me on a picnic along the Murray River to look for platypus, but although we found plenty of their burrows, we saw no living specimens. For this I had to wait until I visited a local naturalist with a miniature nature reserve, complete with a 'platypussary', where I could watch these extraordinary proto-mammals – duck-billed, fur-coated, web-footed and egg-laying, still half reptilian, but secreting milk into a saucer-shaped depression on their bellies, to be lapped up by their newly-hatched young. The creature is a biological jigsaw, a 'missing link' that has managed to survive for over sixty million years. The fact that it continues to be so biologically successful is due, I presume, to the absence of large carnivorous marsupials in mainland Australia.

I had long wanted to visit one of the coral islands within the shelter of the Great Barrier Reef. This ambition had been kindled by the accounts of Captain Cook's voyage up the Barrier Reef in a biological book by Savile Kent, which I had read with excitement at my grandfather's house at Eastbourne, and by the reports of a later expedition by my friend Professor Maurice Yonge – both of which revealed the extraordinary richness of the fauna.

The *Rattlesnake*, with my grandfather on board, had visited many of the islands inside the reef, but at the time, as recorded in his Diary (which I published, with annotations, in 1935), he had been in the grip of a lassitude and indeed depression very alien to his ordinary nature, and had paid little attention to the rich coral fauna. This was in marked contrast to the hard work he had previously expended on the floating creatures of the open sea, such as salps and medusae, which he had dragged up in tow nets on the voyage out, and of which he had sent a long scientific account and analysis to the Royal Society. Instead of working, he spent most of his time reading novels in his bunk, noting briefly in his diary that he felt depressed and morose.

My interpretation is that he was worried about having received no acknowledgement of his manuscript from London, and also that he was suffering from pricks of conscience for having become engaged to Henrietta Heathorn with no prospect of being able to support her. But he was wrong about his scientific prospects: his monograph had been accepted and published in the Royal Society's *Philosophical Transactions*; further, as a result of its brilliance of exposition and interpretation, he was elected F.R.S. *in absentia*, and next year was awarded the Royal Society's Gold Medal for this work at the unprecedented age of 27.

He was to wait seven long years before he obtained a post that enabled him to marry. Meanwhile, it took six months to get a reply to his letters to my future grandmother ...

To return to the Barrier Reef, it is an extraordinary fact of nature, worthy to be ranked with the Great Rift Valley of Africa as a major geographical phenomenon. It extends some 1,200 miles along the north-eastern coast of Australia, enclosing a lagoon 150 miles broad at its widest point. The whole floor of this huge lagoon, as well as the barrier itself and the fringing reefs round the atolls dotted about its enclosed waters, is all made of coral – layer upon layer, laid down as the sea-level was raised by the melting of the ice during the warm interglacials, to a thickness of over 1,000 feet. It is almost incredible to think of these billions of tiny polyps secreting their calcareous cups through hundreds of thousands of years, to furnish the Coral Seas.

I travelled north to Gladstone, and much excited, set off for Heron Island, where a tourist hotel had been built. I slept in a small hut on the edge of the bush covering the island's centre; this provided nesting burrows for the local shearwaters and tree-nests for the handsome and absurdly tame noddy terns, which elsewhere breed on open ground. Every morning I was woken by the shearwaters waddling along the worn tracks through the underbrush and attempting to take off as soon as they saw light at the end of their arboreal tunnels. But, like the northern shearwaters I had seen in Pembrokeshire, they were very clumsy and often bumped against my hut, robbing me of sleep.

Armed with stout gum-boots from the hotel, I waded out into the shallow part of the lagoon – a strange and beautiful sight: the pink and white of the corals; the waving of the sea-fans or Gorgonians, with polyps set along plant-like fronds;

the sea-snails and sea-cucumbers, sea-urchins and starfish; and most extraordinary of all, the slit-like 'mouth' of the enormous bivalve Tridacna, which lies embedded in the sand, inhaling water into its interior and sifting out the minute food-particles. The edge of the mantle cavity of this fascinating bivalve is set with miniature lenses, which not only warn of approaching danger but also concentrate the sun's rays on the algae that live in the mollusc's mantle, thus enabling them to grow and multiply, and by their surplus provide food, which is channelled into the Tridacna's stomach – a remarkable case of symbiosis, valuable to both partners. But one must be careful not to put one's foot in the slit between the valves: they will snap on it like a vice, breaking bones and even trapping the imprudent, to drown in the rising tide.

Later, we went out in a glass-bottomed boat to peer into the deeper water. The parrot-fish were crunching bits of coral as if they were bread-crumbs, the huge groupers ready to pounce at small fish from their lurking-places in the coral caves, and the brilliant little coral-fish darting, at the slightest threat, to take refuge among the stinging tentacles of giant anemones (another case of symbiosis, for the coral fish bring snips of food to their hosts). I even saw the sinister shape of a shark swinging lazily along, scaring all other fish into shelter.

As a human being I loved the beauty of this subaqueous world; as a biologist, I marvelled at the complex web of animal and plant lives, woven through long ages into an interdependent ecological community.

My pockets stuffed with beautiful cowries and cone-shells, I returned to the mainland for another uncomfortable journey, to Townsville, still further north, on the Queensland coast. There, I changed into a little three-seater plane and set off across the base of Cape York, thinking how my grandfather had slashed his way through its forests a century earlier; then on to Darwin, over a semi-desertic plain, which appeared to be a vast graveyard dotted with red-brick tombstones. Actually these were innumerable termite nests, fabricated from the reddish soil below and rising to four or five feet. I calculated that the termite population of Australia's Northern Territory must be many times larger than the human population of the whole earth.

Termites owe their biological success to a strange partnership with a microscopic protozoan which lives in their gut and produces an enzyme enabling them to digest crude wood and other cellulose materials like paper, and turn them into assimilable food-stuffs. These diligent insects, the size of large ants (though the queen is huge, as large as a fat caterpillar), are one of the greatest pests in tropical countries, devouring wooden beams, furniture, books, anything not mineral, and covering the land with their strange architectural monsters – up to seventeen feet high (I saw one with all the massive quality and swelling contours of a Henry Moore sculpture). The big nests are almost indestructible, made of earth cemented with a glue-like substance secreted by the workers.

Darwin is the last outpost of civilization on the north of the continent. I found it depressing: so, it seems, did most of the inhabitants. There was nothing much there but the telegraph station, then the only channel of quick communication with countries to the north and west. Almost all the sea-going trade of these countries went to Perth, while Australian wealth and trade was concentrated in Adelaide, Melbourne and Sydney. The only recreation was bathing, but the water was almost tepid and I had to be very careful not to get stung by the numerous Portuguese men-of-war floating around. Tree-ferns and Pandanus palms border the shore, but the kookaburras fail to laugh; the joke is that they have nothing to laugh about. Actually, they belong to a different subspecies from those in the south, and their call is much less boisterous.

I met some cheerful abos on Melville and Goulburn Islands. On the latter, a remarkable missionary had established a mission farm, where he succeeded in teaching his charges to grow wheat and do carpentry, making paddles for their canoes and souvenirs for tourists. They were excellent craftsmen when given the chance. The only trouble was the immemorial tribal urge to go on 'walk-about' into the wilds of Arnhem Land. After all, why not? We, in so-called civilized Europe, have an

112

annual urge to take our holidays in different surroundings, and the abos' walk-about gives them a valuable contact with the mysteries of their own race and of nature.

On the borders of Lake Oenpelli, I saw what I took to be a tree covered with white and pink blossom. On nearer approach it exploded into a flock of galahs, beautiful but destructive small cockatoos, with orange crests, pale-pink wings and white bellies – an unforgettable sight.

My next port of call was Alice Springs. I set off with an abo driver on the 1,000-mile journey along the bitumen, as the Australians call macadamized roads. A few miles south of Darwin, something went wrong with the car, and while the driver walked back for a spare part, I wandered about in the forest, where I found the largest termitary I had yet seen, eighteen feet high. There were a few cycads, those strange, primitive plants, halfway between ferns and palms. (They are also found in South Africa and South America, supporting Wegener's theory that the three continents were once united and later drifted apart.)

This is confirmed by other biological evidence: the southern beech, Notofagus, which I saw growing in the forests of Tasmania and southern Queensland, is also found in Chile; and both Australia and Africa possess the beautiful Proteas, as well as those strange, bulbous trees, the baobabs. Nor must we forget that marsupial mammals are found only in Australia and South America, while egg-laying mammals exist only in Australia. This last fact indicates an early date for the isolation of that continent, at least 200 million years ago.

Idly reflecting on these strange, earth-shaping phenomena, I fell into a doze, from which I was awakened by a gentle touch on my hand. I opened my eyes and there was a gorgeous tropical butterfly, spotted with bright colours, slowly making its way across my palm, putting out its proboscis to search for sweat. In these hot regions, every drop of fluid is precious to insects, especially saline fluid like sweat, to prevent desiccation and to replenish the body with precious minerals like chlorine. The velvety touch of the creature's frail limbs and questing proboscis was charming, and it was a delight to see the beautiful wings folding and opening at every step, only a few inches from my eyes.

At length the driver returned, the fabulous butterfly flew off, and we resumed our journey. I must say that it was monotonous, driving along that thousand miles. There were only three interesting incidents in the three days of that journey. One was the passage of an immense swarm of budgerigars, migrating from the plantations and forests in the north (which they had doubtless ravaged, bud-nipping like our bullfinches) in search of new areas to strip in the southern hills. They came in vast numbers, like a swarm of locusts, right over our heads. I was able to time them by our speedometer: they were flying at thirty-five miles an hour. It was very difficult to equate this devastating horde with the pretty little parakeets in our birdcages at home; but there they were, one of the plagues of the Australian continent.

The other main indigenous pest of Australia is the flying fox, a great fruit-bat with a wing-spread of over two feet, which does great damage to Australian orchards. Francis Ratcliffe had been set the task of controlling them; but, as he told me in Canberra, there was not much that could be done – there were just too many! One could scare them off particular spots with bonfires or try to reduce their numbers by shooting up their roosts. But there were always plenty left to reproduce and continue their destructive work. Their damage is slightly offset by one benefit: they pollinate the flowers of the trees whose fruit they later devour.

Another outstanding natural history event for me was a flock of giant black cockatoos with scarlet crests; but that was in the south, after our long drive.

Next day, we passed several abandoned cattle-stations, doomed by recurring droughts in this semi-arid waste. At evening we arrived at a mission station, where a number of abo children flocked round us in their primitive nakedness. Their mothers, in ugly Mother-Hubbard dresses, hovered in the background. One little piccaninny came up to me with a smile and took my hand. The velvety touch and the trustfulness reminded me of the butterfly on my hand the day before, and

I hoped that the Australian Government would not default on their trusteeship for the natives.

Up till then, the abos had too often been treated with contempt, save in rare instances when they made themselves useful as trackers or cowboys; vast tracts of the tribal lands they used to roam were denied them, and they were now confined to reserves or mission stations – just like the North-American Indians.

I had urged in Canberra that they should be helped, but though 'integration' was proclaimed as a policy, little was being done to restore their self-respect or help them to earn their own living. Today, I believe, things are much better. They are no longer officially regarded as inherently inferior, but are being given much greater opportunities for bettering themselves through education, and by practising many crafts and trades from which they were formerly barred.

Of the other two memorable sights I saw on the three-day drive from Darwin, one was a solitary hill called the Abo's Leap, because of a legend that an abo woman, spurned by her lover, had committed suicide by throwing herself over the cliff. I had seen a similar isolated butte in Wyoming called the Indian's Leap, where the same legend prevailed – a romantic parallel between two remote peoples.

The other was the so-called Giant's Marbles. These resembled one of the Dartmoor tors, except that here the 'marbles' were huge, rounded granite boulders, piled up to a formidable height instead of lying scattered on the ground. The desert winds must be enormously powerful, for this one-time solid mountain of stone had been converted into a mass of separate boulders, their surface etched by driven sand.

Deep memories are sometimes rooted in physical discomfort – Benvenuto Cellini's father must have known this, when he beat his son to imprint on him the memory of a salamander playing in the flames: a curious story, for human eyes have never seen such a sight. I remember Alice Springs partly for the hunger I suffered there: under union regulations, no restaurant was allowed to feed travellers after five o'clock. I wandered along dusty streets in vain search of a meal, having missed my lunch on that interminable journey. I finally found a shabby corner where they gave me strong tea and meat patties – for which I was thankful.

But I remember it also for its landscape. This was truly fantastic: red sandstone cliffs fading to purple at sunset, and gleaming gold and orange when touched by beams of the rising sun; miniature canyons in the cliffs, with ivory gums growing in the dry torrent-beds; these are among the most beautiful of all Eucalypts, with deep-green canopy on stems of purest white, contrasting strikingly with the russet of the canyon walls.

Melbourne was in some ways the most old-fashioned town in Australia, in spite of its prosperity. There were more of the Victorian wrought-iron balconies here than in Sydney, and the Club had been left untouched since late-Victorian times: the leather armchairs outdid those of the Athenaeum, and gaslight was provided in the original glass globes.

I heard many interesting stories from my host, Sir Mac-Farlane Burnet, the distinguished medical man, head of the Federal Medical Services, which included the unique 'Flying Doctor' system for the sparsely populated outback.

One tale I particularly remember concerned a great forest fire that had broken out a few years previously, just north of Melbourne. The weather was very dry, and there was a hot wind from the desert. The resinous eucalyptus trees were, of course, an easy prey for the flames. But in one place, where a cliff reflected the hot wind, they did something which I thought impossible – they burst into spontaneous combustion.

Not all the forest was destroyed. I was taken out into its depths by Jock Marshall, zoologist at the University (whom I got to know much better when he lived near us at Hampstead, while preparing his remarkable book on bower-birds and their habits). He showed me the largest non-coniferous trees in the world, a Eucalypt actually topping the 300-foot mark.

I had much wanted to see a cock lyre-bird displaying his amazing lyre-shaped plumes, which he erects in a foam of white and bronzy-purple when dancing on his special display-mound. But, alas, we merely heard his song. He uses a wonderful range of notes and often snatches of song mimicked from other birds. Nobody seems to know what this vocal mimicry signifies: perhaps a challenge to mimicked birds, a warning not to trespass?

Later, in the New South Wales National Park, I saw the most extraordinary bower, marking the display site of the satin bower-bird. This creature, like most other bower-birds, decorates its bower, in this case a tunnel of twigs, with gleaming objects – small shells, feathers, bits of bone and of bright metal, even stolen jewellery, with a preference for blue and purple (matching his own blue eyes). So among the white and shiny objects he places blue feathers and flowers, and has been seen stealing blue-bags from laundries. To cap all, he paints his tunnel-run, through which he chases potential mates, using the juice of blue berries as pigment, with a twig in his beak as brush. He is thus one of the half-dozen non-human creatures known to use a tool, and probably the only one to become an artist ...

Koala bears are not, of course, true bears, though they look so like toy teddy-bears, with button eyes and short leathery snout. They are arboreal marsupials, related to the sloths in South America, and like them, swing slowly from branch to branch suspended by their hooked claws. They live entirely on a few species of eucalyptus, now much depleted on the mainland, and vast numbers of the harmless little creatures had also been killed (mostly to make gloves for arctic trappers!). So the State Government made Phillips Island a sanctuary and transported 100 koalas there. I saw quite a number of them clawing their way up the trunks and eating upside-down. They are extremely tame and seem affectionate but I was warned not to startle the one I held, for its claw-like nails could rip one's face open.

Hobart, as I have already mentioned (Vol. I, p. 15), was another link with my ancestral past, for my maternal grandmother was Julia Sorell, daughter of the then Governor of Tasmania. Julia was the belle of Hobart, and I often wondered whether both my grandfathers had danced with her there – Tom Arnold while he was courting her, and Tom Huxley at the ball given in honour of Captain Stanley of H.M.S. *Rattle-*

snake and his officers. At any rate, I have a double connection with southern Australia, and both my Christian names, Julian and Sorell, commemorate my Tasmanian ancestry.

On my way to Lake Sorell, I was struck by the 'Englishness' of the scenery. Gorse had early been introduced to the island and had spread all over the slopes of the pretty valley, which might have been anywhere in Britain.

Among Tasmania's attractions are the fairy penguins, with their main breeding-grounds in an east-coast bay. They are the smallest of all penguins. While the females are sitting the males go fishing, returning in the evening with fish in their gullets to regurgitate to their mates and chicks. This nightly return is quite a spectacle, and when we went to see it, there were a number of Tasmanian families picnicking on the shore, waiting for it. Hundreds of the little creatures, driven by the strong wind, got tumbled on to the sand by the breakers, but they picked themselves up as if nothing had happened and started to make their way inland, ridiculous but charming with their rolling sailor's gait and flippers outstretched for balance. Toddling on through the dunes, they reached their burrows, where they indulged in a regular orgy of vocal greetings, a duet of grunts and cackles, not musical but heart-felt, for penguins are very loyal and affectionate to their mates and much enjoy each other's company.

From Hobart I was taken out into the rain-forests to the south-west, composed of strange and spectacular trees, known locally as 'horizontals'. These put out horizontal boughs which not only continue to branch laterally, but send down suckers, which root and turn into new stems. The space beneath this branched roof is so encumbered that it is difficult for a man even to crawl through it, and the flat surface of inter-twining side branches looks so solid that cars and even lorries have been fooled into driving over it, only to crash down into the under-brush.

This forest covers the whole south-west quarter of the island, up steep hills and across deep valleys so impregnable that they have never been penetrated except by a few rash prospectors. The area is the last haunt of the Tasmanian Devil, the vicious marsupial carnivore that looks rather like a small bear. Killed off elsewhere because of its depredations on poultry, conservationists feared that it had become extinct. At last, this year, a few have been spotted and I should imagine that the forest will continue to protect them.

I had wanted to see the beautiful black swans of Australia in their natural habitat, so I was taken by Mountfort and Mawson, the Antarctic explorer, to the Coorong, a huge sand-fringed lagoon south of Adelaide. There, on the far side, we could see a black line extending for at least a mile, which resolved itself, after we had embarked in our little motor launch, into a tremendous horde of black swans. When they flew up at our approach the spectacle was overwhelming – I estimated their number at 2,000–3,000; the swish of their pinions and the clangour of their whistling note assaulted our ears, and their black wings, touched with a bar of white, were like a beautiful thunder-cloud over our heads.

A large colony of pelicans also nests on the Coorong, and the great birds came flopping down within a few yards of us to feed their young. They regurgitate the fish into their own pouches, which then serve as soup-basins for the hideous young, patched with tufts of white down.

At Perth University, in Western Australia, I met Professor Pearson, a zoologist who takes a keen interest in the Australian fauna, that unique collection of pouched mammals which has evolved since the continent was isolated from the rest of the world.

We spent a final day visiting a National Park in the wooded foot-hills to the south. I carried away two vivid memories. One was of a gigantic iron-wood tree, a species of Acacia – so big that it took ten men to encircle its trunk. The other was the carpet of flowers under the forest cover – Leschenaultia, flat and star-like, of a wonderful azure blue.

It was a fitting end to my naturalist's journey round this strange island-continent.

CHAPTER 8

To the Philippines, Indonesia and Thailand

THE Philippines, in spite of nearly fifty years of American occupation, and all the educational and material benefits that it had conferred, were, at the time of my visit, in a state of near-war between two opposing groups. Indeed, internal conflict was, one might say, endemic in the archipelago, even after it had become independent at the end of the Second World War.

The major reason for my visit was to attend an International Conference in Manila arranged by IUCN, the organization for Nature Conservation I had founded and built up while at UNESCO (p. 46). This seemed a pleasant duty; but I was still badly overtired by all my Australian journeyings, with the night flight from Perth on top of it, so it was not welcome to receive a message from my old friend Harold Coolidge, head of the American section of IUCN and chairman of the Conference: he was sick, and would I please go in his place to inspect a new dam-site in the northern mountains and report on its effect on the scenery.

I felt I had to accept and went off on a gruelling trip in a jeep. The mountain forests were beautiful, but there were rebel guerrillas lurking in them and an armed guard had to be provided for us. Luckily nothing happened, and we climbed safely to where the ricefields were terraced up the steep slopes, their glistening emerald strips in sharp contrast with the dark crown of the forest above.

The dam, built by American engineers with the reluctant help of local labour, was situated in a fine wooded gorge. When completed it would provide vast quantities of electric power, and irrigation for the lower rice paddies; it would also, I felt, enhance the scenery of the area. However, I heard later that the project had been abandoned, leaving a half-finished mess.

The Conference opened the same afternoon. I fear I slept through most of it, but it made important decisions, setting up one National Park in the north and another in the south.

My next stop was some thousand miles south-west, at Kuching in Sarawak, where I met my old acquaintance Tom Harrison, now Director of the Sarawak Museum. He was devoting part of his energy to collecting relics of the tribal past – war canoes, shields and spears – journeying into the interior to interview the savage inhabitants about their legends and customs, and photograph their splendid barbaric ceremonies.

He and his wife were also interested in conservation and were active in protection work. One of their concerns was the edible swift, whose nest, made of straws gummed together by the bird's glutinous saliva, is boiled to make the famous bird's-nest soup so esteemed by the Chinese. They were also trying to save the turtles breeding on a beach to the west, and had just succeeded in making the area a reserve. But their main concern was to save the orang-outangs. The adults were being killed by Dyaks when they raided the tribal crops, and the young were captured, often after their mothers had been killed, for zoos all over the world. Furthermore, conditions in the ships transporting them were often bad and many died in transit.

It was tragic to think that this rare and peaceable relative of man was being thus decimated – another in the long list of species in danger of total extinction.

From Borneo, I flew south-west again, across the equator, to Java, where I met Juliette.

Here we had our first real introduction to tropical ecology, with its fantastically exuberant vegetation, its trees with bunches of leathery leaves, shaped like giant hands, like plates, like plumes, cut out of green metal; huge scarlet flowers, Judas-trees, Bougainvillaeas, frangipanis, mangoes, cannon-ball and bread-fruit trees. Sheets and pennants of vital chlorophyll draped on arboreal armatures, climbing through alien branches to explode in improbable flowers high up towards the open sky; giant trunks anchored in the soil by splayed roots or buttressed with flanges. And all prepared for the great rains which wash and polish the green metallic foliage, and drench the jungle soil into a steamy sponge. Above and between this incoherence of nature rise man's orderly paddy terraces, with their strips of shiny water and their delicate green growth, subtly following the contours of the mountain.

The heat became a major fact of life, all pervading, night and day. Crowds of people bathed in the numerous canals of Jakarta, which they also drank from (and used as sewers). Cyclists pedalled furiously along the highway, while streams of pedestrians crowded every street and lane – an exuberant population matching the exuberant vegetation.

After a visit to Jogjakarta in the centre of Java, we crossed the narrow straits to Bali.

It is impossible not to rhapsodize over this enchanting and enchanted island. In 1953, Bali was still to all appearances a small and perfect paradise, with people of great personal beauty and grace, highly cultured and creative. The Dutch occupation had interfered as little as possible with the island's traditional beliefs and customs (a blend of Hindu theology and ancient pagan ritual). They had actually forbidden the entry of missions of any denomination – a ruling reversed when independence came to the Dutch East Indies. One of the results of the missionary influx which then took place was a veto on women's naked breasts; henceforth they were to be covered with a blouse over their batik sarongs. Luckily it was not always enforced: among a people of such universal grace and poise, bare breasts were natural and lovely, enhancing the women's sculptural beauty – caryatids carrying baskets on their heads, or mothers 'wearing' their babies straddled on the hip, their bodies slightly bent to accommodate the stress.

The men, bare-chested, wore short sarongs and were slim and handsome. In fact, I do not think we saw one ugly person during our stay. Neither did we see anyone not engaged in some creative or expressive activity – singing in the rice-paddies, weaving, carving, dancing, playing the gamelan, making the elaborate offerings for a religious festival, shaping flowers and birds out of coconut flour. Even a shell we picked up was promptly housed in a little leaf-box deftly plaited by a child.

We stayed in the palace of the ex-Rajah of Oebud, a small and gentle man demoted at independence, who made a living by using his ancestral dwelling as a hotel. It was a collection of pavilions with carvings over doors and windows, simple but comfortable furniture and a lean-to attached for bathing facilities, consisting of a large tub from which one spooned out enough water to shower oneself. Juliette mistook the tub for the bath, and with some difficulty climbed into it. She remarked on this curious arrangement to our escort, who was shocked.

Our pavilion had a slightly macabre history: it was used in earlier times for initiation rites, among which was the very painful filing of teeth. There had been some grim sides to this gentle paradise ...

We met a procession carrying a corpse to be burnt on a funeral pyre. Even this sad event was an occasion for beauty, with moving song, brightly-painted banners commemorating the virtues of the deceased, and every mourner garlanded with flowers.

The highlight of our stay was a traditional play, commanded by the Rajah. Troops of men and women came in at dusk from the nearest village, five miles away, though they had been working all day and would have to be up at dawn next morning. The principal dancers were little girls, 7 or 8 years old, arriving in the uniform of their mission school – white blouses and short navy skirts. We went into the tent to watch their theatrical transformation: their little bodies were swathed in long rolls of white cotton, compressing them to animated tubes. Over the moulding cotton came the brocaded bands, stiff collars of painted and gilt leather, elaborate head-dresses of high conical shape. Their little faces were daubed with rice-flour, their eyes surrounded with kohl, eyebrows drawn in a fine line, lips rouged. Impassive under their masks, the little girls danced, their chrysalis-like figures arched over knees bent apart, poised with straight backs, hands flexed with incredible suppleness expressing a whole gamut of meaning. The village orchestra accompanied the dancers in perfect unison, without the help of a conductor, changing the rhythm with each phase of the ballet, introducing variations of infinite subtlety, every instrument unerringly combined. There were drums, one-stringed fiddles, sithars, a series of resonant pots, and the great gamelan, a contraption of assorted pieces of wood, supported on a frame and beaten with wooden mallets. They were carefully cut to give an ascending scale of twanging quarter-tones, very different from our European scale.

There is no written score for Balinese musicians – they learn by long practice and co-operate as if by instinct, the whole group improvising on the spot, while children learn by joining the group.

The climax was terrific – the wicked witch, masked like a Tibetan devil armed with huge claws, leapt on to the stage to cast her spells on the warrior-hero. The chrysalis girls whirled with hands outstretched in supplication against the witch's creeping approach, while the circle of villagers raised their arms in loud incantation, symbolically chasing away the witch and all evil influence. Then, suddenly, there came a hushed silence, broken by a great sigh of relief from the crowd, when the warrior struck down the devil-woman, followed by a final bout of tremendous applause.

The whole troupe then changed back into their everyday garb, packed up, and tramped back the five miles to their village.

Next night we saw the unforgettable monkey-dance under a banyan-tree, with a high lamp illuminating the players' quintuple circle, 150 of them, sitting cross-legged with bare torsos, light glimmering on dark-gold skin. It starts violently into action, all the men swaying and shouting 'Tcha, tcha' in perfect unison, expending a forceful energy from their sitting position, their raised open hands all pointing to the high centre while their bodies tensely sway. For three-quarters of an hour we watched absolutely entranced; and carried away the vision of those 300 hands stretched out in stark supplication – or denunciation – of a dark mystery, with the unending shouts of 'Tcha, tcha tcha'. There was no music.

Looking across the narrow straits to Lombok, the next island in the chain, I recalled that this marked the so-called Wallace Line – the sea-gap where the Indian fauna and flora from the west give way to the plants and animals characteristic of New Guinea and northern Australia. Later research has largely justified Alfred Wallace's conclusion, though the separation of the two faunas and floras is not quite as sharp as he supposed.

*

Back in Java, we visited the shrine of Borobodur, one of the most amazing temples in the world. It towered before us, a huge stepped pyramid consisting of no fewer than nine terraces running round the conical building, their walls decorated with elaborate sculpture commemorating notable scenes in Buddhist theology and history. Even the foundation walls had been richly carved with demons and devilish figures, and scenes of the hellish underworld, although they were originally buried in the earth.

We circled from terrace to terrace, performing the sacred rite of nine perambulations. On the parapet of the ninth circle stood nine stone bells, perforated so that worshippers could see the statues of the Buddha within. But at the top of the centre of the ninth platform stood a single perforated bell containing – nothing. A wonderful symbol of the ultimate goal of Buddhism – Nirvana, the all-embracing nothingness of absolute peace, its very emptiness more eloquent than any man-made image.

Borobodur is now, as so many great monuments of the past, on the danger list, its foundations giving way under the colossal weight they support. UNESCO has set up a fund and a team of experts to save it.

And Bali? A new Hilton is being built there; Japanese transistors are ousting the music of the gamelan, and I expect that mass-produced plastic flowers will soon replace the delicate artefacts lovingly created for the great festivals. Alien ideas and techniques are sweeping in, destroying the unconscious paradise we saw. Is it the inevitable price of material progress? Or can we reharness mankind's creative skill and will into new but equally satisfying activities?

At the University of Jogjakarta we also witnessed the depressing sight of a large assemblage of students, some crowded out of the big Aula Magna on to the steps outside, taking down in their note-books a lecture on law, delivered at dictation speed by the invisible professor. This mechanized so-called higher education was very depressing. We found the same sort of thing in India – there are just too many students, and they are not given the chance of any original thinking.

From Java, we crossed the equator again to Singapore, where

we were the guests of Malcolm Macdonald, then High Commissioner for South-East Asia.

Malcolm, who has always got on very well with people of every race, invited a charming Chinese millionaire, Loke Wan Tho, and his beautiful wife Christine to meet us at dinner. It turned out that Loke, like myself and Malcolm, was keen on natural history, especially birds. He later took us to an amazing tropical swamp and forest which he had bought as a nature reserve. Here again there were orchids of many kinds, from tall ground orchids to climbers and bird's-nest types coiled round tree branches, their fantastic flowers suspended in mid-air. There were fresh-water turtles in the swamp, and enormous tropical butterflies, gaily coloured, flapping slowly away. We caught one, and Nelson, the local naturalist, whom Loke had also invited, showed us the tufts of evil-smelling hair at the tip of its abdomen, to deter possible predators, as did the brilliant coloration. No wonder Wallace spent nearly eight years in the Malay Archipelago – even in this tiny marsh there were marvels enough. A flying squirrel, *Galeopithecus*, was clinging to a tree-trunk; as we approached, it scrambled higher, spread the skin membrane joining fore and hind limbs and glided gently to a more distant tree. Even more remarkable, we saw the same aerial trick practised by a reptile – the large flying lizard, *Draco volans*, which extends a frill of scales along its flanks when disturbed, and glides almost as far as the flying squirrel.

Then there was a large frog so beautifully camouflaged that it was indistinguishable from the surrounding leaves; the little green herons (the same species I had seen in Louisiana); the racket-tailed drongo, the elongated tail-plumes of the males ending in oval discs – and, great triumph for Loke, a flock of the rare needle-tailed swifts, speedier and more agile even than our own large species. And so I could continue ...

The culmination of our stay was a dinner given us by the Loke Wan Thos in their pent-house on top of Singapore's highest sky-scraper. He had inherited a fortune from his father, who rose from cooliedom to riches when in charge of the catering for a railway-building enterprise. Loke himself was a shrewd businessman, but also an artist in living; he had amassed a splendid collection of jade and Chinese porcelain, and was an amateur photographer of no mean talent, as well as a keen naturalist. Alas, he was killed in an air accident a few years later.

I seldom remember the details of my meals, though I enjoy the evanescent pleasure of eating them. But this dinner was a high point in gastronomy, being composed of bird's-nest soup, gelatinous but crisped with noodles cooked in chicken broth, subtle-tasting, very smooth in texture; then ancient eggs, black and slightly rubbery, served with bamboo shoots and ginger, each just one mouthful, but with a complicated taste, to be savoured slowly and thoroughly; an entrée of bamboo shoots and mushrooms stewed in delicious soya sauce, very tender; then chicken, cut small enough for chopsticks, eaten ungarnished; and then a wonderful fish, pomfret, cooked in mushroom gravy and covered with very finely shredded ham, mushrooms and onions, tender yet crisp, a real delicacy. Each new dish was twice proffered, our host saying: 'This is the last-but-one course, you must have some more.' As Malcolm Macdonald once remarked: 'A Chinese meal is a series of penultimate courses.' The last course of all was a great dish of rice with eggs, chicken, mushroom and various condiments – the host's ritual apology for the insufficient nourishment he provided: we declined this. The meal was washed down with a delicious half-dry liqueur, then a sumptuous red wine, and finished with a bowl of fruit, tasting like scented flowers.

After our brief stay in Singapore, we continued north, across the Gulf of Siam, to Thailand. Here I was to help Sir Charles Darwin and his assistant, Mr Gee, in a report to the Thai Government on scientific research and teaching in the country.

The weather was still very warm, even in mid-December. We stayed at the old Oriental Hotel on the river and enjoyed the mixed pleasures of watching the gondola-like boats plying up and down, mostly rowed by women, and eating pleasant food, while being in turn devoured by mosquitoes.

Besides visiting schools and laboratories with Sir Charles and his assistant, and discussing the need for introducing more biology into the school curriculum, we also 'did' everything that a self-respecting tourist should do.

The old city of Bangkok is full of palaces and pagodas – an enchanting mixture of fairy-land and film extravaganza: palaces whose doors and windows are decorated with intricate eyebrows of gilt carving, pagodas entirely covered with small mirror mosaics and ceramics, leaping into the sky with a series of ever smaller, tilted roofs, each corner tipped with an upright tongue of gold. As Somerset Maugham once wrote, Siamese architecture makes one laugh with delight that anything so fantastic should continue to exist in this humdrum world. I felt the same delight as we wandered through this forest of golden spires, guarded by imposing stone warriors with lion heads, or by mythical Garuda birds.

We dined with Prince Prem, great-grandson of the famous King Chulalongkorn (of *The King and I* fame): it was a large gathering, mostly of businessmen and diplomats, at which the guests were received by Prince Prem's mother, an old lady in a pale-blue two-piece suit, sitting in a low chair and accepting homage as the oldest surviving member of the royal line. Prince Dahni, whom we had met in Paris in UNESCO days, while he was Regent to the young King, prostrated himself before her on the floor and touched it three times with his forehead – as did several princesses of the blood. Her R.H. just sat and mumbled a greeting. After drinks, brought in by servants crawling on their knees, a buffet supper was served: delicious shredded vegetables and curry, followed by a sweet course of egg-yolk beaten with cream and squeezed through a fine sieve, with fresh fruit and jelly. All the Siamese ladies wore unattractive European-style dresses made of Siamese silk; none of them was as beautiful as the Javanese we had met, nor did they have the Javanese warmth and friendliness. The furniture was also disappointing, being mostly heavy European, except in bedrooms, where some of the lovely traditional Siamese carved and gilt pieces were kept.

Bangkok is a sort of Venice, with the difference that the canals, called *klongs*, are crowded with houseboats and a flourishing population; the water, as in Jakarta, is used for all purposes, with no dire results, owing, we were told by scientists, to its containing bacteriophage virus – so long as the balance between fresh and polluted water is kept in safe proportions. We heard the same thing in India, especially at Allahabad, where sick people often die in the Ganges. When the balance of effluents is exceeded, as in the North-American and Swiss lakes, the remedy is almost beyond reach.

Darwin and I went to visit the Minister of Agriculture and were told of the improved methods of rice cultivation, and then taken to see them near Ayuthia, the old capital. It certainly looked as if Thai rice would continue to be abundant, so long as improved strains were planted and efficient cultivation practised. Fish-ponds were also being made and stocked with Tilapia fish from East Africa, a useful supplement in a country with an insufficiency of animal protein.

The ruins of the deserted city were very impressive: instead of Chinese-style pagodas, they were dotted with so-called *dagobas*, steeple-like pinnacles on top of large hemispherical mounds of earth, erected over the ashes of past kings and nobles. In the centre, a great empty palace rose from the middle of a lake, with ruins all round it, like a sad dream.

Darwin told me that women students did better than men at Bangkok University. The explanation was simple enough: all Buddhist males, including the King, are expected to enter a monastery for at least a year, and many stay longer – some even permanently; for monks are exempt from military service, and monastic life is easy-going and fairly comfortable. Yet the monks have to beg for their daily food, and are obliged to do so from rich and poor alike: they sometimes fail to get anything but the humblest fare. The only examinations monks have to undergo are religious, concerning the teaching of the Buddha and his disciples. I suspect that they are just as farcical as Divvers at Oxford (which luckily has now been abolished).

Today I read, with surprise and horrified admiration, that Buddhist monks in south-east Asia have become politically minded, and have registered their protests against the Vietnam war by burning themselves alive, besides organizing violent anti-war processions.

I cannot even list all the schools, colleges, universities and

129

technical projects we visited. Suffice it to say that the Thai authorities were trying hard to foster science teaching and to apply science to benefit the common people; but we felt that they were not differentiating properly between the role of school and university, not insisting enough on research, nor stressing the importance of biological as against physico-chemical studies.

Our Report was well received. One immediate result was the detachment of a member of UNESCO's Regional Science Office in Manila to serve in Thailand. And if long-term results were satisfactory, Thailand's future seemed assured, until war or over-population began to damage the economic and social system of all south-east Asia.

Juliette and I took a long trip – twenty-four hours by train – to Chengmai in the north, through vast forests of teak on both sides of the line. In spite of the tiredness with which I had left Bangkok (I shudder when I look at my notebooks and see how many visits I had to make), the cooler atmosphere refreshed us and we were full of new energy. First, we set off to see the work of the Forestry Department, felling teak with the help of elephants. We saw a troop of them coil their trunks round the heavy logs, carry them up the bank and stack them with expert precision. One large elephant found a log too heavy and trumpeted for help: a young beast was sent to his aid, and together they hauled the mighty tree with much bulging of muscle under their thick, elastic skin.

At Chengmai itself we were met by the aged Abbot of a peaceful monastery: he surprised us by talking perfect English and even by recognizing me as former head of UNESCO. But then I reflected that pre-Reformation abbots of the great English monasteries had often occupied important posts as governmental advisers, and that it was natural, therefore, in a deeply religious country like Thailand, for religious dignitaries to be conversant with mundane affairs.

The monastery was approached by a splendid flight of stone steps. Most of its numerous shrines had gilded umbrellas on their roofs and plaster tigers flanking their doors. And some of the elaborately gilded window-frames were adorned with painted plaster snakes devouring plaster dragons.

A river flowed past the foot of the temple hill, crossed by a bridge of bamboo joints suspended on rattan lianas. It swayed dangerously as we made our cautious way across it. The monks, however, rode bicycles over it, their orange robes flapping in the wind. The lake from which the river flowed was exceedingly lovely, with grotto shrines cut into its deep, forested banks. Its fish were sacred and grew to vast size in their protected waters.

After returning to Bangkok, we made the short flight to Angkor, just beyond the Cambodian border. We flew over dense forest, followed by a vast swampy lake and sluggish rivers meandering vaguely across a semi-submerged plain. Then, on higher ground, but still within what seemed to be un-inhabited forest, rose the complex group of temples and palaces of Angkor, once the capital of the land of Khmer, now Cambodia.

All the buildings were on a fantastic scale, apparently built between the ninth and mid-thirteenth centuries; then the Khmer kings were expelled by invading Thais and their buildings abandoned, the commoners' wooden houses left to decay, the royal palaces and temples to be devoured by voracious Ficus trees and lianas. When the ruins were discovered by the French missionaries in 1860, the process had gone so far as to allow the huge trees to root themselves in the defeated masonry; much of this vegetable excess was removed and the walls restored, but the French archaeologists, with a sense of the dramatic poignancy of this colossal battle between rampant nature and the perishable works of man, left one area untouched. Here, long, grey root-tentacles had squeezed through the mortarless shrines, crushing apart architrave and pillar, choking the graceful rhythm of a frieze of dancing *apsaras*, cramping their ligneous muscles on to the crumbling walls, which yet are held together by the still-growing trunks of the great trees, anchored by out-growing buttresses. One walks in shocked amazement through long vistas of leaf-roofed passages, the green bowels of the invading forest, with here and there a forgotten Buddha brooding in the shadows. Lattice windows of stone, clearly derived from wooden originals, open on small courts choked with tumbled masonry, with the wing of a Garuda bird and the fat

131

belly of Ganesh, the elephant god of prosperity, with fragments of decorative panels like our Renaissance volutes. We had an impression of reckless exuberance, both in the intricate carvings and splendid architecture, and in the fierce vitality of the embracing vegetation.

Angkor Thom was the original and very sacred city of temples, while Angkor Wat, built 300 years later, was both temple, sacred palace and monastery. It has been described in Osbert Sitwell's admirable book, *Escape with Me*, as the Versailles of south-east Asia. It rises from the centre of a lake full of pink lotus and water-lilies, across a grand causeway bordered by huge and sacred Naga-cobras, each with seven heads.

The vast façade encloses a great court, with pillared corridors lined with relief carvings of the battles of the builder king. Within, a series of pillared terraces flank the stone mountain, culminating in a central tower, legendary centre of the world. As we emerged from porticos leading upwards, we would catch glimpses of the topmost tower against a sky of tumbling white clouds. We gazed enthralled at the jewel-like chiselling of this great aspiring cone, to be suddenly shaken by the sharp pleasure of colour – a yellow-robed priest standing theatrically in the black entry of the tower. When we finally reached the top of the steep steps, we found a group of young priests chatting in the cool shadow – a welcome sign of life.

The Bayon temple is very different: our first impression was of a jumbled cluster of rocky towers; gradually the eye perceives these rocks to have a smile, a haunting profile. Faces appear and separate themselves, and one sees that every tower has four visages covering the four points of the compass. There are fifty of these towers, ascending to a larger central one, built upon encircling terraces. Buddha[1] gazes to the four corners of the universe, serenely smiling his multiple smiles. It is an awing and impressive conception, beautifully carved and grandly designed.

As we emerged from the forest coolness into baking heat, our minds over-charged with wonder and an almost religious awe,

1. Probably ideal portraits of the builder king, as incarnation of the Buddha.

I thought of Gibbon's meditations on the fall of Rome as he walked through its empty Forum. But here the forest's green silence was more impressive, and the tree-tangled shrines evoked an even stranger story.

CHAPTER 9

And so to India

OUR main destination, as enjoined by my acceptance of the Kalinga Prize, was India; and there we now flew. Indeed, we went twice to this extraordinary country, and I shall here treat of both these visits.

Our first stop was Calcutta – and Calcutta shook us, as it has shaken many travellers before and since; I counted over 100 sacred cows on one side of the street in the six minutes we drove to our hotel: lying on tram-lines, strolling on pavements, sitting by traffic policemen at street crossings, grazing off vegetable stalls and dust-bins, gentle, mild, impervious to screeching brakes and honking horns, their large drooping ears flapping to the buzzing of flies. Some had docile calves with them, early inured to traffic problems. Thanks to their protected status, India's cattle were increasing even faster than her people, and now, I hear, there is a movement to fit them with contraceptives. Their bodies are sacred, but man may tamper with their reproduction.

And the people! It seemed that all India's poverty, misery, despair, and homeless vagrancy – indeed, the general unwantedness of the swarming population – was centred in these wide, ugly streets. Though we later found horrible slums in other cities, Calcutta was the worst. At sundown, these homeless humans lie anywhere in the streets, on pavements, in side alleys, covered only with their cotton dhotis, the small bundle of their possessions serving as a pillow – and God knows what despairing thoughts in their heads. Refugees, outcasts, unemployed – the sight of these lost human beings filled our hearts with unbearable pity and anger. And all through our journeys in India, beneath the magic and enchantment of an immense variety of impressions, of unique sights and, of course, some wonderful people, whose warm friendliness endlessly delighted us, there was this aching problem, this cruel over-population of cities, set against huge areas of sterile soil, deserts of sand we flew over, dry river beds – a deforested and worn-out land.

I was thankful to see India for the first time after it had achieved Independence. To have witnessed this misery under British rule would have shamed and distressed me. Yet to see it now also left me guilty, helpless though I was; it has remained one of those insoluble burdens which time does nothing to lessen. I have just read that population in India increased by 17 million people in 1969.

The phobia against killing animals in general (even mosquitoes) and cow-slaughter in particular has some ironic consequences. Though the sacred cows overgraze the land, their droppings could be valuable as manure; but so serious is the shortage of wood and charcoal that the cow-pats are plastered on walls to dry in the sun, later used to cook the villagers' food and provide a little winter heat, in spite of their vile and acrid smoke.

In Delhi, I walked out of our hotel on our first evening and was surprised and delighted to see a flight of green parakeets swooping down to roost in one of the busiest squares. I recalled the chattering flock of starlings that used to sweep down to roost in Westbourne Square, our old home, and the much vaster hordes that now descend on central London to find sleeping perches. But these were tropical beauties, and it was wonderful to see them fluttering like emeralds in the lamp-light. Their shrieking and cackling was much louder and more cacophonous than the murmuration of our starlings and made conversation difficult. It was in any case difficult enough, with street vendors bawling their wares and excited crowds endlessly jabbering.

After a few days we accepted the hospitality of Flux Dundas, the representative of the British Council in India, and he and his warm-hearted wife Joy were most helpful in arranging excursions and interviews in Delhi. He obtained permission for me to read in the university library, and in preparation for the millenary celebrations of Avicenna in Iran on our way home, I spent many hours there, mugging up everything I could find out about the great Persian polymath – physician, chemist, philosopher, historian and sage.

Among my interviews was a private one with Nehru, that great fighter for India's freedom – charming and well-bred, besides being formidably intelligent. He showed me my first Indian sunbird, glittering as it hovered before a flower in his garden, and told me how much he had learnt and written while jailed by the British – just like Patnaik.

He also spoke of India's problems: of bringing good water, health and education to the half-million villages scattered through the land; of recurrent famines and of the Government's attempts to check erosion by planting trees; and of the regulation that compelled doctors (who receive their medical education free) to spend at least a year in a village before setting up in more lucrative city practice.

When I went to take my leave at the end of our stay, I told him frankly that I believed over-population to be the greatest threat to the country's prosperity. He pooh-poohed this, and said that India's prime need was industrialization. This was also the view of his President, Radhakrishnan, the tall, handsome sage who had been India's representative on UNESCO's Executive Board. In 1959, however, basing himself on official figures, and staggered by the multiplicity of students clamouring for places at universities, not to mention the recurrent famines, aggravated by overcrowding, Nehru not only agreed that the problem was urgent, but took the chair at the opening session of the Population Conference in Bombay, organized by that formidable Parsee, Lady Rama Rau. He also ordered the Department of Health to get a move on with measures for controlling population.

On a later visit to Madras, we realized that this was having some effect, for we found that men who had fathered four children could be sterilized by the harmless operation of vasectomy (which still permits pleasurable sex) and were even paid a few rupees for their consent. Now (1969), I read that the bribe has been increased by the offer of a transistor radio – fewer people, but more noise!

Birth-control for women incurs greater difficulties. With both Muslims and Hindus, any contact of a woman with a male doctor is unthinkable, and the old mother-in-law too often believes that the whole business is unnatural and will do her best to prevent any young woman relative from being fitted with a satisfactory appliance. The pill was a step forward, but it will take time to popularize it.

Whatever the cause, birth-control in India has not been much of a success. At the time of my first visit, the population of India and Pakistan was well over 400 millions. Today it is nearer 600 millions.

New Delhi was, of course, full of reminders of the British – the statues of British personages remained (until later the Indians replaced them with their own heroes). But Old Delhi has kept its character and its history, in its forts and palaces, its bazaar and busy market places, its extraordinary iron pillar at the Qutb, erected in the third century B.C. by that remarkable king, Asoka. The first Indian prince to embrace Buddhism, he became so disgusted by the slaughter of his triumphant campaigns that he determined never to fight again. His reign is one of the great examples of history, and the iron pillar which he built, among other surviving edifices, is a superb piece of workmanship and technology. By a method which I believe has never been explained, the iron has resisted some 2,000 years of exposure without a trace of rust.

The Muslim invasion of India, during the fantastic explosion of Arab power, led to the establishment of Islam as the official religion of northern India, and the Emperor in Delhi as well as the Moguls in neighbouring states all became Mohammedans. As they were forbidden by their religion to make representations of human forms, they decorated their palaces with elaborate mosaics inlaid on marble, representing flowers and leaves and occasional birds, against a brilliant background of blue and gold. The Red Fort in Old Delhi is especially rich in these dehumanized decorations, executed by Italian craftsmen specially imported for the work. Water in stone runnels refreshed the great halls, wide courts conferred spacious majesty on this wonderful palace, while the marble windows, delicately fretworked to admit the slightest breeze, were both lovely and functional.

We saw the same versatile architecture in the Red Fort at Agra, and in Fatehpur Sikri, the noble palace erected and then abandoned by Shah Akbar. These were among the flawless creations of Mogul India, and made us realize the immense power of this vital Moslem culture, grafted on Indian roots. For not only did Babur and Akbar fuse the conquered religions with their own beliefs and social systems; they also contributed their own magnificent style of architecture, both religious and profane.

We relished the Muslim sense of proportion which opened vast sunny courts or cool chambers to the eye, promised seclusion and meditation in small uprising pavilions, secret delight in dark inner bath-chambers panelled with small mirror mosaics, reflecting pin-points of light like a multiple eye. Threads of water wove in and out with a gentle tinkle, even more precious in that sun-baked land than in the hills of Granada.

The most notable of all Islamic monuments is, of course, the famed Taj Mahal, built by Akbar's grandson, Shah Jehan, in memory of his beloved wife Mumtaz. It was certainly impressive, with its huge cupola and slender minarets, sparkling in white marble, the whole reflected in a long pool bordered by dark cypresses. It remains in our memories as one of the world's jewels, but not, I must add, without some reservations: it fills the eye with wonderment but leaves the heart cold, with its functionless expanse of inner space.

These grand palaces called for, and contained under Akbar, an amazing civilization, a court life where East and West met and discussed everything. Akbar, like his contemporary, our own Queen Elizabeth I, strove to unify his dominions and even to create religious unity within them, discussing theology and ritual with Jesuit missionaries and Jain and Hindu saints, as well as Muslim priests and devotees of yoga; he was surpassed in his humanism only by the great Buddhist monarch Asoka (p. 137), whom H. G. Wells considered 'the greatest king in the world'.

Alas, Akbar's influence lasted but 100 years. His successors were vain and cruel, often tyrannical. His great-grandson Aurangzeb finally destroyed Akbar's legacy of enlightenment, defaced many fine paintings, suppressed music and dancing, and became the bigoted Calvin of Muslim India.

*

On the way back to Delhi we stopped at Bharatpur, itself a picturesque little fortified town, with wild peacocks grubbing about the streets and a gaudily caparisoned elephant passing through the city's main gate. We were on our way to a nature reserve created by the Rajah of Bharatpur on his estates. It turned out to be more of a shooting preserve, though the Rajah explained that he personally limited his bags to a reasonable figure; in the old days, when the British were there, his predecessors had organized veritable massacres. Some tablets recorded these special triumphs of killing; on one occasion, when the Viceroy was present, the bag exceeded ten thousand duck, with hundreds of snipe, woodcock, wild swans, and even herons and cranes of various kinds.

It was a pleasant place: we saw a few blue herons, some little green bitterns and painted storks, and there were songbirds in the trees. But on the main, wide lake there were only a few hundred duck – no wonder the Rajah limited his own bag!

Every year in January, Hindus of all castes unite for prayer at a gathering called Khumb Mehla at the junction of the sacred rivers, the Ganges and the Jumna. This year was particularly auspicious, being the last of a twelve-year cycle. We flew to Allahabad, over the wide sandbanks of the Ganges, flowing sluggish and grey-brown in its restricted bed, and were taken to the Mehla by Colonel Ratan Swami in his jeep.

The site of the sacred festival was like a fairground, the number of worshippers fantastic – our Colonel estimated it as at least a million. A temporary township had been created to accommodate this multitude, with tracks traversing clusters of grass huts, tents of canvas, or of blankets, shelters of rags. There were also first-aid marquees and observation towers, as well as a very necessary police station. Along the lanes sat patient pilgrims wrapped in white cloths, eating, cooking, mostly just squatting. We went through an area of huts with long bamboo poles tipped with coloured pennants portraying devices of slippers, baskets, tridents – the various symbols of the saddhus, the professional holy men – round which clustered groups of disciples in search of learning and second-hand sanctity. And everywhere, as far as the eye could reach, the slowly pulsating mass of pilgrims wandered in their flowing draperies, ant-like in their multitudinous rambling. They were like the grains of the sand, turned into human insects.

We threaded our way, first by jeep and then on foot, among the people, scanning their absorbed faces and seeing that their almost identical garb concealed vast differences; for these people, rich and poor, had come from all over India, on foot, in trains and planes and private cars. Moved by imponderable but compelling faith, they come to the rivers' purifying waters. They cast aside all but the need to wash away their sins, and daily, whatever the cold or heat, perform their ritual ablutions. Some nights are especially propitious because of the conjunction of stars, and in the surprising cold of this season, they stand for hours in the nocturnal waters. After this immersion, which they do in sari or dhoti, their wet garments are replaced with the dexterity and modesty of people accustomed to bathing in public. The women then wash the clothes and hang them on every available guy-rope, spread them on the sand, or merely hold them out to dry in the breeze.

Long-haired fakirs, clad only in a loin-cloth, smeared all over with ash and white and ochre paint, shout slogans. 'Cow murder must stop' is one of their favourites. Child fakirs, looking like miniature Buddhas in meditation, squat immobile for hours, their small bodies blotched with ash, to be rewarded by the faithful with a few annas. Other fakirs lie on beds of thorns or nails, strewn with flowers dropped on them by admiring worshippers.

Some old or sick people come here to die; their ashes are then thrown into the river for added sanctity. As I wrote before, these rivers are said to carry self-generated viruses which destroy bacteria, and tests have shown that the noxious effluence produced by the multitude is neutralized after flowing three or four miles. It would need to be, I thought with a shudder.

Enormous, swaying elephants carrying loads of saddhus timidly tried a pontoon bridge; one panicked and reversed into the packed crowd behind, causing a crush in which a number of pilgrims were killed. Our Colonel told us how easily such a tragedy could occur in this compacted congregation; how easily, too, anger could flare between rival processions and how quickly swell to danger point.

We hired a boat and went out on the broad river in the afternoon heat. Even to float on the surface confers sanctity: the whole expanse was dotted with craft of every kind. Many of the pilgrims were singing, while others were throwing their garlands into the river, as a symbolic sacrifice of themselves. Evening fell as we returned, past the frowning bastions of the old fortress dipping straight into the water, with a beautiful sunset reflected in the oncoming stream. Relative peace had descended on the vast fair-ground, a faint cloud of dust floated over it, and crowds of pilgrims made their way to their tents. The small fakir boy we had noticed earlier in the day was still squatting like a statue, but now repressing a tired yawn: poor little fellow – he was still earning his keep.

We left Allahabad feeling that in India all things are possible – holiness and squalor, fakirs who are fakers, religious hostility, and above all confusion and unpredictable violence.

Farther down the Ganges lies Benares, holiest of all Hindu cities. With memories of Kipling's *Kim* in our minds, we made our way along the Great Trunk Road, still shaded by avenues of British-planted mango trees, here and there replaced by the Indian Forestry Department with young saplings.

This gave us a very good impression, an impression which was confirmed when I later met one of the chief foresters in Calcutta. The Department had a huge programme for reforesting the barren plains of north-west India, and for planting shade-trees in the villages. Luckily this latter aim was reinforced by religious feelings – the peepul tree (a banyan-like species of fig) was considered sacred, because the Buddha had been converted to saintly life when, as a young prince, he had rested during a hunt under a bo-tree, as the peepul was then called. The tradition has lingered for over 2,000 years, and it was considered a duty to plant a peepul tree in a village, where it has the additional function of providing a shady refuge for the discussions of the village elders.

The Director of Forestry was also responsible for wild-life conservation and National Parks. This was a heavy assignment, for in the wooded areas villagers were always trespassing into the State forests to cut firewood, and poachers in the Gir Desert in the Rann of Kutch were killing off the few remaining lions as saleable trophies. They were also shooting Indian rhino for their horns, regarded here, as in Africa, by obvious Freudian transference, as agents for restoring male virility. However, the Department was aided by some of the rajahs – our friend at Bharatpur had restricted his bag of duck, and the Maharajah of Mysore had set aside a huge tract of his own jungle-lands as a sanctuary for tigers, elephants and the little woodland deer.

To return to Benares, innumerable sick people come here hoping to be cured by a dip in the holy (but dirty) Ganges, or if that fails, to wait patiently to die, achieving transcendence by having their corpses burned on the banks of the sacred river, which will then receive their ashes.

We saw several such burnings – the pyre lit by the mute and impassive next of kin, the slow fire revealing the blackened corpse to our shocked European eyes. For the Hindu, acceptance blunts the horror of the burning-ghat, and they are denied time for long mourning, for in this climate the dead must be burnt immediately. It was all part of the river-side activity – pilgrims taking their ritual baths, beggars, vendors under large umbrellas, women carrying loads on their draped heads, looking like caryatids in their beautiful draperies. Laundering goes on all the time – men and women slapping wet clothes on flat stones or beating them with a stick, then spreading them to dry on sand or step in a pattern of gay colours.

Beggars everywhere – I still recall the tragic creatures, exhibiting bodies eaten away with disease, pursuing with relentless avidity. And the beautiful gold and silver saris, exquisitely coloured and woven in startling designs, sold in squalid *souks* while beggars nudge for alms.

Aldous went to India in 1925, and wrote *Jesting Pilate* on his travels (which included visits to Burma, Malaya and North America). He was as bewildered as we were by the fantastic mixture of creeds, architecture and styles, cultures and languages in this 'blotting-paper' sub-continent, which has absorbed innumerable invasions, so many races, divinities and cultural influences.

About Hinduism he wrote:

Admirers of India are unanimous in praising Hindu 'spirituality'. I cannot agree with them. To my mind, spirituality (ultimately, I suppose, the product of the climate) is the primal curse of India and the cause of all her misfortunes. It is this preoccupation with 'spiritual' realities, different from the actual realities of common life, that has kept millions upon millions of men and women content, through centuries, with a lot unworthy of human beings. A little less spirituality, and the Indians would now be free – free from foreign dominion and from the tyranny of their own prejudices and traditions. There would be less dirt and more food.

The vast number of strange divinities made visible in every kind of form, the caste system, the taboos and superstitions, the vagaries of the innumerable cults (including the erotic explosion of Tantric Buddhism); it all adds up to what? – an impenetrable fog of custom, belief and ritual. And I agreed with Aldous that it was the sort of luxury which India least of all could afford. Yet I could not help being moved by this climate of intense religiosity. The genius of the Buddha had cut through religious tangles and found a great and liberating answer: strange that such a magnificent religion should have dwindled in India, and lost its meaning – until one remembered the power of the Brahmins and the appeal of the complex and legendary polytheism of the Hindus.

One of the strangest sects is sited at Puri, in Orissa, where the temple of the god Jagannath raises its imposing complex, closed to all but Hindus. We watched it from the roof of the public library – where *Encounter* and the *New Statesman* were on display to students.

Pilgrims and beggars were thronging the temple entrance and disappearing into the buildings: for Jagannath is munificent to his devotees and feeds thousands in his vast kitchens, while he himself – or rather his triune self, for he has a brother and sister – has at least 4,000 attendants on the pay-roll. They bathe him, wash his painted teeth, change and feed him four times a day, and escort him to his summer palace, to which he is drawn in a grand wooden chariot made new every year, his brother and sister in their own smaller ones. There is a myth that 'the car of Jagannath' crushes human beings – a myth which has penetrated into the English language in the word Juggernaut, to denote a blind power mercilessly sacrificing human lives. This is not based on fact, as even a drop of blood pollutes the god and his priests. What struck the first travellers was the frenzied eagerness of the pilgrims to be allowed to pull the god's chariot: some fell and were crushed by its huge, solid wheels.

The nearest we got to see the 'Lord of the World' was in the market-place, where plaques of tin were on sale, embossed with garishly coloured figures of the god with his brother and sister. We bought some, impressed by their crude magic. These must be primeval deities, dating back long before the Aryan invasion; they are represented by grotesque figures, scarcely human, with arms growing out of ears and blind, staring eyes.

But what matters is that the cult is one of the most thriving in India and continues to attract tens of thousands of pilgrims, and valuable alms. The famous Koh-i-nur diamond was formally bequeathed to Jagannath by Rajah Ranjit Singh, but the gift was never actually received.

The primary fact on which Jagannath's popularity depends is that he welcomes all Hindu castes, and feeds the hungry, whatever their position in India's status-ridden society. This has a parallel in Christendom, where until recently society was divided into privileged and unprivileged. It is still true in India, where civilization is only a crust spread over ancient rites and systems, an amazing crust, sprouting scientists and mathematicians of the first order, lawyers and artists, philosophers and mystics, as well as a rich upper class of highly cultivated men and women; but it is only a crust, covering an ever-increasing mass of poor peasants, low-caste people and outcasts plunged in ignorance, wretched victims of superstition.

As guests of Mr Patnaik, we had a wonderful time in Puri. We all stayed at the old Railway Hotel on the beach, and walked across the sand to bathe in the huge breakers which come tumbling their foam into the curving miles of shore. Swimming is not easy – barely a stroke before the next translucent mass rolls in, throwing one about like a match-stick. The great game is to dive right through this liquid arch and emerge on the other side, as Patnaik taught Juliette to do. In spite of his reassuring support, we were attended by a number of very dark-skinned guards, recognizable by their conical white hats. These agile Dravidians are also fishermen. Launching their long boats through the breakers is a remarkable feat, which we watched with admiration – and with interest in the strange creatures, even including sea-snakes, which they brought back.

As I wrote before, Patnaik is also an ace airman. Driving his Studebaker as he might fly a plane, he took us the fifteen miles to Konarak, the Black Pagoda, on a track which was being 'improved' with blocks of solid earth and was still unrolled. The car bounced at speed over every bump, leaving various parts of its chassis behind. The silencer was torn off, the door handles came away, and finally the exhaust pipe. This was retrieved red-hot by the chauffeur, who grinned resignedly.

Four years later, such was our enthusiasm for Konarak, we returned, again with Patnaik. This time he took two jeeps and followed the coast-line. The tide was up and the estuary a great expanse of water. Nevertheless, we drove on and in, until the tidal flood came up to our feet and the cars stopped in the middle. But the Patnaik magic worked again – he just shouted into the empty distance and within minutes we were surrounded by a swarm of strong fishermen and peasants, who pulled us through.

Konarak was worth all the trouble imaginable. Built in the mid-thirteenth century, it was to have been the largest Hindu temple in the north-east; but the central pyramid, rising to over 200 feet, was so vast that it began to crack and the building was never entirely finished.

It is dedicated to the sun-god Surya, whose image rises magnificent in green chlorite stone, driving one of his four chariots, with worshipping attendants at his feet The wheels of the chariots are 10 feet high, the stone chiselled like woodwork with infinite detail. All round the vast structure, in richly decorated niches, there stand statuettes of sensuously beautiful couples engaged in love-making – a sculptured text-book of amorous anatomy. One walks around spellbound by their ballet of passion, by its tenderness and abandonment. The English guide-book warns that much of this is 'licentious'. To us it was a beautiful expression of physical love, free from prurience and frankly explicit, carved with admirable skill.

Climbing the steep steps to the upper storey, one finds this amorous scene accompanied by dancers in lovely poses, and on the higher terrace, enormous blossoming figures of female musicians. In the court stand gigantic figures of war-horses, ready for the god, while a superb elephant holding a struggling man in his trunk symbolizes the god's gigantic power. The style of these fine statues is strangely reminiscent of Chinese art in the Tang period.

We later visited other 'erotic' temples, notably the famous Khajuraho group, where the act of love is forcefully expounded with the same lack of reticence, again and again, in temple after temple. Perhaps it was our satiety with this curious style, perhaps the sultry heat and the fatigue of having flown there at dawn, but here we felt rather bored, protesting to our secret selves that this was definitely not an act of worship, no symbolical union of soul and body, but merely a sophisticated explosion of primitive fertility rites.

But Konarak remains in our mind as an especially beautiful witness to this exotic and erotic cult.

Still in Orissa, there was much to see and to digest. Bhubaneshvar, only a few miles from Puri, has more temples than any tourist can enjoy, nearly 400 of them. Here one can see the proliferation of the Hindu's need to worship in solid stone, in profusely decorated carving, in erotic 'auspicious couples'. One wonders what wave of religious fervour swept over the country to create these elaborate and costly buildings, what need they supplied and what propitiation they demanded.

No doubt an Indian seeking after Truth would feel the same confusion if he were to study the Old Testament for proofs of pure divinity – for the roots of faith are buried deeper than reason can expect to delve, and he would be as bewildered by the cruelty of Old Jehovah as we are by the unalloyed eroticism of Hindu sculptures.

Patnaik also took us up country to visit tribes settled before the days of the Mahratta invasion – and probably much earlier. These aboriginal tribes form about 40 per cent of the population of Orissa and still live a wild and primitive life. We were told many strange stories about them by Mr Das, the District Magistrate.

A particularly strange one was about a tribe whose chief crop was turmeric, a member of the ginger family. The roots are dried and powdered to be used as a condiment or dye, varying from yellow to dark reddish-brown. The tribe preferred the red variation, which in their tradition grew better after a blood sacrifice. This involved the capturing of a man from a neighbouring tribe, who would be sacrificed, when the auspices were right, on the turmeric fields. The ritual was particularly revolting: the victim was chased from field to field, with the farmers slicing off a small piece of his flesh at opportune places, while his pouring blood soaked the earth, until he died. This practice was ended by the British, who got the tribesmen to substitute a water-buffalo, this increased the blood, but also the horror as the animal took longer to die, and a dead buffalo was unacceptable. Finally the practice was entirely forbidden, much to the chagrin of the tribe. The District Officer then set out to demonstrate how good red turmeric could be grown without blood. By using artificial fertilizers, he produced a bumper crop of the best turmeric. 'You see,' he told the farmers, 'a little science does more for your crop than all your blood magic.' But the tribesmen stuck to their old beliefs. 'You are Government,' they said, 'so of course you can get all the blood you want.'

We travelled on through miles of hilly country, hot and deserted, where it would have been no surprise to see wild animals prowling. For lunch, we stopped by the enchanted lake Chilkha among green pastures and shady trees, now a National Reserve; then on to Patnaik's constituency, where he was greeted and garlanded by eager crowds, expectant faces, ebony eyes. A new school is to be built, his gift, now merely a hole in the ground, which he duly consecrates. Speeches and songs and dances, and then we rise and with difficulty make our way back to the car, inch by inch through the thick mass of boys and men, their eyes fixed on us, straining to penetrate our foreignness. At last we are released. Patnaik is silent, obsessed with this terrible poverty, ignorance – and pathetic trust. He gives all the help he can, but is that the right way? For centuries these people have relied on rajah, warrior chief, or British sahib, and done next to nothing for themselves. When will they wake up and assume responsibility?

We were to see this poverty, this apathy, all over India. The impetus given to the nation by Independence, the promise of great changes, the hope of progress, of freedom from poverty – where are they now? The giant inertia of the huge subcontinent still blocks their achievement.

We spent evenings with Patnaik discussing ways and means, and miracles; today, in 1970, something has been achieved – unrest is fighting inertia and changes are on foot. One still hopes.

We left our friends the Patnaiks, and Puri, with great regret – it had been a wonderful fortnight – and in early March arrived in Madras. It's a fine city with many 'Regency' buildings, left by the British, wide roads and pleasant gardens, well-tended cattle, with their horns painted and pointed with copper, and few beggars: an air of prosperity, and to us, because we saw mostly academic people, the feel of a liberal city in control of its problems. When I gave my lecture at the University, Dr Mudalyar, the Vice-Chancellor, in white-and-gold turban, introduced me in a speech both eloquent and learned.

We had a fascinating breakfast with the Chief Provincial Minister, Dr Rajagopalachari, an urbane and scholarly gentleman for whom conversation was an art, full of a rare culture and charm. He asked me whether my brother Aldous's book, *The Doors of Perception*, in which he told of the transcendent and usually beautiful visions induced by mescalin and lysergic acid, was really serious, or was it intended as a parody of Indian yoga? I was able to assure him that it was indeed serious – a real contribution to our knowledge of the capacities of the human mind when suitably stimulated, whether by psychedelic chemicals, by fasting, or by meditation. I added my own private comment that the use of these methods *could* be dangerous.

Of our sightseeing, I must just mention our visit to the sacred site of Mahabalipuram on the coast near by. Here a whole stony valley has been carved, into miniature temples, religious halls, thatched huts, life-size, free-standing elephants and sacred bulls, and, most extraordinary of all, a whole cliff called 'The Descent of the Sacred Ganges', but really celebrating the multiplicity of creation, a fantastic conglomeration of life-size elephants and other mammals, snakes, birds and holy men, enmeshed in foliage, with angelic beings above – the largest single sculpture and the strangest interpretation of Genesis in the world.

From Madras, we continued south to Ceylon, where we visited the ruins of its ancient capitals, Anuradhapura and Polonnaruwa. Ceylon was converted to Buddhism by missionaries sent by the great King Asoka (p. 137) about 250 B.C., and at Anuradhapura the landscape is dotted with white-painted stupas – immense steepled domes like huge handbells, poised ready for the grip of a giant god. These structures appealed by their strangeness rather than by their beauty; as did the forest of naked granite beams, bare skeletons of many-storeyed buildings once inhabited by swarms of Buddhist monks.

There was a Chinese touch in the carvings of the granite stones at the foot of stairs – called moonstones – smooth, concentric reliefs of elephant, lion, horse and bull, surrounded by geese, each goose holding the lotus flower in its beak, with a central pattern of 'baroque' foliage – a lovely piece of design and workmanship.

The whole complex of ruined prayer-halls, hermit cells and small temples, clustering round the stupas, covers at least six square miles – the size of Richmond Park. Asoka sent seeds of the famous bo-tree, whose offspring flourish in Ceylon's sacred places.

Polonnaruwa, further inland, founded later to escape from Tamil invaders, is smaller. There are the ruins of the king's palace, built of thick brick walls seven storeys high, with an abundantly decorated 'erotic' pavilion near by; further afield, many temples, one said to have housed the famous relic, Buddha's tooth; and cut in the living rock, three gigantic stone statues – Buddha lying asleep while his faithful disciple Ananda keeps watch, and a great standing figure, a Buddhist sage, bearded, high-capped and reading from a palm-leaf book. The heat was almost unbearable, especially as we had to walk bare-foot over the sacred terraces.

But what really kindled our imagination was Sigirya, the fabulous rock fortress, engineered in the late fifth century by a guilt-mad king, seeking refuge after his parricide. The anchoring of his palace on the summit of this mushroom-shaped rock, 600 feet above the surrounding plain, was no mean achievement: tank, brick palace and gallery of frescoes – besides warehouses. One climbs the steep ladder to see the frescoes painted under a protective rock overhang – a frieze of leisured ladies with opulent breasts and tiny waists, lovely Sinhalese faces and flower-like hands, full of a haunting but unnatural beauty.

All round the fortress-palace lies the thick jungle-forest of tropical Ceylon, though one can still see the remains of the original royal city at the foot of the great rock.

We longed to know more about this king, Kassapa, who lived at the end of the fifth century. He must have been impregnable on his high perch, yet he descended to give battle, twenty years after he had made his escape, to an avenging brother at the head of an army. He was beaten and killed – and Sigirya became deserted, a place of legend. The pressure of guilt and fear created this fantastic retreat, unique in the world.

It was too late to climb to the top and see the ruins of the palace complex. As we regretfully descended, dusk was falling and swarms of little white-rumped swifts were flying home to their nests in the cliff above the frescoes. Tumbling and whirling, in a symphony of aerial motion, they filled the darkening air. We could hardly tear ourselves away, bewitched by the place and the excited birds, a moving foreground to the silent paintings.

Frescoes are perishable treasures, and it is wonderful that so much of this extraordinary flowering of the golden age of the Gupta period has survived in central and southern India as well as in Ceylon. Perhaps the most complete of those in India are at Ajanta, where the walls of shrines and places of religious assembly, carved out of the living rock, are all covered with majestic paintings, both of royal courts and religious figures.

Ellora, which was achieved a few hundred years later (eighth century), is a stupendous architectural and sculptural creation, with its Kailasha Temple, a piece of the tall, sandstone hill carved into a huge two-storeyed edifice, symbolizing, of course, the sacred snow-peaks at the source of the Ganges, with enormous elephants and mythical monsters sculptured on its pediments. I was delighted when, in spite of the terrific heat, I climbed the surrounding cliffs to get an over-all view – and discovered an Egyptian vulture nesting on one of their pinnacles, as well as enormous mud-nests of wild bees clinging to the sheer walls of the cliff. These bees are extremely dangerous if disturbed – they can sting one to death.

Meanwhile, I had been invited to attend the meeting of the Pakistan Association for the Advancement of Science in Karachi. Before its opening, I had just time to see the fleet of dhows beached on the mud, fishermen drying huge prawns, and the many species of duck and shore-birds on the mangrove-fringed harbour lagoon; of these, the pheasant-tailed jacana, that glorified moorhen, was perhaps the most remarkable.

It was an impressive gathering of scientists, not only Indians and Pakistanis, but myself from Britain and Nuzhdin from the USSR, a disciple of Michurin and Lysenko, a firm believer in their false theories of heredity. He attacked everything I said on genetics so violently that I challenged him to a debate next morning, to be held in Karachi's largest hall. However, I needed to refresh my memory by getting hold of my book on the subject, *Soviet Genetics and World Science*, written after I had heard Lysenko himself expound his nonsense (Vol. I, p. 282). The hunt seemed hopeless, until luckily a bright young man on the staff of Karachi's paper, the *Star*, managed to get hold of a copy.

Next morning the hall was full, with students out in the corridors and swarming within. In spite of a rather poor interpreter, I demolished Nuzhdin's arguments. This is not mere boasting, for the *Star* came out with a banner headline: 'Huxley versus Nuzhdin, Huxley wins'.

It was good to have won – Nuzhdin now had no chance of

persuading the Pakistani agricultural authorities to embark on futile projects based on Lysenko's false premises.

I wanted to see as much of Pakistan as possible, so headed north up the Indus Valley; first to Hyderabad, with a really magnificent turreted building overarching the intersection of its four main roads, like the Tetrapylon at Palmyra; then on to the great Lloyd Barrage, one of Britain's benefactions to this thirsty land, and to the ruins of Mohenjo-Daro close by. This was the main city of the so-called Indus civilization, dating back to the third millennium B.C.; it bore many resemblances to the coeval Sumerian civilization of Mesopotamia, probably through trade contacts. Even the sculpture was similar in style. Now I had seen the remains of all three of the earliest civilizations – in lower Egypt, Sumeria and north-west India – all based on great rivers.

Next came a dash far up the Indus to Peshawar – a place of lovely gardens, dense orchards and overcrowded bazaars. Near by lies Taxila, with the great reliquary reported to contain some of the Buddha's ashes, not only beautiful in itself, but remarkable for its mixture of Graeco-Roman and Hindu-Buddhist motifs. Indeed, all the art round Taxila has this mixed origin. It was strange to see Buddhist saints with classical Greek features – until one remembered that Alexander had penetrated far up the Indus before his troops refused to go further into this unclassical land.

And of course I had to see the Khyber Pass, still an important caravan route to Afghanistan and beyond. All I recall is the valley's stony desolation, the grim fortresses on its rocky spurs and the local tribesmen with long old-fashioned muskets on their backs – while I remembered what I had read as a boy about the disastrous Afghan war, over a century ago, when a solitary medical officer tottered into Peshawar, sole survivor of the large British-Indian force that had vainly tried to capture Kabul.

Very different was another approach we made to the northern frontier, this time to the high foothills of the Himalayas, at

Darjeeling, on the border of Sikkim. It was also a pilgrimage to the Anglo-Indian past – the town is almost British in appearance and the Grand Hotel, with its sham Gothic, might be in the Scottish Highlands. We arrived in a typical Scots mist and never saw any of the great mountains, let alone Everest or Kangchenjunga. We visited various laboratories, and a farm run by Mr Bee, who was trying rather desperately to provide milk for Darjeeling in a land devoid of pasture, amid its great forests of cryptomerias and rhododendrons, magnolia – and bracken, that most ubiquitous of plants. He grew a coarse canary grass and fed his cattle on this, as well as on bracken shoots and magnolia leaves. But his chief trouble was getting new bulls to keep up the quality of the herd – involving half a dozen ministries and endless paper-filling. Since the war, he had failed to achieve any success.

Juliette, like me, had been much impressed by his gallant effort. Attending a gathering that evening at the English Club, she sought him out, as she thought, and said, quickly getting to the subject, 'I have been thinking of your problem: why don't you use artificial insemination?' A look of shocked horror descended on his face – she had picked the wrong man in her haste; instead of Mr Bee, it was a travelling dentist we had met earlier ...

Another delightful trip was to the state of Manipur, by the Burmese border, where we visited, among other things, the man-made floating islands on the lake near by, moving from one to the other in a canoe, each squelchy islet supporting a large hut, a lean-to for chicken and goat, and a flourishing family. They reminded us of the floating islands of Xochimilco in Mexico.

But I realize that descriptions of our journey through India could fill volumes. It is true that writing about it gives me the renewed sense of discovery which so pleasantly enhanced our days. A sense also of understanding the ancient (but still present) conflicts of a land divided by many races and religions, languages and customs, immensely divergent and apparently irreconcilable. As Jack Haldane once wrote: 'The world is not only queerer than anyone has imagined, but queerer than anyone *can* imagine.' And that, we felt, applies particularly to India.

The synagogue at Cochin, down in the south-west corner, resists my blue pencil. It was so surprising to find that a colony of Jews had been here since the second (or at least the third) century A.D., when the discovery of the monsoon winds facilitated voyages from Egypt and Arabia to India and the spice islands beyond.

And I must mention Trivandrum, a little further south, where we visited a holy sage called Krishna Menon (a name as common in India as John Smith in England), recommended to us by Roger Godel, our French medical friend and expert on mysticism. This sage had certainly attained true peace and had set up an ashram, or school of disciples. But I found many of his philosophical ideas unmanageable, probably because of my lack of familiarity with a difficult mode of expression.

The scientists we met were outstanding – among them, the ebullient and restless Dr Bathnagar, Director of India's Council for Industrial and Scientific Research, who was putting into practice the then new method of using sun-heat for cooking and general heating (later used on a large scale in Israel). In a country so devoid of fuel and so exposed to solar heat, this could be very useful – yet he found strong resistance among the common people, always afraid of novelty.

He was succeeded by Dr M. S. Thacker, with whom we had stayed at Bangalore; eminent not only as a scientist but as manager of a large Government department.

Then there was Dr Hora, head of the Zoological Institute in Calcutta, an authority on Indian fish; Dr Chatterjee, the ambitious Director of Calcutta's wonderful Botanical Gardens, who proudly showed us his proliferating banyan tree, which already covered three acres; Salim Ali, the remarkable author of Field Guides on Indian birds; Dr Chandrasekar, whose pioneer work on India's population has now been recognized as of crucial importance; and many other dedicated men of science.

The most brilliant of all, we felt, was Dr Homi Bhabha, Director of the Atomic Research Institute in Bombay, Foreign Member of the Royal Society, a scientific genius, as well as a fine painter and discerning art-collector, and a tremendous worker. Alas, he was killed in his prime in an airplane accident.

We went to see Jack Haldane and his wife Helen Spurway, while they were still working at Professor Mahalanobis's Statistical Institute in Calcutta (Mahalanobis was its founder and inspirer, an exceptional man). He had offered the Haldanes important posts when they decided to leave England, and they found, at first, a splendid outlet for their ideas and their work at the Institute. We asked Jack what message we should give his mother, then still alive in Oxford. 'Tell her', said this stormy petrel of British science, 'that at long last I am able to do some constructive work, without being hamstrung by bloody red tape.' Alas, he did not escape trouble, usually of his own making, but finally found a refuge at Bubhaneshwar, under the wing of our friend Patnaik.

That Jack should have chosen India for his final refuge, rather than the USA or some European country, is a measure of the liberal treatment accorded here to science and technology. He was able to make some important contributions and initiate many projects, and found happiness and fulfilment in his Indian home until he died.

I have said little about India's wild mammals, for the simple reason that I saw little of them: ground-squirrels and mice, monkeys and mongoose, and a few deer at Bharatpur. In any case, large mammals were scarce – lions nearly gone, tigers[1] confined to the jungle, and the great Indian rhinoceros (the species drawn by Dürer) confined to a few localities in the delta area of Bengal. But the birds were wonderful. Sunbirds were everywhere (like humming-birds, they prefer scarlet flowers). Then there was the smallest owl I have ever seen, a scops owl, no bigger than a starling; spine-tailed swifts; a variety of cuckoos, including the maddening 'brain-fever bird'; mynas everywhere, and the cheeky house-crows; kites, eagles and vultures, soaring at different times according to their weight; and the most beautiful birds I have ever seen, the blossom-headed parakeet, with plum-coloured head, red and yellow beak, bright green back with scarlet 'epaulettes', and the paradise fly-catcher,

1. The World Wildlife Fund estimates that under 2,000 tigers now exist in the world.

with crested, blue-black head, silvery white body and spreading tail.

Curiously enough, we never saw a wild snake – except the cobras in the snake-pit at Singapore, where a man was collecting their venom by making them bite into a spoon: the serum produced was sent all over the Far East. I am ashamed to say that although Juliette went into the pit swarming with cobras, to watch venom-collecting at close quarters, I preferred to stay outside. I'm not repelled by snakes in general, but the deadliness of cobras was too much for me.

We began to make our way home through Iraq. After flying over the desert, lit by flowers of flame and belchings from the oil wells, we thought we had arrived at the edge of the sea, for Baghdad and the country round it was flooded, the worst flood in human memory. We spent two days in the teeming city, and were then off to Teheran for the millenary celebrations of Avicenna. Using the notes I had made in Delhi, I wrote my speech in the plane.

The meeting was opened with great *éclat* by the Shah himself, in a splendid pale-blue uniform. There were many speakers from all over the world, under the presidency of Dr Hekhmat, once a delegate to UNESCO. From France, Matignon was there, the great orientalist, a man of culture and finesse; Henri Laugier, our old friend from Paris, and Professor Massée, also Jean Thomas, earlier my Assistant Director; and from England, Professor Reuben Levy and Dr Frankfort, both notable orientalists and speaking fluent Persian.

While I praised Avicenna for his inspired curiosity, his vast learning in history and philosophy, and his surprisingly advanced knowledge, both theoretical and practical, of theology and medicine (indeed, it was extraordinary how his medical precepts were still being followed in the modern Muslim world, after he had broken the spell of Galen's authority), I also mentioned his unfortunate addiction to alcohol and to women, which seems to have hastened his death. This shocked some of the Iranians; but I believe, I think rightly, that one must present the whole man, and show how his faults had not prevented his attaining true greatness. He could truly say, like the Venerable

Bede: 'I have resolved all the problems which lie from the centre of the world to Saturn. I have been able to undo all the knots – excepting the knot which ties us to death.' And he proclaimed that 'the human soul is a lamp whose light is science and whose oil is divine wisdom.'

Besides the learned meetings, there were many entertainments: we were invited as a group to meet the Shah and his Queen Soraya, in the New Palace in Teheran, full of fairy-like walls of mirror mosaics, reflecting in myriad glittering points the row of crystal candelabra. The Queen was lovely, not unlike Ingrid Bergman, but overcast with sadness. The Shah had a clear-cut face, fine eyes, and a very attractive expression of intelligent interest. He spoke to me about the reforms he was introducing to curb the power of the great landowners, and his problems about modernizing agriculture.

Finally, we drove the 200 miles to Hamadan, on the site of ancient Ecbatana, where Avicenna spent many years and where, according to tradition, he was buried. As the Shah and his Queen were expected, the villages along the road were decorated, and goat or calf was held in readiness to be sacrificed as Royalty passed, leaving floods of blood on the road, then cooked and eaten by the festive crowds. We saw many interesting flowers and my favourite hoopoes, brilliant bee-eaters and rollers, soaring kites and vultures and – strange in this remote land – a large rookery in the poplar grove at Qasmin.

The road climbed on through ancient Median country – winding between grim boulders, both river and road cutting through the savage beauty and desolation of its high places. At the foot of snowy mountains sprawls the large Turkish city of Hamadan, with a brand-new Avicenna Hotel, comfortable and elegant.

Wrapped in pink silk ballooning in the breeze, the statue of Avicenna stood ready to be unveiled by the Shah-in-Shah. Interminable speeches followed: Avicenna has returned to Hamadan after nine centuries – but not to Ecbatana. Nothing is now left of that luxurious city, nor any traces of Alexander's conquering march.

Soon we were on our way to Beirut and Damascus. Damascus was now a large and thriving city, suddenly blossoming in a crop of luxurious villas and blocks of flats and offices. But there were still, tucked away inside the clefts of the mountains behind it, vestiges of a more primitive past. Malula was a cliff-village of stone houses incrusted on the crest of a ravine, with little terraces carefully irrigated and growing wheat and fruit-trees. About 1,500 Christians (Greek Orthodox) lived there, refugees from early Muslim persecution, safe in that almost inaccessible cleft, some even living in caves reached only by ladders. It reminded me of the Siq at Petra, for its approach was through a crack in the pink wall, along which flowed the torrent that brought life and livelihood to the village.

The priest offered us a delicious glass of wine and we talked about his double isolation: not only physical, but chronological – so extraordinary as to be almost unbelievable. But he appeared serene and untroubled, hardly conscious of the hectic modern world on his doorstep.

We were now on the last lap of our journey. We stayed in Beirut with our old friends, Emir Chehab and his charming wife, who took us to see the Cedars of Lebanon, another survival from the past – and to a memorable lunch of mashed aubergines with yogourt, and fresh mutton pounded with wheat, tasting of herbs and legend, washed down with arak. All too soon we were airborne in a plane well-named *Argonaut*, the map of the world below narrowing to the pinpoint of home and all it represented.

'As the Spanish proverb says, "He who would bring home the wealth of the Indies must carry the wealth of the Indies with him." So it is in travelling; a man must carry knowledge with him, if he would bring home knowledge', reported Boswell of Dr Johnson.

I am not sure that I altogether agree. It is true I took some knowledge with me, of biology and history, and this did enable me to enjoy things I might not otherwise have done; but I gained infinitely more. I count myself enriched by wonderful memories, and also by a new and precious sense of understanding, an enlargement of my awareness and general curiosity, and an increased appetite for more knowledge. I confess to being a voracious traveller.

CHAPTER 10

Mostly Transatlantic

THE rest of the year, 1954, was full of work, articles, pleasant week-ends with friends in the country, and in the autumn, Aldous's yearly visit. We had much to tell him about our travels, especially in India, for which both Juliette and I felt a great sympathy, but one not shared by Aldous. In fact he hated India when he went there in 1925, long before Independence and partition. He had seen only the dirt and poverty, the nuisance of the sacred cows, the hopeless peasantry and degraded city proletariat, not realizing that the Indian élite, inspired by Gandhi and led by Nehru, was soon to force the British to grant Home Rule, and that an independent India would undergo a swift blossoming in science, literature and the arts – although these still covered a basic layer of poverty and ignorance.

It was now that Aldous told us about Maria, who had stayed in Paris with her sister Jeanne; she had had a serious operation for cancer, and was having treatment which would necessitate their early return. But he seemed unworried – at least, unwilling to talk about it – as if silence would help the situation. We were very much concerned, but rather left in the dark. It came therefore as a bomb-shell when we had a letter some six months later telling of Maria's critical condition. 'Think of her – think of me', he wrote; and even before we had time to answer came a cable announcing her death.

Maria had been my sister-in-law for thirty-five years. At Aldous's suggestion, I had met her in Naples during the last year of the First World War, on one of my leaves from the Italian front. She was staying there with her mother and sisters, still refugees from their home in Belgium – a gay and lovely creature. But I doubted Aldous's choice of her as his future wife.

In answer to my reaction, he replied:

As to what you say of Maria, I think I realize her faults clearly enough. The fundamental fact about her, I think, is that her aesthetic sensibility is very great: she has – hideous expression – the artistic temperament to an advanced degree. Aestheticism is a dangerous thing; in fact I don't believe that anyone who lives wholly on sensations is safe; it leads almost inevitably in the end to a sort of corruption and deliquescence of the character. What I have tried to persuade Maria to do is to centre her life on thought rather than on sensation, to adopt some fixed occupation, involving a certain amount of effort and mental concentration, and not merely to live on the aesthetic sensation of the moment ... I think she will grow up all right. 'Grow up' for you mustn't forget how absurdly young she is, only nineteen. When one considers how infinitely half-baked, jejune and unhealthy one was at that age, one's surprise is, not that she shouldn't have achieved more, but that she could be as developed as she is. I only wish I was with her, for I think I could be of help to her in growing up – not to mention the fact that she would help me out of the curiously unpleasant slough of uncertainty in which one seems to wallow so hopelessly these days. I have spared you more lyrical effusions about her, not because I don't feel lyrically, but because it would be so tedious for you. One's aim in leading the life of reason should be to combine the lyrical with the critical, to be simultaneously Shelley and the *Edinburgh Review*. I have only given you my *Edinburgh Review*'s opinion about Maria; for the rest, see my Works *passim*.

I have quoted this passage in full because it illuminates Maria's essential character, and also the need that Aldous had of her. Strangely balanced and fulfilling was the relationship between these two contrasted but loving and understanding beings. For Maria did indeed 'grow up'. She became Aldous's eyes, his antennae, his intermediary with the outer world. It was not important that her intuitions about people were not always right: what mattered was that there was this curiosity, this ability to link up with experiences which Aldous would have shunned, shutting himself up in forbidding silences, those withdrawals which could be so paralysing. His blindness made her his guide, his chauffeur, his secretary. She typed his manuscripts for him, she read to him for hours every day, she nursed him devotedly. She was also a chronicler of their varied and interesting life, writing enchanting letters to her friends, and keeping a detailed journal of their doings. It is a real tragedy that this diary was burnt a few years later, in the fire that destroyed Aldous's house.

We knew how lost and desperately unhappy he was when she died – 'It is like being amputated', he wrote.

His second marriage, a little over a year later, did not altogether surprise us. It was a great relief to know he had fallen in love with a young and gifted woman, a former concert violinist, Laura Archera, who had been a friend of Maria and himself for two or three years. He was to die seven years later, and Laura wrote an account of their lives, *This Timeless Moment*. It contains much which we feel should have been left unsaid, but certainly is an important document for these last years of Aldous's life; it confirms my feeling that they were filled with new love and new vitality, in spite of the unforgettable sorrow of Maria's death. But I am anticipating.

Earlier that year, I had been approached by Dr Rhoades, Secretary of the Sloane Kettering Foundation for Cancer Research in New York, to lecture on cancer from the angle of a biologist. I knew very little about the subject, except the fact that Peyton Rous, on my first visit to the USA over forty years earlier, had shown that sarcoma in domestic fowls and poultry was caused by a virus. But I thought of my mother's too early death from that frightful disease, and now Maria's, and accepted – in the hope that any knowledge about tumours in lower organisms might help in combating this horrible enemy, born of our own bodies. By dint of much reading in the libraries of the Royal Society, the Royal Society of Medicine and the Royal College of Surgeons, as well as consultations with men like Sir Alexander Haddow and Dr Pio Koller at the Chester Beatty Cancer Research Institute in London, and with many of my biological colleagues, I was able to give two lectures on the subject to the Sloane Kettering Foundation, but not till the next year, 1955.

In these, I dealt with the occurrence of cancer in lower animals and plants as well as in man, the various agencies that were known (or guessed) to initiate or halt its progress, the occasional regression of the tumours, the change from benign to malignant growth – in short, what can be called the comparative biology of cancer. My initial postulate was that cancer was not a particular disease, any more than fever. Fever is a symptom of many infections; cancer is the result of many disorders of cell growth and multiplication, initiated by many different agencies.

The Board of the Foundation were pleased – they not only published the lectures in their periodical, but asked me to amplify them for publication in a journal of more popular appeal. In order to achieve this, I obtained a grant from the Rockefeller Foundation to spend four months in 1956 in the USA, mostly at Wood's Hole, Massachusetts, whose biological station has the world's most extensive collection of reprints on general biology.

That summer, therefore, Juliette and I led a curious life in a somewhat Spartan apartment, I fetching the milk and the paper every morning before breakfast and spending at least four hours every day in the library.

We made friends with interesting residents, such as Szent-Gyorgi, a brilliant scientist who, in his late 70s, still regularly sailed through the Sound, tanned like a red Indian, and vigorously continuing his researches, and also shared many an afternoon's peaceful sunning with old Dr Oskar Loewi.

Loewi was retired, but liked to spend his summers in his old haunts, reminiscing about his past. I remember a curious story he told us. He was working in Vienna, a young, obscure researcher, trying to find the link between nervous impulses and muscular contraction. This gave him long hours of frustration, for the answer kept eluding him. One night, however, he dreamt he had the formula: it was all there, clear and bright; he woke in delighted recognition of something definite at last, and promised himself a wonderful day in the laboratory testing the idea. But when he got out of bed in the morning, nothing was left in his memory except the certainty that he had been given the right answer and had lost it. A few nights later, the dream recurred. This time he switched on a light, and grabbed the first paper available, a flimsy scrap, on which he hastily noted down the magic formula. Now he had it for sure – but, to his horror next morning, the paper he had written on was so crumpled and torn that it was impossible to read what he had written. It was too much: he walked round the city in despair. But, miraculously, the dream came again: this time he left nothing to chance; he leapt out of bed into a pair of trousers, ran all the way to the laboratory, and in the small hours verified his dream-given solution. His colleagues found him re-checking his successful results. 'You have got a Nobel!' they exclaimed. And so, indeed, he had – a beautiful example of subconscious intuition co-operating with conscious reason.

Back in London, I worked up my notes into a book, published in 1958, entitled *Biological Aspects of Cancer*. In my preface I wrote – and it was no exaggeration – 'I can truthfully say that its preparation involved me in more hard labour than anything I have attempted since I took my Final Honours examination in Zoology at Oxford', which was nearly fifty years back. I added that it might be a good thing for a few elderly scientists to be free to devote themselves to such general surveys; and finally pointed out that I had ended by realizing that cancer was not merely of medical concern, but a key subject for the advancement of general biology.

To return to 1955, an invitation came out of the blue that year from Cyrus Eaton, to fly to Nova Scotia to attend one of his discussion meetings at Pugwash.

Cyrus Eaton is an extraordinary man – a prominent industrialist, Chairman of the Chesapeake and Ohio Railway, discoverer of a valuable source of iron ore in a high-latitude Canadian lake (iron which was of great importance for steelmaking in the Second World War), and a passionate believer in the possibility of reconciling the communist East with the capitalist West; and I should add, not only believing but acting on his belief, exchanging visits of goodwill with important members of the Soviet hierarchy. He is also an ardent rationalist, devoted to the memory of the great biologists of the nineteenth century, like Darwin and my grandfather.

For many years, college presidents, professors and other intellectuals interested in world problems were his chosen companions on summer vacations in Pugwash, the small fishing village in Nova Scotia where he was born. It was the second of these meetings that Juliette and I were invited to attend. I remember among the guests Dr Julian Boyd, Librarian of Princeton University; Dr James, President of McGill in Montreal; Wiggins, editor of the *Washington Post*; the social historian, Professor Commager; Dr Wilson, an Egyptologist, and some others. It was August, and the small village was pleasant in the sun, with bathing and fishing and various excursions.

The meetings were stimulating, with the assembled company discussing problems arising out of the new orientation of ideas in general, as well as the threat to peace and conservation posed by atomic technology.

The ground was thus prepared for what was to become an important series of conferences, for in 1957, Bertrand Russell, Albert Einstein and Albert Schweitzer were invited to attend a meeting to discuss the problems of atomic warfare. As a result, Russell asked Mr Eaton to sponsor international meetings of scientists to warn the world of the hazards of nuclear warfare. The first Conference on this subject was convened at Pugwash in July 1957. Initiated by Bertrand Russell in a manifesto in 1955, now known as the Russell-Einstein Manifesto, the Conferences continued under the name of the Pugwash Movement, with Lord Russell in the Chair. By 1962, ten Pugwash Conferences had been held – in Canada, the United States, the Soviet Union and Britain. The cumulative effect of these meetings helped to pave the way for the 1963 Nuclear Test Ban Treaty, by which the USA, the USSR and the UK agreed to discontinue tests, except those conducted underground. As Bertrand Russell wrote in the third volume of his superb autobiography:

The Conference was called the Pugwash Conference of Scientists and for the sake of continuity the movement has continued to be identified by the name Pugwash. It established among other things a 'Continuing Committee' of five members, of which I was the Chairman, to organize further conferences. More important, it established a form that future conferences followed. A number of plenary meetings were held at which important papers were read. There were a great number of meetings of the small committees set up at the start, at which particular aspects of the general subject were discussed and decided. Most important of all, it was held in an atmosphere of friendliness. Perhaps the unique characteristic of this and subsequent Pugwash Conferences was the fact that the members consorted with each other in their spare time as well as during the scheduled meetings, and grew to know each other as human beings rather than merely as scientists of this or that potentially inimical belief or nation. This most important characteristic was in large part made possible by the astute understanding by Cyrus Eaton of the situation and what we wished to accomplish and by his tactful hospitality.

It was typical of Cyrus Eaton to devote a considerable amount of his capital to the furtherance of this campaign.

Juliette and I were fortunate in becoming close friends of this remarkable man and his second wife Anne, a brilliant and lovely woman, handicapped, but not in the least subdued, by early polio.

At first destined for the Church, Eaton retained throughout his strenuous career a missionary spirit, combined with personal gentleness and social tolerance. A chance encounter had brought him in touch with the elder Rockefeller, who, rightly assessing the potential acumen and economic flair of the young man, offered him a post in his financial empire. Eaton made and lost a fortune, and remade a bigger one. He achieved success by his calm appraisal of situations, his extraordinary grasp of possibilities and his capacity for bold decisions.

We have often stayed at his home in Acadia Farms near Cleveland, where he rears a special breed of cattle as a relaxation from business. He still rides round his estate on horseback at the age of 86 (I accompanied him on several occasions) and his book-lined study has been the scene of many fruitful discussions between divergent minds, brought to a tolerant understanding by his wise handling.

Ever since my early days at the Rice Institute, pre-First World War, I have been lucky in being able to keep links with the United States, and enjoy solid friendships with a variety of Americans. My many visits there have been happy and stimulating, and my lecture tours strenuous but rewarding – not only in financial terms, but especially in accrued knowledge. For the United States is a land where (except in dark times like the McCarthy era) ideas are given a chance to flourish and many basic discoveries are made. This is perhaps due to the juxtaposition of men of many races and cultures, permitting minds with different backgrounds to exchange ideas and attitudes.

On this visit (1955), I was much impressed by the Atomic Energy establishment at Oak Ridge in the Great Smoky Mountains, though my lack of background knowledge of physics interfered with my understanding of the fantastic progress being made there. The mountains themselves, with their tremendous forests of wild rhododendron, were pure delight.

Week-ends with the Ernst Mayrs, on the slopes of the Boston hills, stand out with rich memories – of bird display, notably that of the American woodcock drumming on his territorial flight, rather like a snipe; we hastily crawled to the spot from which he had taken flight, to see him plummet down to land close by on the Mayrs' lawn; of the beavers in the neighbouring lake, with carefully made lodges as evidence of their constructional mania, and many trees, especially birches, felled by their sharp incisors.

Thanks to the foresight of residents like Ernst, many parts of New England are still wild – with traces of the early settlers in the woods, just a stone chimney-breast, with perhaps a lilac or a rose-bush planted by those gallant colonists who strove to extract a living from this poor soil, thinly spread over the harsh rocks. No wonder the discovery of the Middle West, with its 6-foot depth of rich black earth, pulled them out like a magnet, leading them to abandon their shacks in this granite land.

I went to several biological congresses – and was astounded by the number of participants; one had at least 2,000. As a result, I was always rushing from one lecture hall to another and even missed many interesting discussions. What a change from my early days in the USA forty years back, when Biology was just emerging as a discipline in its own right, instead of being split into Zoology, Botany and Physiology.

In New York, I failed to get a grant from the Rockefeller Foundation for further research and study of what I called *Idea Systems*, which I had started earlier at PEP in London. The surviving documents on these discussions still await investigation, but who will give the time for that?

We then sped across the continent for a good visit to Aldous and his new wife Laura, perched high above the smog and vistavision of Los Angeles – in a house which, alas, was later to burn in one of those brush conflagrations so common on these dry hills.

Aldous took us to the University of Los Angeles, to see some remarkable experiments on influencing the behaviour of rats by fine wire electrodes implanted in different regions of the brain. The researchers had discovered the existence of a 'pleasure centre' in the hypothalamus. Its stimulation must certainly have given the rats pleasure, for they spent so much time pressing the key that released the current that they neglected food, drink and even sex, until the experimenter removed the seductive wires. We were stirred by a mixture of fascination and horror at the sight of these poor creatures acting under a compulsive spell, and wondered when the same experiment would be tried out on human subjects. Was Aldous's *Brave New World* moving a step nearer?

We also saw John Lilly's experiments with dolphins. He had demonstrated not only that these large-brained aquatic mammals could find their way and communicate with each other by 'sonar' – sound-waves, of their squeaky and grunty language, reflected back from obstacles – but they could understand and act on simple commands given in human speech; that they attempted to communicate with men, making sounds that imitated human speech, deliberately produced at the customary human pitch – about an octave lower than that of their own 'language'. These aquatic creatures, it seemed, could learn human words more readily than man's much closer relatives, the chimpanzees.[1]

Though perched on the heights above Los Angeles, Aldous was far from leading a hermit's life. While we were with him, there was a stream of visitors – Linus Pauling, Gerald Heard, Christopher Isherwood, Romain Gary (then French consul at Los Angeles, author of that fine book on wild Africa, *Racines du Ciel*) and his wife Lesley Blanch, also a writer (we loved her book, *The Wilder Shores of Love*), Professor Harrison Brown, population expert, Dr William Kiskadden, once a virtuoso surgeon, now turned to population control as a more important

1. This engrossing adventure into the dolphin world has continued, and Lilly has published the results in *The Mind of the Dolphin* (Doubleday, 1967).

problem, Bertalanffi, Alistair Cooke, and others. In all these diverse encounters, Aldous was the fulcrum of the conversation – knowing so much of every subject and putting the intelligent questions it required. He seemed to radiate what journalists now call *charisma*, which added quality to the moment, as we sat around on the terrace of his little house, watching the wide evening sky.

There were also long expeditions by car on the great speedways of California. Juliette was often driving Aldous's leaping car with her heart in her mouth, amazed at Aldous's grasp of the map and his perfect direction: he had an unfailing memory of the landscape and of the maze of Los Angeles' motorways. We thus went to San Diego Zoo, whose enchantment culminated in a baby orang-outang cuddling in our arms; and to the new Salk Institute at La Jolla, built and financed by Dr Salk from the profits of a new vaccine. It was, Dr Salk told us, an 'idea factory', where Salk himself had charge of the physiological side and our friend Bronowski was studying the history of scientific and technological theories.

From California and its super-sophisticated way of life we set off to New Mexico, where we were to stay with Dr G. G. Simpson, the palaeontologist, at his ranch near the town of Cuba. Unfortunately, however, he had met with a severe accident while finishing some research in South America – being badly crushed by a huge tree clumsily felled. He recovered after years of pain and many operations, sustained by his heroic determination; but for the time being, he could not be our host and suggested that we should stay with his sister Martha and her husband Bill Eastlake, the writer, who had a ranch not far away.

This was our first visit to that hallucinating country, and we were able to see a great deal of it: the mesas, rising like giant fortresses in flat deserts of rust-red sand; the well-named Painted Desert, its coloured sands and cliffs more variegated and brighter even than those of Petra; petrified trees, their wood miraculously converted to onyx, fossilized mimics of the living forest where they lay; and piles of fossil bones of animals extinct for over two million years – a multiple and fabulous experience.

At Taos we found the same sculptural but arid beauty. In the midst of the town clung the adobe houses of the Indians, flat-roofed and scale-like, mercifully preserved from modernization. We had an enchanting visit with Juliette's old friend Dorothy Brett,[1] and talked of Garsington days of long ago. She has elected to stay in that pleasant oasis town in the heart of the timeless desert, painting Indian rituals. We were sorely tempted to do the same.

René d'Harnoncourt, the genial Director of the New York Museum of Modern Art, arranged for us to stay with the Lippincotts at Santa Fé. This was another pleasant interlude, filled with trips to the deserted cliff villages of legendary Indians, clinging like scattered honey-combs to the cliffs of Chelle Canyon; as well as to the Hopi and Navajo Reserves, where modern Indians strive to keep alive their ancient traditions and their dance rituals: a task which I fear is doomed to end in failure, since they have lost the mode of life which originated them. Maybe the Indians will find a way to complete integration into the American Way of Life, but in so doing they will lose much.

Autumn was ending in a blaze of gold and flame as we arrived in Montreal, where I was to give a series of lectures to the English (and Protestant) McGill University. It was during this stay that I was able to speak at the French Catholic University in vindication of Teilhard de Chardin (see p. 24).

One of our cherished memories of the visit is of meeting the great brain-surgeon Dr Penfield. He was then in the midst of his fantastic exploration of the brain and the functions of its various regions. Paradoxically, brain-tissue itself suffers no pain, so he could operate without anaesthetizing his patients. Thus they were able to answer his questions on what they experienced when he electrically stimulated different parts of their brains. He was able to localize the physical seat of various functions, including memory, inducing total recall of some aspect of the patient's childhood. We spent a stimulating afternoon listening to his experiences. Today, thanks to his work, many more mysteries of our brains are being explored.

We were also taken down the St Lawrence River to see the

1. See Vol. I, p. 114.

congregation of migrating snow-geese – a fantastic spread of wild white birds over the green fields and brown mud-flats. For the benefit of ornithologists, I will add that these were a mixture of greater and lesser snow-geese, and that the lesser had an admixture of blue-grey. In point of fact, the blues are merely mutants: but why the percentage of blues varies geographically is still a mystery.

We finally got back home in time for me to be asked by the Royal Society to give a lecture in February, on the occasion of the Queen Mother's admission as an Honorary Fellow. I was delighted by this distinction, since, with many others, I had long been a devoted admirer of Her Majesty's charm and simplicity. I chose as my subject 'Bird Display and Bird Behaviour', and had plenty of amusing and interesting slides to illustrate an hour's talk, as well as stuffed birds with fantastic plumage, evolved by the operation of selection to stimulate the opposite sex, to proclaim ownership of territory, or to cement the pair-bond between mates.

Among my examples was a slide of the male Argus pheasant displaying his ocellated tail, so vast that he has to peep between the huge feathers to see how his dowdy mate responds; I also had an actual Argus pheasant tail-feather from the Natural History Museum, in itself an object of wonderment. It seemed fitting, at the end of my lecture, to present the Queen Mother with this miracle of evolution; and having obtained the necessary permission from a Trustee of the Museum, who was present at the gathering, I was delighted with the pleasure it gave her.

A second and even more gratifying occasion for me was the award of the Society's Darwin Medal, given to those Fellows who had been especially successful in following up Darwin's work on evolution and the methods by which it operates. I was pleased by the President's citation of my having extended Darwin's theory of sexual selection (which he applied only to species in which the males display their bright plumage) by introducing the concept of mutual selection, where both sexes are brightly coloured in the mating season, and stimulate each

170

other by joint display (curiously enough, not even mentioned by Darwin).

An amusing incident took place at one of the dinners of the Royal Society Dining Club. An acquaintance had been made the executor of a rich old lady, and in the course of his duties had found a locked box containing some peculiar objects, clearly designed as condoms, but made of a mysterious substance. The question was what? I remember the puzzled faces of eminent scientists as I handed round a specimen with the port. Finally, Professor J. Z. Young, the distinguished anatomist, thought he knew, but would investigate.

He discovered that they were made of the caecum (blind gut) of a sheep, and later inquiries by Young and myself disclosed that they were the usual 'armour' for the amours of eighteenth-century men (Boswell records washing his 'armour' in the lake in St James's Park after a disreputable night).

I found that they were also mentioned in Grose's *Classical Dictionary of the Vulgar Tongue*. After explaining that they were called *condom* after their inventor and exploiter, a certain Colonel Cundum of the Guards, Grose adds: 'These machines (*sic*) were prepared and sold by a matron of the name of Phillips, at the Green Canister in Half Moon Street. The good lady having acquired a fortune retired from business: but hearing that the town was not well served by her successor, she, out of patriotic zeal for the public welfare, returned to her occupation in the year 1776.' Among the English names for these objects were the classically disguised *Posthocalightion* and *Cytherian Shield*; and in French, *Redingote Anglaise*, *Gant des Dames* and *Peau Divine*!

A note I published in the *British Medical Journal* was rewarded by a letter from a Canadian doctor saying that objects made of sheep's caecum were still on sale in western Canada.

CHAPTER 11

My King Charles's Head

EARLIER on, I referred to over-population and conservation as the two faces of my King Charles's head; I should have included a third: evolution. At any rate, these three closely related subjects continued to absorb me and determine much of what I did – and wrote – and since they enabled me to indulge my delight in travel, I was happy that they should.

The highlight of 1956 was an expedition to the Coto Doñana in southern Spain, undertaken at the request of the rich Spanish owners of the area, to see whether it should be recommended as a National Park, or safeguarded as a special Wildlife Reserve. This (like two previous reconnaissances) was led by my old friend Guy Mountfort, prominent both as ornithologist and man of business. His book, *Portrait of a Wilderness*, illustrated by Eric Hosking's splendid photographs, gives a vivid account of the place and of the expedition's work.

On our way to the Coto, we spent a few hours at Jerez de la Frontera and were taken by our sponsor, Don Mauricio Gonzalez Diez, to a large Bodega owned by the Gonzalez-Byass family company, where the ancient ritual of sherry-making takes place. Vast-bellied casks filled the dim vaults, with dates and sometimes dedications to famous people (I was proud to have one inscribed with my name, alongside Churchill's). We learnt that sherry matures well in whisky casks, and that empties from Scotland are regularly shipped to Jerez to serve as ripeners for the best sherry.

We were also shown an amusing side-line in the form of sherry-addicted mice. It happened that the old night-watchman got bored in the small hours and invited some venturesome mice to share a nip of sherry with him. At first the sherry was lapped from a saucer, to their evident relish; soon the watchman put the sherry in a glass and made a miniature ladder to give access. The mice queued up, regaled themselves and made way for the next in line, nimbly jumping off. Older mice, we

172

were told, carried their liquor well, but young ones lurched about with every sign of inebriety. Sipping our own delicious 'copita', we watched the show with surprised pleasure, while Eric Hosking took photographs.

The Coto had earlier belonged to the dukes of Medina Sidonia, and its *Palacio* had been used by them (and by its present owners) as a luxurious hunting lodge, to which the Spanish kings had sometimes been invited. In memory of the last, King Alfonso XIII, his bathroom, much the best in the house, had been kept inviolate, so that the other – whose plumbing left much to be desired – had to do for our large party.

There was no timepiece in the Palacio nor on members of its staff. Early breakfast, booked for 7.30, might appear at 9.00 or later. James Fergusson-Lees, one of the best ornithologists of our team, had an appetite larger than his mastery of French, the language we used with the staff. 'Où est le mange?' he demanded, on such occasions of delay.

An ornithological inquest was held every night in the great hall. A list of birds was read out, and species ticked off when absolute evidence of identity was obtained. I remember the severe grilling of a rashly optimistic member, who claimed he had seen a two-toed eagle; he finally had to relinquish his claim.

The Coto harboured about half the known species of European birds. Our expedition identified over 200, including such rarities (for Europe) as flamingoes, great bustards, purple gallinules, stilts, three species of vulture and four eagles, including the rare Bonelli's eagle.

On top of a stone-pine in the lee of the dunes, an equally rare short-toed eagle had made its nest. We built a pylon of prefabricated tubular scaffolding, with a cloth hide opposite the nest. Braced by guy-ropes, it was to be inhabited by Eric Hosking for the best part of every twenty-four hours, armed with sandwiches and a battery of thermos flasks containing his only addiction – tea; and there this dedicated artist watched and took splendid photographs of the family life of these royal creatures. He was able to record that the single chick took half an hour to swallow the three-foot water-snake his parents brought him, yet managed to devour a second later in the day.

173

Baby birds have no fun in their young days, though presumably swallowing enormous quantities of food gives them pleasure. They just crouch in the nest, helpless and ugly, until their feathers grow and the miraculous gift of flight liberates them.

The general ecology of the place was interesting. The largest sand-dunes in Europe, nearly fifty miles long, two to five miles broad and up to 300 feet high, were piled up by south-east winds, moving slowly inland and engulfing the stone-pines. I felt like Baron Munchausen when I hitched my horse to the upper branches of a pine sticking up through the sand.

I was specially interested in the marsh-bordered lagoons, some brackish and frequented by flamingoes and seashore waders, others by fresh-water birds. A colony of spoonbills were trying to nest on muddy ground below the nesting bushes of herons, among marks of wild boar trampling and rooting. I saw no boar myself; nor any mongoose (though they have been recorded here, testifying to the recent separation of Spain from North Africa). And no one saw the lynxes that earlier expeditions had recorded. The red deer also eluded me, but one morning before breakfast I got a splendid view of a herd of fallow deer, the palmate antlers of the males proudly glistening in the early sunshine.

The only other large mammals on the Coto were domestic cattle, roaming about as if wild. The cows were tame enough, but the bulls were large and their behaviour unpredictable. Eric Hosking had trouble with one, and Juliette and I were pursued by a very large bull along the shore of one of the lagoons; we only escaped his attentions by hiding in a clump of rushes.

The flowers were varied and interesting, and while we searched the sky for birds, Juliette, the expedition's official 'botanist', scanned the ground for her collection.

I rejoice to know that, as a result of Guy Mountfort's reports, this little paradise of the Coto Doñana has been saved from exploitation and is now one of the best Nature Reserves in southern Europe.

Another valuable expedition headed by Guy Mountfort, in

which I took part, was to Jordan in 1963. As I wrote in my foreword to his book about it, *Portrait of a Desert*: 'When Guy asked if I would support him in organizing the expedition, I agreed whole-heartedly, but countered by asking if I might come too. He agreed and asked me to report on its archaeological aspects, as well as on conservation in general.'

It was an unforgettable experience. It took us to such strange and memorable places – to the vast expanse of black stony desert, to the scenic extravagance of Wadi Rum, the unique desert palaces of the Ummayad Arab potentates from our eighth and ninth centuries, my first sight of the Dead Sea, and of the spectacular canyons in the rift wall on its eastern side, and to a renewed acquaintance with fabulous and incomparable Petra.

It was remarkable, too, because of its aim. It was focused on the ecology and conservation of this strange land, nine-tenths of it desert – and largely unoccupied desert – the remaining tenth watered by springs and unexpected streams, like Moses's river, the Wadi Musa, bringing fertility to desertic Petra. We used birds as ecological indicators, for most of the team members were expert field ornithologists, including my old friend Max Nicholson, naturalist, planner and sociologist, and Eric Hosking, the finest bird photographer of our time.

After being submitted to the Jordanian Government, our report was handed to the International Biological Programme, and proved very valuable to its Director, my old friend Barton Worthington.

Yet no one except myself had been trained professionally in biology – and I had been asked to deal with non-biological matters! We were all amateurs – and the results of the expedition again showed the importance of the amateur in field science. One thinks above all of Darwin, of Fabre's work in France, the ecological studies of Cyril Diver, and the many amateur field workers who have given us knowledge of spiders and their habits; and in scientific ornithology, of Eliot Howard, Landsborough Thomson – and Mountfort himself.

Our journeys were made possible by the loan of land-rovers and cars by the Jordanian Government. For young King Hussein (whose grandfather Abdullah I had met on a previous visit), and his chief Ministers, realized the importance of our mission for the country, too much of it deforested, eroded, arid and goat-infested.

Our first long stay was at Azraq, whose ancient fort had been occupied from earliest antiquity, and later by the Romans, the Turks – and T. E. Lawrence. It boasted a large lake, varying from fresh to brackish, whose shores were haunted by innumerable migrant birds of many species, from familiar blackcaps to exotic hoopoes, fan-tailed warblers and thrush-nightingales (both new to me), and of course many marsh and aquatic birds – grebes and herons, egrets and storks, ducks and gulls (of a rare species).

Azraq was also a site for great gatherings of camel caravans; and a few miles to the west were the remains of the strangest and most beautiful of Ummayad desert castles, Quesr al Asma, once furnished with a Turkish bath and still decorated with remarkable mosaics, including the first known representation of the starry night-sky on a dome.

We speedily decided that this should be our first recommended region as a National Park, Nicholson adding that he hoped camel-racing would be encouraged as an extra tourist attraction. Later, in Wadi Rum, we staged a race between two cameleers of the Jordanian Frontier Force – a wonderful combination of the exciting and the ludicrous.

There were many other Ummayad castles – especially the Qualat al Hasa on the great desert highway (probably Moses's route) in the south, with fields of purple-black iris all round. Here our driver triumphantly brought us a fragment of chain-mail from the moat – relic of some battle between Arabs and Crusaders.

There were also Crusader castles from the twelfth century: Monreal, not far from Petra, and the terrific fortress Kerak, perched on the rift-edge further north. From it we looked down on Alpine swifts in the vertiginous hollow of the rift; and I again wondered at its enormous and formidable glacis.

We went to Jerash, perfectly preserved, with hollyhocks growing wild in the near-by valleys, and later to Gadara (now Um Quais), a frightening place, with strange black buildings

176

of basalt, including two Roman theatres. But the neighbouring pine-woods were full of flowering shrubs, like the maquis of southern France.

To me, as a biologist, the most interesting fact was what evolutionists call adaptive variation in the larks: we saw no fewer than ten lark species, each filling some particular ecological niche. Three were especially interesting – the hoopoe lark, with long curved beak, for prying insects from under desert stones; the thick-billed lark, with beak almost as large as a hawfinch's and fulfilling the same function, of crushing hard fruit or berries – in this case, the fruits of the desert spurge; and the horned larks, whose striking, yellow-and-black faces bordered by feathery brims, doubtless added to their distinctiveness and prevented quarrels between species.

Hawks and eagles were plentiful; not long ago, an elderly sheik told us, he flew his falcons at Houbara bustards and sand-grouse – now there were no Houbaras and only a few sand-grouse.

One great surprise was the abundance of sunbirds – of many species, bringing Africa and India into this strip of the Middle East. There were dozens of chats and wheatears, and, most interesting, two species of crag-martin, one dark, one pale, adapted to nesting on differently coloured rocks. Ravens were represented by three varieties, including the unique fan-tailed raven, which curiously enough behaves like our rook.

There are (or have been until recently) many links between the fauna and flora of south Jordan (and Israel) and those of north-east Africa. Some plants and animals could have crossed the Isthmus of Suez recently, but most of the migration probably occurred before the Red Sea was formed, by rifting, well over 100 million years ago. We found dung-beetles apparently identical with the sacred scarabs of Egypt; and an extraordinary plant called Caralluma, a new species of a well-known African genus: it was pollinated by blow-flies, attracted by its disgusting carrion smell, and at close quarters by the wriggling hairs, simulating small flies, on its purple and yellow flowers.

There were crocodiles, of course, in the Jordan in biblical times – Job's scaly and terrible Leviathan – and not long past, the desert chiefs tamed cheetahs and used them to hunt gazelles and the so-called 'unicorn', the Arabian oryx, closely related to the African species, whose pair of nearly straight horns look single in profile. Keats in *Endymion* speaks of 'Asian' elephants, lion and panther, and of Bacchus's attendants riding 'unicorns'; while the sober Xenophon, in his account of his great journey across Asia Minor, records ostriches, lion, and many kinds of antelopes.

No ostriches or cheetahs can be seen today, and almost all the oryx have been killed, mostly by rich Arab sheiks in fast jeeps, using murderous tommy-guns. King Hussein was shocked when we told him of this destruction, and instituted heavy fines and penalties for killing any rare creatures. But the slaughter continues.

On our visit to Petra, as amazing as ever, I managed to clamber up the rough and very steep track to the High Place of Sacrifice, in spite of my seventy-three years and the heat – over 100° F. Eric Hosking later complained that I had worn him out, dragging him all over the opposite slopes to photograph special tombs.

But our high spot was the Rum area. We were all bowled over by its grandeur, the unimaginable magnificence of its 2,000-foot red cliffs and their snowy caps of white sandstone.

I could write much more about our trip, but must refer the reader to Mountfort's admirable book.

On our return to Ma'an, we proposed a number of measures to King Hussein and his Ministers. First, to prevent further erosion, and further gains by the desert from cultivable lands, we recommended an end to tree-felling and increased afforestation; the prohibition of haphazard driving by motorized vehicles in arid regions, which converts them to real desert; the drastic reduction of the swarms of goats; and their replacement by sheep wherever possible.

To increase food-production, we recommended the setting up of a land-use plan (here Nicholson's experience was essential), allotting some areas to agriculture, others to sheep-farming, some to water-conservation, and still others as Reserves and National Parks.

We proposed three Parks: the Desert Park, centred on

Azraq; Petra, together with some of the magnificent canyons in the rift-wall north of it; and the whole Rum area, where, Mountfort wrote: 'I experienced a more profound sense of peace and beauty than anywhere else in the world.' We asked that all motor vehicles should be banned in the Jebel Rum, and that visitors' accommodation should not clash with the scenery (as did the new 'modern' hotel at the approach to Petra). This was agreed and we later heard that the Rum 'hotel', at the entrance to the canyon, was a glorified Bedouin tent, roofed with black skins – an attraction in itself.

We also proposed two smaller areas as Reserves: one in the beautiful and surprisingly fertile canyon of Zarqa Main, ending in a lovely oleander grove (oleanders are goat-proof), on the shore of the Dead Sea; the other, the forest-maquis region round Ajlun, north of Jerash. And we naturally pressed for strictly-enforced laws against killing rare and interesting mammals and birds, especially gazelle and oryx, bustard and desert courser, but with shooting areas for hunters once the fauna had recovered.

We also recommended the restoration of historical sites, including the Ummayad and Crusader castles. Finally, we pressed for the conservation of all wild fauna and flora, rightly believing that their strangeness and variety would add to the revenue from tourists.

Our proposals were welcomed and the King personally thanked us for our work. Since then, all our recommendations have been implemented, and Jordan has become not only better known, but financially rewarded by expanding tourism. As I write this, in 1971, the country is unfortunately going through troubled and dangerous times, but I still hope that eventually peace and common sense will prevail.

To return to 1956, when I got back to London from the Coto Doñana, I was invited to open the exhibition of chimpanzee paintings at the Institute of Contemporary Arts. There were two young anthropoid 'artists' – Congo, a two-and-a-half-year old male from the London Zoo, and Betsy, slightly older, from New York. Interestingly, their styles were quite different, inasmuch as Congo painted with brushes while Betsy used her fingers to spread the paint, producing an almost Van Gogh effect. But both radiated the paint over the paper, betraying a rudimentary but definite sense of 'composition'. One of Congo's pictures hangs in our hall and mystifies many visitors – as it can compare with modern abstract paintings. Betsy's pictures looked like a sea of interwoven grasses, as likeable as Congo's but less flamboyant.

I was amused by the reactions of several human artists at the show, as they contemplated the work of what one of them called their 'rivals'. Sir Charles Wheeler, however, a very academic Academician, said it was ridiculous to call these 'pictures' when they were merely 'swished by apes' paws'. I do not think these experiments have been continued, but the results certainly were fascinating.

What with travel, the writing of many scientific papers and the publication of a book of essays, *New Bottles for New Wine*, dealing with the relations of modern science to our religious and spiritual outlook, I over-exerted myself and had another depression. Once again, however, it was cured by electric shock treatment, followed by convalescence at Dartington.

It was during my breakdown that I was offered a knighthood. As before, the sense of unworthiness that goes with depressive neuroses made me hesitate to accept it, but I was finally dubbed in 1958.

We had so much enjoyed our previous long stay in India that we were delighted to receive an invitation from Mr Patnaik to renew our acquaintance with him and his family, an invitation which happily coincided with the International Conference of Planned Parenthood in Delhi in 1959. I was asked to be one of the main speakers and devoted much thought to what I was to say, glad that at last the Indian Government was proposing to do something about this, its greatest long-term problem.

Its efforts did have some effect – they slightly lowered India's birth-rate in the next five years, but not nearly enough. Today, the net annual increase of India's population has risen to ten million.

It was important that Nehru had at last realized the gravity of the problem. He made the opening speech at the Congress and was followed by its formidable President, Lady Rama Rau, and many foreign and Indian officials, all stressing the gravity of the situation. The gallant but frail and aged Margaret Sanger had a great ovation – her whole life had been spent in fighting, with a ferocious compassion, for the right of women to limit their families; in warning Governments of the irrevocable harm caused by over-population; and in helping the public to realize the danger of the world's plight. Had she but been listened to earlier – she and many others who fought the same battle – our troubles today would not be so dire. They are now immensely complicated by the enormous advances in medicine. Merciful and compassionate though they be, they add extra unwanted millions to an already grim total. I confess to a feeling of deep anguish about the future of our own species, about the damaged environment that we are making for ourselves and about the quality of our very lives.

After the Congress we resumed our exploration of India, with a mixture of pleasure and dejection, of hope and despair. Yet there is a quality of survival, a persistent tenacity of the human race which denies our fears and keeps us striving from day to day. As I write this, the World Wildlife Fund has just held an important session in London. Prince Philip summed up effectively, pointing out that it was not enough to pass admirable resolutions and think that this accomplished anything. 'We must all help, every one of us – if we want to survive.'

Meanwhile, Juliette and I had been invited to attend the celebration of the centenary of the publication of Darwin's *Origin of Species*, at the University of Chicago. We sailed on the *Bremen* in mid-September of 1959, and were put up at the University's Quadrangle Club. We had rather a shock on hearing that it was not safe to walk alone on the campus after dark.

We went out to Libertyville to lunch with Adlai Stevenson, and had a wonderful time with him in a lovely woodland setting. Though extremely busy, he found time for literature and the arts, a true liberal – a cultured man with the crowning gift of a sense of humour. We met but seldom, yet always found the same rare friendship and mutual understanding.

Later on, Adlai, Sol Tax (the Professor of Social Anthropology, who organized the celebrations), Harlow Shapley, the astronomer, and myself appeared in a midnight television performance. These night shows are a deplorable but successful invention of American television, capturing a large audience of people who do not mind keeping awake on Saturdays until three or four in the morning. But I must confess that the questions were topical and keenly interesting, though the whole discussion was larded with commercials, firms being willing to pay enormous fees for proximity to well-known names.

It was during our stay in Chicago that I was summoned to New York for a very gratifying occasion – the presentation of the Albert Lasker Award 'for outstanding contributions to the advancement of Planned Parenthood' (see Vol. I, p. 151). A distinguished company was present, including my old friend and colleague in the cause, Margaret Sanger. She died soon afterwards; but I shall always remember her gallant spirit and the impression of courage and purpose she gave when I first met her in the late 1920s, in my rooms at King's College, London – and the way she had kept it unfaded, for half a century.

The preparations for the centenary celebrations were now in full swing, people arriving from many countries to render their homage to Darwin, in lectures and discussion groups on every aspect of evolution. At one of these symposia I spoke on the 'Emergence of Darwinism'; at others, there were discussions on the origin of life, on the evolution of mind, on the teaching of biology, and on man as an organism – exhausting but interesting, and I think with important results on American thinking about evolution.

Cyrus and Anne Eaton had come from Cleveland for the occasion, and assiduously attended the meetings; he was an out-and-out Darwinian. They also wanted to hear me, as I had been asked to give the special Convocation Address in the University chapel.

I called it 'The Evolutionary Vision' – an extension of the evolutionary view-point to human affairs. It was perhaps not appropriate in a chapel, for I pointed out how Darwin and his successors had made it certain that man was not specially created, but descended from some ape-like creature, gradually becoming more human and more competent during his million years of evolution; that he could no longer 'take refuge from his loneliness in the arms of a divinized Father-figure, whom he himself had created'. I ended with a plea for more exploration and understanding of our own minds and our evolutionary situation. In view of the world's rapidly increasing population, man must try to find the answer to the question, 'What are people *for*?' – to which my reply was: 'for greater fulfilment'.

I had already affirmed this view in various books and essays, but here in Chicago, from a chapel pulpit, it shocked many orthodox Middle-Westerners – and much upset Professor Tax. He feared that the whole celebration would be damaged by my utterance, in spite of the fact that I insisted, here as elsewhere, that some form of religion, some self-transcending experience, was universal and apparently inevitable – and psychologically rewarding – in all human societies.

Actually, I do not think that my preachment damaged the celebrations. Anyhow, a book, edited by Sol Tax and containing a record of all the discussions and speeches, including my 'sermon', was published early in the following year and had a wide circulation.

CHAPTER 12

African Travels for Unesco

Heureux qui, comme Ulysse,
A fait un beau voyage.

IN June 1960, after months of preparation, Juliette and I sailed for South Africa on what was to be a prolonged and memorable trip.

The main reason for the journey was the mission entrusted to me by UNESCO to report on the conservation of wild life and natural habitat resources in south-eastern Africa. But as I had also been invited to take part in the Congress of Education at Durban University, and to lecture in Cape Town and elsewhere in South Africa, I decided we should begin our trip in that country, as yet unvisited by either of us.

On landing at Cape Town, we stayed with Dr J. F. Duminy, then President of Cape Town University, at his hospitable house, looking out at the sheer front, 3,000 feet of it, of Table Mountain, and near the marvellous Botanical Gardens at Kirstenbosch. Here we saw why Linnaeus had given the name *Protea* to this abundant plant genus. It is indeed protean in the varied beauty of its species, and wonderful in its strangeness and multiformity. Kirstenbosch was a revelation to us, and a staggering introduction to the richness of South African flora.

For my lecture at the University (which was just then being forced by the South African Government to close its doors to new 'coloured' and black students) I chose as my title, 'A Hundred Years of Darwin'. It attracted a huge audience, both of students and the general public, no doubt because evolution, especially the evolution of man and his various ethnic groups, was a dangerous subject in this land ruled by racially-bigoted Boers. Some students even perched on the rafters, and I was vigorously clapped. There was poignancy in this applause, for the false evolutionary doctrine and ugly practice of *apartheid*

184

was, and still is, threatening the country, while my lecture emphasized the need for freedom of thought and of all human beings.

We were to see and hear a good deal about apartheid and its results during our stay – the shanty towns, the small cement boxes of African 'townships', the low-paid work and hopeless poverty, the desperate efforts made by non-white students to get an adequate education. We were to hear of the Brotherhood, a powerful secret society sworn to defend the theory and practice of apartheid, opposed only by a handful of liberal whites, who too often suffered house-arrest and even imprisonment for their anti-apartheid beliefs.

We sensed the fear and distrust over the whole of that beautiful country – the tenseness of conditions which only endured because of governmental power working through harsh laws and restrictive regulations, and more directly through the police and the army. Dr Ramsey, the Archbishop of Canterbury, after visiting South Africa ten years later, said that a dangerous and explosive situation was boiling up which boded ill for the land. In 1960, it was already simmering.

A wonderful 700-mile drive through fertile, undulating country with the biologist Professor Scaife and his wife took us to Durban. Dr Malherbe, then Chancellor of Durban University, had organized a large-scale conference on education, attended by students and teachers from South Africa, and with many guests from Europe and America. I remember the sense of keenness, of patient militancy in the large audience; and also the wild applause given to liberal speeches and protests against educational injustice, which showed where the shoe pinched – as it so often does in this divided land.

After briefly visiting Pretoria, Johannesburg and Pietermaritzburg, we began our tour of National Parks and Reserves. As long as I live I shall remember this journey as the most rewarding, stimulating and altogether wonderful of my life. And so will Juliette, who recorded it in her excellent book, *Wild Lives of Africa*, which communicates vividly and accurately

185

the experiences we shared on this trip. I owe much to her powers of observation and evaluation, and shall often borrow phrases of hers in this account.

From my Introduction to Juliette's book, I will here merely quote a list of the places we visited and confine myself to a summary of their impact on us.

When we first went to Africa in 1929, there were only two National Parks in the whole continent – the Kruger Park in the Union of South Africa, first set up as a Game Reserve in 1898 and established as a National Park in 1926; and the Parc National Albert in the Kivu region of the Congo, established in 1925. By 1960, nearly forty National Parks or their equivalents – Provincial Parks, Wild Life Sanctuaries, statutorily established Reserves and Tribal Parks – had been set up in eastern Africa; of these, we were able to visit some twenty-five. In addition, we made a point of seeing as many as possible of the areas which were likely candidates for National or Tribal Park status. This added another dozen areas to be visited.

Besides looking at wild-life areas, we had of course to make contact with as many as possible of the Government Departments, University colleges, research institutions, museums and private organizations directly or indirectly concerned with conservation; and this involved discussions in over a dozen cities.

Our journey took us from Cape Town across the Transkei to Durban; on via Hluhluwe Provincial Park in Natal, to the Kruger National Park in Transvaal, to Johannesburg and Pretoria. Then to the Central African Federation, with visits to Zomba and Lake Nyasa; Salisbury, with Wankie and Lake McIlwaine Parks, Zimbabwe and the Kariba; Livingstone, Lusaka, the Kafue Park and the Lochinvar Reserve; and a side trip to the Portuguese Park of Gorongoza in Mozambique. Finally, to East Africa – Tanganyika, Dar-es-Salaam, and Arusha, the Serengeti, Manyara and Ngurdoto National Parks, the Ngorongoro crater and Leakey's dig at Olduvai; Uganda, with Entebbe, Kampala and Makerere College, Queen Elizabeth and Murchison Falls Park, the Gorilla Sanctuary in the mountains above Kisoro and a meeting on the Congo border with the Warden of the Congo National Park in Kivu Province; and lastly Kenya, with Nairobi, the University College, the Coryndon Museum and various East African research institutions; the Nairobi, Tsavo, Aberdares and Nakuru National Parks, the Game Reserves at Amboseli and Isiolo, the Meru Tribal Reserve; and finally an exciting aerial reconnaissance to Lake Rudolf.

This involved thirteen weeks of criss-crossing the vast area of southern, central and eastern Africa by car, land-rover and every variety of plane ...

It was indeed an exacting journey, and as I look back I wonder how I stood it, for after all, I was nearly 73. However, there is nothing so sustaining as the ever-changing spectacle of natural phenomena, nothing so exciting as the diversity, not only of man and his customs, but especially of the amazingly rich fauna and flora of the region.

I have always been a keen naturalist, and in the African National Parks and Reserves one sees, not only a greater variety of wild creatures than anywhere else in the world, but also a unique collection of larger mammals, a relic from the late Pliocene era, perhaps 2 million years ago, long before man had started to use land for agriculture – and still longer before he had developed the deadly weapons with which he shot the creatures that interfered with his crops, threatened his personal safety, or yielded valuable trophies like ivory or beautiful pelts.

I am especially interested in birds, and here again, Africa is much richer than Europe. To take but one example: the wardens in the Serengeti Park alone have recorded over 400 species of birds, most of them not found in Europe; while the list for Britain, excluding occasional vagrants, comes to about 250. Many of the African species are exceedingly beautiful, like the rollers and touracos, and the crested cranes with their communal dances; others are strange and interesting, like the hornbills with their mud-walled nesting-holes, the whale-headed stork with its absurd boat-shaped bill, the shrikes, whose cock and hen sing duets, and the multitude of large birds of prey – eagles and hawks, buzzards and vultures – now so rare in all but the remoter parts of Europe.

I am also an ecologist, and it is endlessly fascinating to see the ordered ecology of a large wild area. Through the centuries, a wonderful balanced system has evolved – grass supporting the antelopes and ostriches, coarse leafage the rhinos, high foliage the giraffes and gerenuks, marsh plants and grass the hippos; carnivores taking the surplus plant-eaters, so preventing their excessive multiplication, with its consequent damage to their own food-lands and to the environment in general; and scavengers, like hyenas, jackals and vultures, consuming the dead and preventing corruption; along with insect-eaters like aardvarks and many birds, and a rich variety of insects, from driver ants to termites, from malarial mosquitoes and tsetse-flies to huge beetles, tiny midges and exquisite butterflies. And let us not forget the reptiles – the ancient crocodiles, the three-foot monitor lizards, and the great variety of snakes (though these are rarely seen by the tourist); nor the fish, including the huge Nile perch and the fabulous lung-fish of Lake Victoria, which 'aestivate' in mud cocoons when the shallow waters dry out, and so successfully survive to live another of their many years; and the innumerable small species, all playing their part in the food-chain – the whole a miracle of self-regulating order and balance, created by diversity of demand and fostered by diversity of habitat, from wet tropical forest to dry scrub, from grassy plains to high mountains.

For scenery, Africa provides both beauty and wonder – from the snow-capped volcanoes like Kilimanjaro to the forested volcanoes, mostly extinct, in the Kivu area, from the heath-lands of the Aberdares to the vast grass plains of the Serengeti, from drought-stricken areas like the eastern Tsavo to splendid waterfalls like the Victoria on the Zambesi, or that of the Nile in Murchison Falls Park. Lakes of every size and sort, both fresh and saline. And traversing the whole region, the geological wonder of the Rift itself, that gigantic walled crack in the earth's surface, running 2,000 miles from Nyasaland to northern Syria.

Then there is the variety of peoples: the proud Masai in their ochre paint and skin togas that liken them to Tanagra figures; sad to say, ever fewer of them are now to be seen in their traditional dress and adornment, as Tanzania is 'modernizing' them. The Kikuyu, whose interesting features arrest attention; the tall Watusi, with their Nilotic faces and beautiful poise; the Samburu, the Wakamba, the Nilotic Luo and the Baganda; the Zulus and other Bantus, the forest Pygmies and many others – all distinctive.

Since our first visit in 1929, they have mostly discarded their tribal wear and are now, sadly to our eyes, wearing European clothes. This is a natural trend, an essential part of the 'wind of change' blowing all over the world, and a visible aspect of the immense step in the evolution of the African races. Since the independence of former colonies (except those of Portugal), a new type of African is growing up, wanting to make his own decisions, to shape a new destiny for that immense and ancient continent.

But we were engaged on a survey of the National Parks, created either before or after independence. Hluhluwe, in South Africa, was our first. Because it contains no lions or elephants, the rangers allow visitors to dispense with the protection of the land-rover and walk about freely. This is a rare privilege in National Parks and adds enormously to the joys and revelations of the wild bush country. One is let into the private language of unspoilt nature, recognizing animal trackways and spoor, wild shapes and smells, with an exhilarating sense of participating in its life, reaching a better understanding of its inhabitants. Such free curiosity is infinitely rewarding.

Guided by the Warden, Captain Potter, and two rangers, we wandered across this beautiful parkland area, of smooth, grassy hills, river valley with palms and reeds, thorn-bush laced with narrow game-paths, fringes of mountain forest outlined against the blue-crested horizon – an almost undisturbed habitat, harbouring an exciting variety of wild animals.

On this, as on every other encounter, I became utterly absorbed, enraptured by the different character of the multitudes of creatures living free in their own habitat, belonging so absolutely, each according to its kind. This renewed vision of wild nature and wild life revived all my naturalist's appetite – I was in a state of continual enchantment, and every succeeding experience provided further enrichment for us both.

The best time to watch is early in the morning – before the sun has risen on the animals' secret and private worlds – or again in the late afternoon, after the heat of the day has abated. Seeing a herd of impala suddenly alert and poised for flight, then leaping into space – at all angles – to land and rebound again from a bare touch on solid earth – their fluid grace and beauty takes one's breath away. Or a frieze of zebra galloping in a sudden spurt of speed, flaunting their stripes; lolloping gnus; sables with their superb scimitar horns; eland, largest of antelopes, heavy with powerful muscle and great dewlap; wart-hog, dashing away with tails up-right, like diminutive flag-poles to which one longs to attach the flag of liberty. Or the lumbering black rhinoceros, anachronistically armour-clad, yet surprisingly agile when stirred to action. Or elephants, our favourite above all other creatures, indisputably Lords of the Forest, lordliest indeed of all wild creatures – majestic, infinitely knowing and wise, knit together in loving family groups.

Every day, throughout our pilgrimage in this non-human world, our awareness of its multiple and co-ordinated pattern of life reinforced our resolve to do our utmost to preserve it.

I wrote rather fully, in the first volume of these *Memories*, of our earliest journey to Africa, which took us as far as the Parc National Albert on the Congo border. To describe this second trip, and the several that followed, in 1961, 1963, 1965 and finally 1971, would fill hundreds of pages. Moreover, since 1929, going to Africa to see wild life (and writing about it) has become commonplace. Every bookshelf carries its quota of accounts. I dare not indulge in more descriptions – difficult though it is to restrain my enduring passion. Besides, my *Africa View*, printed in 1931, and Juliette's *Wild Lives of Africa*, published in 1963, give an acceptable outline, still valid, of our experiences.

My Report to UNESCO on the mission entrusted to me was published in 1961. I concluded it as follows:

My contacts and discussions during my journey made me very conscious of the number of people – officials, public servants and private persons – actively concerned with the problems of wild life and natural habitats, or interested in their conservation, and of the large amount of thought and effort that has already been devoted to the subject. Unfortunately, constructive implementation has been consistently hindered or prevented by lack of funds – and often by lack of firm government backing. It is in the light of these facts that I make my recommendations.

As Harrison Brown emphasized in a well-documented study seven years ago, and as Professor Roger Heim (lately President of the IUCN) vividly pointed out in a timely pamphlet, the world is ecologically out of joint. During the present century its ecological equilibrium has been radically upset and its balanced ecological pattern has been disrupted, owing to the drastic over-exploitation of its natural resources. This growing disequilibrium between man and his planet will become increasingly serious and will end in economic, physiological and social disaster unless we take immediate steps to check and if possible to reverse the trend ...

My most general conclusion is thus that the question of the conservation of wild life and natural habitats needs radical reappraisal in the broadest ecological context, in relation to the present situation and future development of the region.

CHAPTER 13

West Africa Revisited

THE following year (1961), I made the second of my visits to West Africa, this time accompanied by Juliette. I had been invited to give the Aggrey-Guggisberg lectures at Achimota University in Ghana, and also to speak in several other universities, including some in Nigeria.

In Ghana's lowlands, the heat was moist and inescapable. It is extraordinary that anyone can work satisfactorily in conditions of constant perspiration, besides being plagued by myriads of mosquitoes; but human beings are capable of an astonishing degree of adaptation.

We found it rather trying, but also fascinating. Nkrumah was still at the height of his power and we were invited to lunch with him. The table was laid in a small courtyard outside his office, under an awning. Sir Robert Jackson, a high-powered expert sent from the UN to advise the President on financial matters, and Erica Powell, Nkrumah's faithful British-born secretary, made up the small party. President Nkrumah was awaiting a reply from President Kennedy in answer to his request for help over the Volta Dam: we all know now that it was Russia who footed the bill, not the USA.

Nkrumah was gay and charming; he talked about wild life with warmth, sorrowed about his pet ostrich, which had been shot without his permission after breaking its leg – and gave me his blessing on my efforts to arrange for National Parks in Ghana. The trouble was, of course, that most wild life, even cane-rats and giant snails, had been killed for meat long ago, though there were some areas in the north where a few large mammals survived.

As well as being President, Nkrumah was also Chancellor of Achimota University, and presided, in magnificent robes, when I gave my lecture. This was along my usual lines for Africa – on the need for ecological study, for nature conservation and for population-control, and against too much dependence on too few export crops, here tea and cocoa.

I think it had some effect; for not long afterwards, a very intelligent African, Dr Asibey, was appointed Head of the Ghana Parks Department and established one with a reasonable quantity of game, including lions, at Tamale, north of Kumasi. It was also decided in principle to set up a second, round the artificial lake created by the huge Volta Dam.

We were taken to see the dam by Geoffrey Bing, nominally Attorney-General, but in fact general adviser to Nkrumah. With memories of Kariba and of the beautiful Volta River and its forested slopes in mind, I agreed whole-heartedly about the future Park. I have had no reports on it since then, and only hope that it has become both a conservation area and a popular attraction.

We spent a delightful week-end near Kumasi, where General Sir Louis and Lady Spears lent us their home, perched above the famous Ashanti gold mines. (Sir Louis was, and still is, President of the Company; dear Mary, alas, has since died.) The style of the house, with its painted blue arches, was taken from the Levant, where Louis had spent many years; but here it stood in the midst of tropical greenery, rich vegetation, and with a gentle breeze cooling the hill-top. We enjoyed visiting the mines and the gold-processing factory. Incidentally, we learnt that a good deal of the gold was stolen by the workers, who had discovered that by swallowing gold-dust in small rubber tubes their theft could not be detected by the special screening machine; but we were told by the able British mine superintendent that mining would come to an end if all such thefts were stopped, as this illegal acquisition of gold was the men's major incentive for taking a job at the mine.

Kumasi was a thriving city, much bigger than when I had seen it in 1944. Its market was full of large and very black Africans in beautiful robes and togas, voluminously draped and explosively printed with designs of great originality. Juliette was very keen to buy some and eagerly explored the piled-up bales, only to find that export permits were impossible to obtain. We also learnt to our surprise that most of these cottons now came from Holland and Japan: Lancashire's share of the trade had sadly dwindled.

We paid our homage to the old Ashantihene, once the all-powerful and cruel ruler of Ashantiland, now reduced to retirement in an absurd suburban bungalow with pink nylon curtains. The entrance was guarded by two huge, white plaster lions smeared with paint – or blood? The old man was ill and touchingly resigned to his fate.

At Accra, too, the market took much of our time. As I had found on my first visit, all the business was done by the 'mammies' in their glorious robes and turbans, opulent ladies with ready tongues, hard-working – and making a very good living. They were mostly unable to read or write, but carried the details of every transaction in their heads.

Crowds of shoppers were disgorged from painted buses bearing alluring names – 'A beautiful woman never sleeps in the same bed twice', 'God is my life', 'You lie', 'Home sweat (sic) Home', 'Time tells' and the all-too-appropriate 'Nearer my God to Thee', which we read on an over-turned vehicle in a ditch, one of many accidents along the busy roads.

From Accra, we motored to Ibadan in central Nigeria, along verdurous, steamy roads, through untamed jungly forests – the lush fertility of creepers, splendid palm-trees, shrubs with enormous water-shedding leaves, and towering bamboos everywhere. We passed villages scooped out of the jungle, groups of mud huts with tin roofs, but some two-storeyed houses with elaborate fretwork balconies of concrete. Every spare inch bore a poster advertising some commodity – Pepsicola or radio, sewing machine or bicycle.

The men wore long trousers, over which a voluminous sleeved toga, billowing like a sail, gave them great dignity. A small pill-box cap topped the outfit and their faces often had a Hamitic beauty, reminiscent of the Ife sculptures. The women wore assorted prints, not so striking as in Ghana, but their heads were even more superbly turbaned.

The new University of Ibadan was built by Jane Drew and Maxwell Fry, using a novel type of open-work screen against the heat: it was an architectural break-through for West

Africa, where most official buildings were built in European style, one quite unsuited to the African climate.

I delivered my lecture in the Great Hall, which was even more crowded than at Achimota; I also gave several television interviews, all excellently monitored by Nigerians. We dined with various members of the Faculty, mostly Yorubas, brilliant and well-informed, interesting as well as interested, and deeply committed to their work.

When the heat allowed it, we visited hospitals, museums and churches, and were much impressed by the high level of culture in this thriving city of nearly a million inhabitants – but also by the high incidence of disease and malnutrition, especially protein shortage.

The traffic on the city's recently metalled roads was a dangerous mixture of walkers and cars, and the noise incredible, with gramophones and radios blaring incessantly. No doubt the civil war in Biafra has since brought many changes.

A curious incident interrupted our visit – we came upon an unexpected crowd, shouting and yelling. Our guide explained that a child had been stolen and the people were demonstrating, angrily but hopelessly. Apparently this is not an uncommon occurrence: the kidnapped child is usually taken on as a slave in a rich household.

We were shown to the palace of the Alaki of Abeokuta, now a venerable gentleman of 89, by Miss Lalage Bawn, assistant to Dr Diké, President of Ibadan University. I had made the Alaki's acquaintance when on the Elliot Commission (see Vol. I, p. 268) sixteen years earlier. Now, much shrunk from the superb man he had been, he sat at the end of a long gallery filled with a curious mixture of objects – a big Swiss clock with edelweiss decoration, lots of signed photographs, terai hats covered in beads, and magnificent mitres and crowns of diverse shapes, also embroidered with beads or cowrie shells; even the Victorian-style throne was covered with this beaded upholstery. He shook hands with a smile, sent for his visitors' book when I reminded him of the Elliot Commission, and proudly showed me my signature – 1944. Drinks were offered and visitors arrived, all dressed in fabulous clothes, the women's heads swathed in stiff, upstanding turbans of delicate silver gauze, the men with long brocade cloaks like Levantine abbas billowing round them, prostrating themselves in their sculptural gorgeousness at full length at the feet of their ruler. They were celebrating the installation of one of the Alaki's young wives as a local chief.

We finally took our leave; but I felt the pressing need of a lavatory, and was escorted through the dining-room full of feasting grandees. The trouble was that, having locked myself in, I found I could not unlock the door, and no one seemed to hear my appeals for help. In desperation I managed to climb through a small window and rejoin my party outside, calming their fears of my being kidnapped. The lavatory will have provided quite a problem for future visitors, as I left it locked from the inside ...

Next, we set off to visit the Mental Hospital of Dr Lambo.[1] This interested us profoundly. We were shown round by Dr Lambo himself, well over six feet in height, strikingly handsome and married to a white woman. He has many mental patients – the Nigerians suffer nervous complaints (mostly religious delusions), just as much as Europeans or Americans. He told us that he could never have accommodated them all in an ordinary clinic, and therefore built a mud village round the laboratories and treatment centre. The families of the patients settle in and look after their relatives, who receive treatment either in their huts or in the out-patient clinic. The 'village' provides a familiar environment, and obviates the trauma of 'going to hospital', as well as considerably reducing costs.

But the most interesting aspect of his practice was the fact that he had six herbalists and witch-doctors on his pay-roll. They were invaluable and did not interfere with his modern treatment, but reinforced it with familiar herbs and traditional spells.

He showed us several huts thus occupied by a patient and one or two relatives. Some even had a few hens about the place, just as if they were in their own village. The patients responded most encouragingly to this arrangement, and other centres are being built on the same principle. I thought how much the so-called civilized nations of Europe could learn from this method.

1. Dr Lambo is now an Assistant Director of WHO at Geneva.

We then went back to the coast at Lagos – by now almost unendurably steamy and hot. There we met many Nigerians, quick, clever men doing fine jobs as journalists, architects, scientists. A party of them took us to a famous night-club, the Kakatu, where jazz, improvised with enormous gusto, nearly deafened us. The moon was shining full on the gathering and the dance-floor was crowded. Juliette was invited to do a 'High Life' and promptly joined the throng. It is a simple enough dance, consisting merely of small steps to and fro, hardly touching the partner, and waving arms in rhythm to the music. She got a big hand when she returned to our table.

It was fascinating to retrace the journey I had made nearly seventeen years earlier, and see the differences that time had brought. The most striking was the rapid growth of the universities whose foundation the Elliot Commission had recommended. Thus the University of Ibadan was now large and flourishing under the Vice-Chancellorship of President Diké, a fine scholar, with a democratic outlook. In addition, new universities were being set up, one at Nsukka across the Niger, in what the rebels of the recent Nigerian war called Biafra, with that wily politician Azikiwe – 'Zik' – as Chancellor.

We were present at its inauguration, I armed with a message of goodwill from Harold Macmillan, then Chancellor of Oxford. There was an enormous crowd – chiefs in long, embroidered robes, wearing top-hats or bowlers, usually decorated with two white feathers, or skull-caps set with cowrie shells or silver badges; some had magnificently carved staffs of office and leopard-skin aprons. In equal proportion were women, some in bright local prints and turbans, but others in the latest Dior fashion, with huge fur or feather bee-hive hats perched on their handsome black faces. We specially noticed a lovely woman in a gold sheath-dress, with straightened hair and lip stick, who, we were told, was a very active member of the regional Parliament.

Here, too, the Mammy-waggons sported fascinating names, some puzzling, like 'Wee-Wee', 'Whether-Whether', or 'Young Supper'; others cheery, like 'Oh, Nigeria, why worry'; or ambiguous, like 'The nightmare of Onitsha' or 'Man proposes, God deposes (sic)'.

197

In Ife, I had the pleasure of seeing the fruits of my protest about the famous heads (Vol. I, p. 270). There was now a fine museum, where the bronzes and terracottas, many newly unearthed in the excavations of the old Royal Palace, were shown in safely-locked cases, and from the north, the earlier-dated finds from Nok, of striking workmanship and strange expression. These are as mysterious in origin as the life-size Ife heads, and seem to be unique in type. In fact, the cultural richness of Nok, Ife and Benin art, found in a relatively small territory, leaves one puzzled, though it is clear that Benin sculpture was influenced both by Ife and by the presence of the Portuguese. Maybe the further excavations now in progress will give a lead.

The present-day city of Benin is a sprawling, mud-hut affair, with markets everywhere, and no hint of the unique and curious artistic power shown by the museum specimens. What is not mud is corrugated iron, unpainted and rusty, used for roofs by chiefs and notables; unfortunately it symbolizes high status.

We crossed the Niger to Onitsha, recently a scene of terrible slaughter and destruction. The mile-wide river, with a sandbank humped in the middle, flowed slow and powerful, yellow with mud and thronged with fishing canoes. The ferry was at last loaded – to the brim – with lorries, cars and bicycles, goats and hens and babies and hundreds of people. It made its unhurried way across the fabulous river, with luxuriant banks of trees along its sandy beaches. Onitsha was then a thriving trade and market centre, thickly populated with prosperous-looking people.

From there we travelled to the Muslim north, to Zaria, where the houses of rich citizens are handsomely decorated with painted pargeting, depicting aeroplanes, motor-cars, bicycles, telephones, clocks – anything that serves as a status symbol. Here again the market contained a thriving multitude in brightly coloured cloths, threading their way through narrow lanes of alluring booths. A favourite buy seemed to be enamelled basins, painted with great cabbagey flowers in garish colours, made in Japan, and used extensively, we were told, as dowries. They are embedded in the mud walls of the inner rooms, making a startling pattern; when the need for cash arises, they can just be prised off and resold – a curious bride-price!

We drove on to Kano. Here, the land was becoming desertic, with only sparse and occasional vegetation. As we neared the great city, we joined donkeys laden with wood (sold at high prices in this treeless land), streams of people going to market and gay buses and lorries, bearing, as elsewhere, strange and special mottoes: 'Destiny is indelible', 'No telephone to Heaven', 'SMOG' (short for 'Save me, Oh God!'), 'Mainline express', and so on.

Kano is a large city sprawling round a small oasis. Here too houses are built of mud. This used to be just scooped out from anywhere; now there is a law forbidding the practice, as it was pitting the place with large hollows soon filled with refuse. To-day, if you must repair your crumbling walls after a heavy rain, you must go outside the city for material. Within the houses, the walls are painted and also enchantingly sprinkled with mica fragments, shimmering like sequins on the wide supporting arches.

Kano is the thriving centre of a wide mesh of caravan tracks, leading north across the great desert to the Mediterranean and west to the hinterland of the Ivory and Gold Coasts, as well as remaining a starting-point of the pilgrimage to Mecca. The market is a gathering place of many tribes and peoples – the largest I have seen in Africa, except perhaps for Onitsha. So it has been, no doubt, for hundreds of years, and we relished the vitality, the tang and immense variety of this teeming humanity under the broiling sun.

We had the good fortune to meet Mr and Mrs Sandford – he then in charge of youth in Kano, doing a very good job teaching football and other games. Unfortunately for the young people, who would soon revert to aimless mischief, he had just been recalled for lack of funds. Mrs Sandford, meanwhile, had been doing her bit – having entry to the Emir's palace, she had actually formed a group of girl guides within its forbidding walls. She took Juliette on a visit to the harem, from which, to my sorrow, I was naturally excluded, left to admire the fortified courtyard, with its redoubtable guards bearing indigo-chintzed turbans, full robes and scimitars.

Juliette, as she later told me, was greeted by the Emir's second wife – a charming young woman with many gold ornaments about her person; bride-price enamelled basins adorned her bedroom, as well as an immense brass bedstead. The first wife, an elderly lady retaining great power, was now looking after the young concubines and children, whom Mrs Sandford, by special permission of the Emir, had enrolled as girl scouts under the leadership of the second wife. Many of these were very young, 11 or 12, and much given to giggling. Once in the harem, the outside world is forbidden to them: they remain secluded and their 'scouting' activities strictly limited to the palace grounds. Still, it turned out to be a great success; they paraded with discipline, a small badge denoting their cubship, and gave the cub's call with gusto as Juliette left.

The whole palace is built of mud, painted white on the outside; within, great arches reinforcing the walls, are lofty halls beautifully decorated with paint and sparkling mica fragments.

We left Kano by plane, regretfully, thrilled by the cultural richness of West Africa and the varied enterprises of its inhabitants; I was much cheered by the advancement of higher education, to which the Elliot Commission had given the original impetus. But I fear that the terrible Biafran civil war has shattered many bright projects depending on Nigerian unity.

CHAPTER 14

Conservation in East Africa and Ethiopia

OUR many visits to Africa have created a pattern of love, awareness and gratitude that is part of our lives. In 1963, we were back there again to attend a Conference of the IUCN in Nairobi, which led on to a valuable conservation survey of Ethiopia.

In Uganda, on our way to the Conference, we had a strange encounter on the slopes of Mount Elgon, to which we had made an excursion while staying with the British High Commissioner, Sir David Hunt.

Under a shade spreading tree were a group of young Africans wearing European clothes, all in earnest discussion. We had seen the spectacular falls of Sepi against the blue outline of the upper mountain, the river-bed's green vegetation, the cliffs enclosing it. As we ate our picnic lunch, we watched the group dissolving – all but one young man who wandered our way. Juliette asked him what they had been discussing. Very pleasantly he replied that they were the committee of a new Ugandan Liberal Party, planning its future policy. After she had introduced me, he went off, but soon returned, bringing their President (wearing a check cloth cap and bearing that status symbol, a giraffe-tail fly-switch), and several members of the group. He was charming, fluent and full of ideas, and suggested showing us the place chosen for their new meeting house. We all piled up in their huge Cadillac and landed at the foot of a steep little hill. There, our young friend flourished his switch and ordered his young men to help 'Old Man' and his 'Madam' up the hill – which peeved me not a little. In the end I remarked that if he wanted to show me respect, he would call off his young men from propping me up and leave me to climb this little hill by myself, which I was quite capable of doing. This took him aback, and he explained that in his country old men were venerated for their wisdom and knowledge, and that he and his friends were merely expressing this veneration ...

We reached the top and admired a superb view, while he was talking enthusiastically about their plans for opening up their country, building hotels, bringing industries to this remote and peaceful land. Finally we parted at the foot of the hill and he shook hands with great courtesy: 'Old man, Father of Nations,' he said, 'tell us what you do that we may always remember you.' This was the first and last time I was ever called 'Father of Nations'.

From the Hunts' kind hospitality we moved to Nairobi, where we stayed with the British High Commissioner, Malcolm Macdonald, then working very hard on the final arrangements for Kenya's Independence. Government House was soon to become State House. He again demostrated the rich variety of birds in his garden – and showed us an advance copy of a wonderful book illustrated by Christine Wan Tho (Loke's wife, see p. 126) on the animals of Kenya.

He had the genial idea of transferring from the Coryndon Museum to the future State House a number of Joy Adamson's paintings of Kenyan chiefs wearing their full pre-European apparel, a grand collection of tribal regalia as worn several generations back, beautifully and accurately depicted. Malcolm's white friends in Nairobi did all they could to discourage him from hanging these pictures in their new surroundings – thinking the Kenyans would dislike being reminded of their 'uncivilized' past. But he took Jomo Kenyatta and a few African colleagues to test their reactions, and was fully reassured by their delight and enthusiasm. They recognized each ornament and its quasi-religious meaning, and rejoiced to see these fragments of the past given a place of honour in their new official building.

The Malin Sorsbies were most kind and took us to their newly opened lodge at Samburu, as well as to Tree-Tops, both superb view-points for the fascinating wild life of Africa. Juliette was also taken to their lodge on Lake Rudolf, an exciting station from which to see that desertic lunar landscape.

Meanwhile, Louis Leakey showed us more recent finds from Olduvai Gorge, and we remembered our first visit there, in 1960, soon after his wife Mary had uncovered the venerable early hominid, *Zinjanthropus*, from nearly 2 million years back. Leakey was also beginning to explore the shores of Lake Rudolf, which lately have proved to contain some of the richest fossil beds in Africa.[1]

The IUCN assembled a number of high-powered delegates, who generated a great deal of energy about conservation, reading papers and discussing means of saving habitats and endangered species. Many of its recommendations were implemented – all the East African states realized the financial value of their wild life habitats.

Towards the end of the Conference, the Emperor of Ethiopia invited a group of Conference members to report on possible National Parks in his still little-visited country.

A small delegation was set up, including myself, Barton Worthington, Max Nicholson, two Americans, Gardiner and Smith, and the French polymath from Senegal, Theodore Monod. Juliette and I were fortunately invited to stay at the British Embassy in Addis Ababa, where John and Aliki Russell provided a wonderful and interesting hospitality; the rest of the party had to stay at hotels.

Addis Ababa, capital since the Italian war, sprawled on a high plateau, was caught in the process of changing from a primitive town to a great modern city, and had thrown up some sky-scrapers among groves of eucalyptus; but there were still many mud huts. The air was bracing at 8,000 feet and the place was crowded by Ethiopians in white robes; the city and its suburbs boasted some excellent roads but in many places had to make do with muddy tracks.

We visited the home of the Organization for African Unity, proudly built of the latest materials and very modern in style, and next door to the African HQS of WHO and FAO. We also visited the newly established University of Ethiopia, housed in one of the Imperial palaces. The standard seemed reasonably high, indeed as high as anywhere in East Africa, with the possible exception of Makerere.

The delegation was granted an audience by the Emperor.

1. Alas, Louis Leakey has just died (November 1972) of a heart attack, a sad loss to African paleontology.

Approaching the Palace, I saw his living emblem, a large lion, lightly tethered on the lawn (the Emperor is styled the Lion of Judah and still officially claims to be descended from Solomon and the Queen of Sheba). I hesitated before touching it, but then a white-gowned Ethiopian stopped to pat its royal head, so I did the same, to our mutual satisfaction.

The Emperor received us cordially, but with dignity, on his Imperial throne. African unity, he realized, should include unity in regard to conservation. Speaking in excellent French, he promised us every support for our mission, from transport facilities to material supplies. He then referred us to the head of the Forestry Department, who had established a fine Forest Reserve in the wooded hills west of Addis. We visited it, and decided at once that it should be declared a National Park; it had everything needed – fine hilly scenery, splendid trees and many interesting birds, some species restricted to Ethiopia.

Then we set off to the Awash plains in the east, round the Awash river, which flowed in a deep cleft – an extension of the great African Rift. There were some fine oryx here, many small gazelles, and reports of lions and cheetahs (these latter we did not see; they had retreated before an invasion of Somali-type nomad herdsmen with big flocks of humped cattle).

We next paid a brief visit to the fortified city of Harar, where the main biological curiosity was a series of holes in the walls, designed to let hyenas *in* – they were the city's dustmen and scavengers, and kept the place wonderfully clean. But the sad ghost of Rimbaud had left no trace.

Here we were told of the arid Danakil desert beyond, some of it below sea-level, containing great numbers of active volcanoes, and one of the few areas boasting droves of wild asses. Though we had no time to visit it, we recommended it as a National Reserve, to protect these now extremely rare creatures.

Back in Addis, we were in time for the extraordinary Meskal Festival. The meskal is a species of coreopsis, and the festival is held when the hills are covered with its flaming miniature cornflowers. Officially it is in memory of Queen Helena, mother of Constantine the Great, and her discovery of the True Cross, to which, according to legend, she was guided by the smoke of a fire God inspired her to light. It could also be, and this we felt to be highly probable, the survival of an ancient fire-cult. In addition, it marks the onset of the Ethiopian New Year.

It is certainly Ethiopia's greatest festival. A huge crowd surrounded the great marquee in which the Emperor and his court sat waiting, with native notables and the diplomatic corps, in front of a hugh cone of firewood – the sacred bonfire.

Ethiopia was Christianized early in the fourth century, and crosses of every material, shape and size are worn by every citizen. The largest examples of these fascinating objects were on this occasion carried by a group of priests in full regalia – bizarre vestments and robes of many colours, richly fringed and embroidered, their heads protected by immense coloured umbrellas, also extravagantly fringed. With their silver crosses glittering in the evening sun, the priests circled the pyre three times, widdershins (a sure sign of magic), and then retreated to the city without taking further part in the pagan proceedings.

Next, the Emperor descended from his throne, took a torch, which he lit from glowing embers on a silver pedestal, walked round the pyre three times (also widdershins), and then, entering the hut-like erection, set fire to the high bundles of firewood. As the great pyre went up in flames, an explosion of ululation burst from the crowd.

Meanwhile, a huge procession was winding its orderly way down to the pyre: the Emperor's personal guard, the Household in pale-blue uniforms, then the Emperor's special herd of beautiful small Arab horses, led by grooms; the municipality in white shamma robes, like Roman togas, and branches of the Army and the Air Force, all carrying blazing torches and chanting exultantly as they passed the fire. The words are *Ehoha hababe*, which we were told meant 'The Flower is here' – the little yellow coreopsis. Then came floats with immense stuffed lions, with an elephant twice natural size flapping articulated ears, followed by one with the Emperor's real lion, lying supine and royal; then a group of wild horsemen on frisky Ethiopian horses, beautifully caparisoned with bands of red velvet and metal, their riders wearing a headpiece of coloured cloths and metal expanding in a high pelt, and real lion-mane capes on their shoulders. They rode with the typical Ethiopian stirrup, which supports only the big toe, and carried circular shields, splendid with velvet and silver. The high-spirited horses pranced and shied at the big fire, skilfully curbed by their superb riders. The grand finale came with a float on which men acted the digging up of the Cross, which slowly emerged as it passed the fire, immense and glittering with thousands of red electric-light bulbs.

The torch-lit procession was well over a mile long, winding down from a hill above the city, so that when fully deployed it seemed a huge and glittering snake, its tail rising in this vast, sparkling Cross. At last it passed the bonfire – fiercely burning now – the two symbols linked for a piercing moment.

From the embers of the hallowed fire, people took, and carefully brought home, some of the burning twigs to light their own private invocations.

Our explorations for National Parks took in Lakes Abyata and Langana, still rich in aquatic life, including multitudes of birds, threatened, alas, by so-called sportsmen equipped with telescopic rifles. We also denominated a large semi-desert area where herds of giraffes, Grévy zebras, gerenuks, Grant's gazelles and even the hideous, hairless desert rats survive and flourish.

But in spite of our reports and recommendations, and their formal approval by the Emperor, all is far from well with Ethiopia's wild life. It is a desperately poor country, and much money can be made from furs and trophies, simply by using the old carbines and muskets which wars have left in almost every Ethiopian's hands; but also, alas, from trophies illegally imported from Kenya. Leslie Brown and his brother George have written of their pessimistic experiences. The IUCN is hammering on; but one glimpse of that wild country will cool the greatest optimist.

We saw this savage scenery when we flew to Axum, erstwhile capital of the country. The view was hard to get through the portholes of the old army plane, but we crouched uncomfortably on its steel seats, unable to take our eyes off. Inaccessible by road, depending on donkeys or mules for transport, villages perched on top of crags, on tiny plateaux, which the erosion of the up-heaved mountain range has allowed to survive. There the fields were bright green or flaming yellow from the meskal flower – contrasting vividly with the precipitous rocky sides of the mountains, which descended almost vertically into deep clefts, some with heavily-silted rivers winding between their walls. The rains fall copiously from July to September, and take their giant bite off the vulnerable cliffs. What is left is an endless panorama of fierce crags, of stark unclimbable peaks, a shaggy landscape standing upright, with what seems, from the air, an infinitely small proportion of level soil. Yet this is what two-thirds of the country amounts to.

Our first stop was at Lake Tana – a huge sheet of water five times the size of Lac Léman, navigated by fishermen in papyrus canoes, beautiful, frail shapes, cheap to make but short-lived. Bas-reliefs in the Cairo Museum show their prototypes, unchanged for an eternity. A hydro-electric barrage spreads the white plume of the Tisisat cascade out of the lake, fed by the sources of the Blue Nile. A tiny monastery stands on the only island – and after all those crags, the vast lake gives a feeling of gentle peace.

Then on to Gondar, where we were greeted on touching down by a flock of lammergeyers, who evidently thought that the grounding of the 'great bird' meant a death, and therefore prey for their voracious beaks. Nowhere else in the world could one expect to see such a congregation of these giant vultures – with their fourteen-foot wingspread.

The next leg of our journey was along the west flank of the Semien Range. We were struck dumb with wonder – the cliff is as high as the Grand Canyon is deep, a vertical mile of coloured sandstone, threaded with green ledges, savagely beautiful in its remoteness, vastness and arrogant grandeur. The stupendous scenery was enough to qualify the Semien as a National Park, and when our guides told us that the high plateau (from 11–15 thousand feet above sea-level) was inhabited by two unique animals, the Semien fox and the splendid Walia ibex, as well as the rare, heavily-coated gelada baboons, we felt no hesitation in recommending the entire range as a National Park.

I have recently seen a BBC film of the Semien top, made by Jeffery Boswall. The pinnacled cliffs are even vaster than we had imagined, and the sight of ibex and huge baboons leaping down precipices to fertile ledges was thrilling. A just-motorable track now reaches the high plateau: the Semien Park could well become as great an attraction as the Grand Canyon itself.

Reluctantly whirled on from that unforgettable sight, we landed at Axum. This is a small town, grouped round its ancient cathedral, still containing the imperial crowns of three past Emperors. The assemblage of square stones and pillars near by is the original enthronement court, which every Emperor still must use at his consecration. We thought of it, draped with precious cloths and surrounded by a glittering array of priests and people, when this unassuming pile of great stones comes to its special life: at the time it had a neglected and desecrated look, meaningless and lost. We wandered further, along goat paths, followed by small boys conjuring up a few words of English. They led us to the mysterious high steles on the side of the hill, huge flattened obelisks of granite, carved to represent many-storeyed palaces. There are several of these inexplicable towers; the largest of all, 120 feet high, lies on the ground in two gigantic fragments.

Queen Judith, it is said, stormed the city of Axum in the tenth century and destroyed it. Who was this mighty woman? Where was her Jewish kingdom? Was she moved by fierce religious faith against the people whose steles and dwellings she destroyed? No one seems to know – these huge witnesses of a legendary past are exciting but dumb.

There were also underground stone-houses roofed by granite slabs and a small temple, its cult unknown, up on a little hill. Altogether, Axum was one of the strangest places we have ever seen. We would have stayed there for days, asking questions which could not be answered, trying to penetrate the deep secrets of these fragmentary monuments. All we heard was that a team of French archaeologists were working on the site.

We had to begin our flight back, threatened by a gathering storm. Semien was shrouded in black clouds, its precipices turned to inky threats. The plane rocked and bounced, flying high to avoid colliding with the grim mountain. It was with relief that we landed in a downpour at Addis.

Ethiopia is famous for its rock-cut churches, but unfortunately we had time to see only one, Yekka Mikael, not far from the Embassy. It was never finished and therefore shows the process of its excavation from the living rock.

Our visit was made the occasion of a grand picnic up on the plateau behind the Embassy, organized by Aliki and John Russell, our hosts. In spite of the wretched, so-called road, more like the bed of a torrent, pavilions had been hauled up and magically filled with tables and chairs, a superb buffet laden with delicacies and delicious drinks, and a distinguished company, including several members of the Ethiopian aristocracy. John delighted us all by jumping his splendid horse over groups of tables and chairs, and Aliki's beauty and vitality made the occasion even more unforgettable.

In our report we laid great stress on the preservation of soil and forest, and on including ecology and conservation in the school curriculum (a measure that has been so successful in East Africa), besides recommending the setting-up of various Nature Reserves and Parks under one of the main Ministries, but with a non-Ethiopian adviser.

However, as I wrote before, all is not well with conservation in Ethiopia – and that goes for much of Africa. We have just read that Tanzania has been sending ivory worth nearly 2½ million pounds to China; poachers invade the Parks; and the export of rhino horns, because illegal, has never been properly assessed: it certainly involves many hundreds every year. The prospect is not good.

We left Ethiopia with regret; there was so much more that we wanted to see of this extraordinary nation, whose roots are deep in ancient myths, as alive today as in their fabulous past; whose people carry a proud Semitic beauty unrelated to any nation in Africa; and whose Christian priests still practise old Coptic rites unchanged for 1,500 years, clothed in barbaric splendour, and proudly assert that the Ark of the Covenant, stolen by the Queen of Sheba on her visit to Solomon, still sanctifies their land ...

Its full history is yet unwritten and its legends, dating back to Genesis, are all the more fascinating.

CHAPTER 15

A Last Visit from Aldous

IN August 1963, not long after we got back to England, we met Aldous at Heathrow Airport. We knew at once that there was something terribly wrong with him; he was ashy-complexioned, very thin, and his voice had but half its usual volume. Yes, he said, he was very tired, having just been in Stockholm at a great meeting of intellectuals, trying to discover means to bring peace to the world. He had in fact sat up all night drafting some sort of plan, as nothing definite had been devised by the Committee, and in addition he had caught a cold. He would soon recover, he assured us, and just wanted to spend a quiet month in England, as he generally did each year.

We brought him to Pond Street and settled him down, but soon saw that the promised improvement was failing to occur. In fact Juliette got so worried that she arranged a consultation with the best specialists at Bart's Hospital and took him there, rather against his will. The fact was that he knew perfectly well what was the matter with him – he was dying of cancer – but did not want us to know; indeed, we never had the slightest suspicion of the terrible reality. He merely told us on returning from Bart's that the doctors had advised a quiet spell, and that his voice would soon be normal. We were only too anxious to believe him.

We also thought that he might be suffering psychologically from the loss of all his possessions the previous year, in the fire that destroyed the hill-side of Hollywood where he lived. A spark from a faulty wire had set one house ablaze, and the wind fanning it soon spread the fire all over the area. The fire-brigade arrived after the TV vans, and anyway could do nothing in that tinder-dry landscape. Aldous and Laura had thought their house safe, and drove next door to a friend's home – to rescue a kitten! Then Aldous noticed that the wind had changed; they rushed back, to find the flames licking their roof:

they had some twenty minutes to rescue what they most wanted. Aldous at once collected the manuscript of *Island*, his last novel, on which he had been working for years; he also took a few suits, while Laura was wandering round the pretty house, admiring the effect of the flames on the yet untouched interior. They both seemed to have been paralysed as by a fateful spell – unable to think of the essentials which they still could have saved: Aldous's notes and manuscripts, files of letters from so many interesting people, and especially the precious Journal which Maria had kept for many years. This was an invaluable document, written in Maria's perceptive and enchanting style, covering most of their lives together. Its loss destroyed at one blow all the hopes Aldous may have had of writing his auto-biography – and incidentally also made the labour of his future biographer, Sybille Bedford, infinitely harder.

In less than an hour, all their tangible past had vanished.

The scope of their loss made itself apparent slowly and gradually. At first, Laura wrote, it seemed almost amusing to replace such simple, everyday articles as tooth-brushes and spare shoes – but the irreplaceable records of a life-time are not so easily dismissed. Aldous never complained, but ruefully compared himself with a man who, having lost his past, had also lost his present and the basis for a planned future.

We felt it possible that the shock of this catastrophe had affected his health. We were entirely wrong: Aldous, with his usual philosophical fortitude, had faced and conquered it. What he could not conquer, in spite of his incredible courage, was the seed of cancer which he carried in his throat. He had decided, for all our sakes, not to tell us.

We took him to stay at Dartington, where the Elmhirsts gave us a wonderful time. The gardens were at their best and so were the sights of Dartmoor. I shall always remember his delight in its vast panorama, as he took deep breaths of its windy freedom. At night, the Music Festival in the Great Hall filled us all with joyful peace. There was a delightful incident after one of the concerts, when Nell Gotkowsky, the gifted young violinist, had been playing Beethoven with inspired perfection. We went to the artists' room afterwards, and Dorothy Elmhirst introduced us all to each other. In the confusion of so many new people, Nell Gotkowsky missed their names, but someone told her just as we were leaving that the tall pale man was Aldous Huxley. She rushed out after him and breathlessly poured out her – and her mother's – admiration for him. Aldous, stooping above the fresh young creature who had just enchanted us with her playing, listened with a smile of pleasure, moved under his apparent remoteness, as she gave him her heart's praise. It was an unforgettable moment.

We also took him to stay at Lawford Hall, with Phyllis Nichols.[1] This fine house is at the edge of Constable country, and it was a happy week-end which revived many memories of Philip and of Robert (see Vol. I, p. 142), now alas both dead. It was typical of Aldous that when he heard that Phyllis's son was suffering from sleeplessness and depression, he endeavoured to relieve the young man by gentle massage and help in meditation, spending himself in giving of his hoarded treasure in this most difficult of all arts – the art of living.

Our last visit was to Saltwood Castle, with Kenneth and Jane Clark. This medieval fortress had been made into a wondrous place, the main living quarters being in the modernized keep, from which narrow Gothic windows open on a wide court-yard surrounded by a battlemented wall. At the further end of the courtyard, K. had established his library in a large tower, with a smaller room attached, where he does most of his writing. The library was a place of silence – striking in its harmony and beauty, its scholarly atmosphere and the essence of so much that Aldous loved. It made a deep impression on him – as did the house itself, with all its modern and ancient treasures, and the feeling of continuity with its historical past. It was a great privilege to share this wonderful interlude with our remarkable hosts, and I shall always remember Aldous, tall and so pale, wandering round the rooms and grounds, and stooping to smell the scented roses.

Yet all the time, he was carrying this heavy burden of doom. He never by any hint or murmur allowed us to guess his fate. He had made up his mind that it would be simpler just to ignore

1. Phyllis died in late December 1971.

it – to fight this last battle without distressing us, to let things come as they would. The last we saw of him was at the airport – he said goodbye, and opened his brief-case to take out some papers ...

Soon afterwards the following letter arrived:

California. 29 September, 1963

Dearest Julian and Juliette,

You must be back from Africa, I imagine, by now – but meanwhile Africa has come to us, with a vengeance, in a frightful heat-wave with temperatures day after day of 105, and 80 degrees at night. In my own case, meteorology has been compounded by a spell of ill-health, due to the after-effects of a long course of radiation which I had to take this spring. I hadn't told you of this trouble before, since it hadn't seriously interfered with my activities and there seemed to be no point in spreading unnecessary apprehensions. It started in 1960, with a malignant tumour on the tongue. The first surgeon I went to wanted to cut out half the tongue and leave me more or less speechless. I went with him to my old friend, Dr Max Cutler ... Cutler recommended treatment with radium needles and so did the Professors of Radiology and Surgery at the U. of Cal. Medical Centre at San Francisco, whom I consulted. I took the treatment in the early summer of 1960, and it was remarkably successful. The tumour on the tongue was knocked out and has shown no signs of returning. However, as generally happens in these cases, the lymph-glands of the neck became involved. I had one taken out in 1962, and this spring another mass appeared. This was subjected to twenty-five exposures of radio-active cobalt, an extremely exhausting treatment from which I was just recovering when at last I was able to make the trip to Stockholm and London. Since my return there has been a flare-up of secondary inflammation, to which tissues weakened by radiation are peculiarly liable, often after considerable intervals. Result: I have had to cancel my lecture tour ... Another handicap is my persistent hoarseness, due to the nerve that supplies the right-hand vocal cord having been knocked out, either by an infiltration of the malignancy, or by the radiation. I hope this hoarseness may be only temporary, but rather fear I may carry it to the grave.

What the future holds, one doesn't know. In general these malignancies in the neck and head don't do much metastasizing. Meanwhile I am trying to build up resistance with the combination of a treatment which has proved rather successful at the University of Montreal and the U. of Manila – the only institutions where it has been tried out over a period of years – and which has been elaborated upon by Professor Guidetti, of the University of Turin, who has read papers on his work at the last two International Cancer Congresses, at Buenos Aires and Moscow. I saw Guidetti while in Turin and was impressed by some of his case-histories, and with Cutler's approval we are carrying out his treatment here. When this damned inflammation dies down, which it may be expected to do in a few weeks, I hope to get back to regular work. For the present I am functioning at only a fraction of normal capacity.

Much love to you both from both of us.

Ever your affectionate
Aldous

This letter was the first intimation we had of Aldous's real trouble, and we were deeply shocked. We were even more so when Laura wrote the further terrible truth that Aldous really had terminal cancer and that there was no hope of his recovery ...

He died on 23 November 1963 – and a light went out of our lives.

His last weeks of poignant fighting against the dread disease have been described by Laura in her book, *This Timeless Moment*, terrible pages of his suffering and his courage.

Soon after his death, Laura sent us the last article he ever wrote, commissioned by *Show* magazine on 'Shakespeare and Religion'. He finished it as he lay dying, unable to write but using a dictaphone, and Laura's help in transcription. It is a most poignant document: not so much about religion as about death – Aldous gathering Shakespeare's many haunting passages on death. Brought together in these few pages, they become Aldous's own requiem, his personal charter on the journey he was facing. He knew that, for him, this was to be 'the last syllable of recorded time'.

Many of his friends joined us at a Memorial Meeting at Friends' House, the Quaker headquarters. Kenneth Clark, Stephen Spender, David Cecil and I spoke of Aldous as we knew him, and Yehudi Menuhin very movingly played Bach's *Chaconne*. Later a Memorial Volume was published, containing, as well as these speeches, appreciations from many friends and acquaintances – a form of biography with many merits, reflecting judgements from diverse angles.

This book, together with the large volume of his *Letters*, admirably edited by an American, Professor Grover Smith, gives a vivid picture, not only of Aldous's amazingly wide interests, but of his kindness and generosity, often displayed by his spending precious time to answer queries from total strangers.

Laura and I then set up a search for a suitable biographer. Sybille Bedford finally agreed to undertake this great work, and her book is slowly progressing. The task is formidable, as all biographers' tasks must be: but Aldous was a very complex being, a mystic without a God, reaching out towards transcendence, endlessly searching for the sense of security and certitude which illuminates saints and martyrs; projecting his incisive mind into a multiplicity of fields where some gleam of mental and spiritual light might be found.

He never lost the intense feeling of wonderment at the strange and fantastic experience of life. Not long before he died, he wrote Juliette a letter finishing with these words:

Do you find, as I do, that the older one gets, the more unutterably mysterious, unlikely and totally implausible one's own life and the universe at large steadily become? For practical purposes, one tries to make a little scientific ethical sense of it all; for non-practical purposes – aesthetic and 'spiritual' – one cultivates Wordsworth's wise 'passiveness' and opens oneself up receptively to the *mysterium tremendum et fascinans* within and without.

He was an artist in style without vanity at his success: what he achieved was purely to satisfy his own integrity as thinker and writer. The world he strove in, as again he wrote in Juliette's book, was 'a world of enormous deserts, with here and there a fountain, a bird in the wilderness singing; a world of brute hard work and occasional inspirations'.

There are, throughout his writings, so many pregnant thoughts which shine for us and also reveal his inner being and the quality of his courage. I quote these lines from *Orion*, a long poem, published in *The Collected Poetry of Aldous Huxley*:

The choice is ours, the choice is always ours,
To see or not to see the living powers
That move behind the numbered points and times.
The Fly King rules; but still the choice remains
With us his subjects, we are free, are free
To love our fate or loathe it; to rejoice
Or weep or wearily accept; are free,
For all the scouring of our souls, for all
The miring of their crystal, free to give
Even to an empty sky, to vacant names,
Or not to give our worship; free to turn
Lifewards, within, without, to what transcends,
To squalor of our personal ends and aims,
Or not to turn; yes, free to die or live;
Free to be thus and passionately here,
Or otherwise and elsewhere;
. . .
The choice is always ours. Then let me choose
The longest art, the hard Promethean way
Cherishingly to tend and feed and fan
That inward fire, whose small precarious flame,
Kindled or quenched, creates
The noble or the ignoble men we are,
The worlds we live in and the very fates,
Our bright or muddy star.

CHAPTER 16

Ritualization and a Visit to Israel

IN 1965, the Royal Society, as mentioned earlier (p. 74), asked me to organize a Conference on the Ritualization of Behaviour in Animals and Man – presumably because I had been the first to use the term *ritualized* for the display of the great crested grebe, and later of other birds and some mammals. There was trouble about the title, which some Fellows wanted long and comprehensive, but the Society's admirable President, Sir Howard Florey (famous for his work on penicillin), insisted that we stick to a single phrase.

Then came the difficult business of selecting the speakers. Some choices were obvious: Konrad Lorenz for a general treatment of the subject; Robert Hinde for monkeys; Thorpe on bird display and on song-ritual in birds; for children's play, Mrs Molly Brearley; the American psychologist Erik Erikson on the development of 'ritual behaviourism' in man, including compulsive habits and symbolic ritual, from babyhood on; my son Francis on the function of Voodoo and ancestral rituals in Haiti; Professor Gombrich, head of the Warburg Institute of Art, on ritualized gesture and facial expression, as well as formal composition, in painting and sculpture; while Maurice Bowra (now, alas dead) gave a brilliant paper on Ritual in Dance, Drama and the Spoken Word. I also secured Desmond Morris on 'forced movement' rituals in captive animals, and the rigidification of their behaviour; J. A. Ambrose on the ritualization and consequent strengthening of the human infant–mother bond; as well as contributions on ritual in religion, education and international relations.

It was one of the most demanding tasks I had ever undertaken, but very rewarding – not only in the personal contacts made with many interesting people from Europe and America, but above all in establishing that the study of animal behaviour was relevant to human affairs.

It also opened a new horizon to sociologists and psychologists by demonstrating what an important part of our lives is dominated by ritualized gestures and formalized habits.

The meeting took place in June before a crowded audience in the Zoological Society's new lecture room, and late in 1966 the results were published in a special number of the Royal Society's *Philosophical Transactions*. I wrote the Introduction to it, with descriptions of display ritual, sexual or aggressive, in various birds, monkeys and apes, fish, octopus and spiders, and concluded that ritualized animal behaviour had two functions, one as an immediate signal for sexual, aggressive or flight reactions by other members of the species, the other as a long-term method of securing a firm pair-bond between male and female, as in my grebes.

With some trepidation I pointed out that ritualization played an important part in man – in the sphere of greeting and what we call good manners, in dress, and even in art and literature, where the elements of paintings and poems are deliberately arranged so as to enhance the viewer's or reader's response, and to communicate the author's or artist's message (or his underlying ideas) more effectively. I also touched on ritualized play – festivals and test matches, traditional children's games; and, of course, on the important role of ritual in state and religious functions.

My trepidation was unjustified – the Symposium was a great success, and later works, on both animal and human behaviour, have often drawn on its findings.

Not surprisingly, I felt exhausted after the Conference. But it had been successful in bringing people in so many disciplines into fruitful contact, and I was happy about the result.

I felt entitled to a holiday and we decided to revisit the Lake District, taking our time driving there. On the way we stopped at Chester and called on the farmer then living in the old house, the cradle of the Huxleys, still called Huxley Hall. Surrounded by open farmlands, it stands within a modest moat, with a Jacobean porch in the front garden. There is a tradition that one of my ancestors once owned the place; anyhow, the cemetery at Chester is full of Huxley graves, and many Huxleys crossed into Wales and became Puxleys – ap-Huxleys – but I do not think that any of my forebears had any exalted past.

We then went to Malham Cove, that extraordinary limestone amphitheatre, with a river emerging from the centre cliff, leaked subterraneously from the tarn above, and bordering rocks looking like Henry Moore sculptures, carved by wind and rain. We asked Henry if they had influenced his art, but he remembered them only very dimly from his childhood days. Malham Cove was painted by Ward in the romantic nineteenth century, and the picture, now in the Tate, has always fascinated me with its towering cliffs and herd of cattle below, a wonderful expression of brooding grandeur.

In the Lakes, we stayed at Keswick and radiated from there to the Wordsworth country, full of his poetry, which I have always loved. Our visit was a sort of pilgrimage, taking me back to the early days when we stayed at Fox How with dear Aunt Fan, last of the Arnold sisters. Grasmere and Rydal, Ambleside and Windermere, Helvellyn and Glaramara, Scafell and Borrowdale, Buttermere and Langdale – all are magic names to me, and magic places, their beauty unimpaired and my love for them unaltered.

We ended our visit with a few days at the house of Alec Carr-Saunders, my old friend and colleague from Oxford days, and his wife Teresa. It was the last time we saw him, for he died soon after. He was a strange man, of immense erudition, great administrative talents and a visionary genius in educational affairs. Juliette was slightly awed by him, and I sometimes shared her feeling. But it was a happy visit to a little-known, secluded valley, which Alec enjoyed revealing to us.

The year ended with a journey to Israel at the invitation of the famous Weizmann Institute at Rehovoth. Our old friend Israel Sieff had suggested it, and Juliette and I were delighted (especially as no lecturing was involved).

What were the chief impressions we gained? First, the sharp contrast between Arab and Israeli enterprise. The hard-won expertise of the Israelis had made the desert blossom, while the Syrians and Jordanians had made desertic conditions worse by tree-felling and the swarms of goats of their nomadic Bedouins.

219

Secondly, the amazing vitality and determination of the Israelis, and in most of them, a warm friendliness towards non-Jews. It is only in Jerusalem among the Beit Sherim, those prisoners of ancient tradition, that the foreigner feels a sense of rejection and disapproval, sustained by Old Testament tradition and persistent taboos. In such a modern state as Israel, this all-too-powerful sect is anachronistic, a sadly reactionary force in Israel's life and politics.

Dr Weisgall, the ebullient and very efficient chairman of the Executive Board of Rehovoth, showed us round the Institute. He was a compulsive talker and oscillated between information, funny stories and laying down the law. After one of his outbursts against someone who was pushing for an interview, I murmured something about his being 'a bit of an old Jehovah': I was promptly ticked off for speaking that sacred name.

The Weizmann Institute is housed on a pleasant site. The work done in the various laboratories there is first class – much of it in biochemistry and biophysics, physiology and scientific medicine. I was greatly impressed by the team of pure scientists who were working there, united by a common scientific ideal and a shared patriotism.

But our most exciting time was spent in the company of General Yoffe, Director of the Nature Reserves Authority. He gave us the best part of a precious week to show us his side of the country. We liked each other at once and built up a lasting friendship.

Abraham Yoffe is the son of Russian immigrants, a Sabra, meaning that he was born and bred in Israel. He is a big man – a gentle giant with a gift of words, of enthusiasm and efficiency. Above all, he has a deep passion for his country, its scenery and history, its fauna and flora. He began to see life young, by joining the anti-British campaign as a teenager in the early days of the Mandate; then, when the Second World War broke out, he joined the British Forces – after all, we were fighting the same enemies. He did well there, and learnt fluent English.

After that war, he was in the Israeli Army, fighting Arabs; he rose to the rank of General, but retired from active service at the age of 50. Then came his great opportunity: he was put in charge of conservation in Israel, at last enabled to apply constructively his remarkable knowledge and love of nature.

On the journeys he took us, down in the Negev, up into Galilee, to the sea-coast, to remote kibbutzim on the frontier, he always amazed us by his extraordinary knowledge of everything round him. He also seemed personally to know everybody, whether Bedouin, Arab or Jew – and was on the best of terms with all of them.

During the Six Days War, he rejoined his brigade and led a tank corps right across the Sinai peninsula, driving hard all the way along a forgotten track, and reaching the Suez Canal in record time. Returning after the astonishing success of the expedition, Yoffe took time to explore more of Sinai, equipped with boundary notices for new Nature Reserves, with warnings not to shoot gazelles or pluck flowers – and incidentally discovered an unexpected site for a new Reserve, a flamingo-haunted lake in the desert.

Israel, small as it is, is a microcosm of strange, almost unimaginable landscapes, as well as a panorama of 4,000 years of history. We reached the Negev Desert soon after leaving Beersheba, its seven wells still functioning, as they have since Abraham's time. Its desert surface covered with stones, the Negev is harsh in colour, ruthless with its browns and undertones of black, brightened here and there by the yellow Salsola flowers, a sort of ragwort which turns into tumble-weed ('the weed before the storm' of the Old Testament), and by the desert broom, Retima, also yellow. There were few birds: little flocks of desert partridges trotting like ambulant pebbles, and lovely small black-and-white wheatears, *Oenanthe lugens*.

The eroded hills seemed to groan with defeat, to sag with resignation, but the sky was softly blue over the desolation.

Suddenly a streak of blue-grey light shone beyond a cliff – the Dead Sea itself, soon revealing its expanse, the grey now startlingly bluer, of a saxe-blue that lay insolently delicate between the sterile walls of the desert Rift. The Mountains of Moab across the Sea shimmered in the heat, pale amethyst. We got out of the car to gaze our fill, before descending to the southern end among strange shapes, 'Lot's wives' in silent multitudes – salty pyramids in deeply eroded valleys half-filled with debris, their grey-gold limestone set with stalagmites – a wildly, indeed immoderately fantastic scene in this land of rifting and volcanic chaos. It is also a formidable mineral world, with a long list of chemical treasures – phosphates, an overabundance of common salt, potassium, calcium, silicon and iron; ammonia, sulphur, magnesium, aluminium and many other elements and compounds.

We reached the level, wide shore left by the ever-shrinking sea, under which lie the remains of the infamous city of Sodom. Unlike that of Gomorrah, its name remains on the map, and its particular sin in our vocabulary. What was Gomorramy? I have often wondered ...

In November, the climate was warm but pleasant; in summer, however, the heat may be terrible, up to 120° F, with no spot of shade in this sun-blasted land – stark and accursed. One is so conditioned to that legendary cathartic wrath of the Lord, which caused Him to wipe out Sodom and Gomorrah, that unconsciously one accepts the apocalyptic punishment; a cataclysm which was in fact, according to the seismologist in Jerusalem, Professor Bentor, a violent earthquake. The main outcome of this turmoil, besides the destruction of the Cities of the Plain, was the blocking of the outlet of the Sea, into which flows the Jordan with its four springs, and the cargo of chemicals brought by it and the rare torrents on the cliffs.

Dr Amotz, who accompanied us with General Yoffe on this remarkable trip, is an expert geophysicist, and explained to us the Dead Sea's strange history. Originally a much larger body of water, some 200 miles in length, filling the whole Jordan valley from north of Lake Tiberias to beyond Sodom, its surface level with the Mediterranean, it has now shrunk to 47 by $9\frac{1}{2}$ miles and has fallen, presumably by faulting, to nearly 1,300 feet below sea-level. In this hot cleft, its water steadily evaporates, leaving an ever higher concentration of its rich mineral content. It is also, of course, the north end of the Great Rift Valley we had first seen in Africa, one of the world's most fascinating geological features. That alone would have made it for me a spectacle of immense interest – but added to this was its fabulous history, and its present unimaginable and ghostly lineaments.

The Israelis have made the area an important source of revenue by exploiting its mineral wealth with the latest scientific know-how; however hard to come by, they need to use every asset to make their nation viable. We were deeply impressed, everywhere we went, by this passionate urge to make the best of their little country – not quite the size of Wales – and its natural resources.

At Masada, towering over the road, another legend became real: here we saw the hill where the besieged Jewish rebels committed mass suicide rather than surrender to the Roman legions, when their refuge, Herod's fortress-palace, was at last taken by assault.

But the magical place on the Dead Sea, for us, was Ein-Geddi. It was one of the most ancient cities of Judaea, a green and lush oasis in the midst of desolation. Clear, cool water gushes out of springs in the cliffs, cascades into pools and brings greenery to the oasis before descending into the salty sea; more springs ooze out of the limestone, untainted by any chemical elements, and all the near-by land is fertile loess. Below was a flourishing kibbutz, irrigated by these untainted waters, where valuable fruit, vegetables and flowers ripen long before anywhere else, thanks to the heat at this low altitude.

We climbed up the cliff, to the Spring of David. The ravine is green with spiny acacia, fleshy Capparis (desert capers), more blue than green, jujube and carob trees, maiden-hair ferns and 'pampas' grasses. It was a steep climb, winding with the capricious carvings of the stream. We reached the foot of David's spring gasping with exertion – and with surprise: the water tumbled from 500 feet above us, almost vertically – then spread into a shiny pool at our feet. The spray created its green foliage of ferns dangling thick over the entrance to a cave. This, it is said, was David's hiding place 'in the wilderness of Ein-Geddi', where King Saul, to quote the Old Testament, went with 3,000 men,

to seek David and his men upon the rocks of the wild goats. And he came to the sheepcotes by the way, where was a cave; and Saul went in to cover his feet: and David and his men remained in the sides of the cave. And the men of David said unto him, Behold, the day of which the Lord said unto thee, Behold, I will deliver thine enemy into thine hand, that thou mayest do to him as it shall seem good unto thee. Then David arose, and cut off the skirt of Saul's robe privily.

Thus Saul, all unaware, a sitting target (he was, in fact, relieving nature), was spared by the young and chivalrous David.

Did David remember the 'wilderness of Ein-Geddi'? Did he return to the secret place to drink of the spring named after him? Did he perhaps bring Bathsheba, once the wife of Uriah the Hittite, and their small son Solomon, to play in the orchards which Solomon praised in his manhood, when he sang: 'My beloved is like a cluster of camphor in the vineyards of Engeddi.'[1]

In the semi-circle of golden cliffs draped with green foliage, we stood riveted with fascination and speculations. It was a timeless moment.

It is probable that the conquest of Masada and the final rout of Bar Kochba and his rebel zealots led to the destruction of the settlements along the Sea of Salt – a destruction made permanent by its further shrinking, its increasing salinity and the spread of aridity along its cliffs. 'Its groves of palm-trees are now like Jerusalem, a heap of ashes', wrote Pliny.

I wish that Pliny could have been at Ein-Geddi with us, that lovely afternoon in November. We would have deplored the burning of the living trees by the Romans, and later by Arabs and Mongols – crimes of human folly added to the geological disasters of long ago. But we could have rejoiced together over the new plantations, the dates and figs and vineyards, the fields of artichokes, asparagus and many-coloured roses.

Back at Sodom and its mineral works, our General borrowed a land-rover. We wandered over one of the many other dried-out Dead Seas, covered with a powdery sand called *lissan*, searching for the opening to another natural phenomenon, the Nahal Pratzim. This is a narrow canyon cutting deep

1. According to modern translators, this passage should read: 'My darling is like a bunch of henna flowers in the garden of Ein-Geddi'; these are white and sweet-smelling.

into the plateau, winding between white-pillared cliffs of gypsum with layers of variously-coloured earths compressed into fantastic solid waves on its steep sides – almost as strange and beautiful as Petra. There was no need to make this an official Nature Reserve: it was an inviolable and fierce wilderness. A few raven circled around, in quest of the desert mice which tunnelled their nest-burrows in the friable gypsum.

We emerged rather dazed, as if admitted to some occult mystery of nature. Few people can resist the attraction of such cataclysmic geology, the point where fact becomes fabulous. The same holds for the Grand Canyon; it is much larger, but not more wonderful. Such lunar and frightening regions, visibly expressing the non-human power of nature, are often chosen as holy sites, of worship or sacrifice, as if man could thus approach the elemental divinity of the untamed world.

It was certainly so in the Negev. 'Put off thy shoes from off thy feet, for the place whereon thou standest is holy ground', said the Lord to Moses on Mount Horeb. A vast number of other sanctuaries and altars, temples and monasteries proclaim this fact all over the land of Israel, from chalcolithic shrines of forgotten gods to the ruins of Jewish synagogues and Christian churches, even bare little caves and shelters – places where 'men and women have tried to escape from the tormenting consciousness of being merely themselves', as my brother Aldous wrote.

A recent article in *The Times* was devoted to the exciting re-birth of Nabataean agriculture in the Negev. Thanks to our General Yoffe, we were taken over one of these remarkable farms on the bare hill top of Avdat, a city of bleached ruins. This royal city was originally built by the Nabataeans to dominate the caravan route from Aqaba, Egypt and Arabia through Petra to Tyre and Sidon, and on to upper Judaea, just as Petra was founded to dominate the twin route to the East from the Red Sea to Damascus and Palmyra.

The Nabataeans had to feed Avdat's hungry mouths, in spite of the aridity. Professor Evenari, of the Hebrew University at Jerusalem, was given the job of finding how they did it. This was a venture after my ecological heart.

Evenari studied old maps and records of the region, as well

225

as every foot of the ground where ancient ruins spelt past human occupation. The annual rainfall of less than three inches, most of it falling in sudden bursts, was certainly far from sufficient to provide farms with the water they needed.

The Nabataeans discovered that the loess soils of the area form an almost impermeable crust when wet, thus increasing the run-off. Evenari exploited this phenomenon. The hillsides, impermeable after a rainstorm, acted as catchment basins, and the water was funnelled off the slopes by means of stone guide-walls, on to the cultivated bottom lands. Each run-off farm was divided into terraces, equipped with cisterns to store surplus water.

Using this ancient method, which must have been practised by the earliest settlers of the Negev long before the Nabataeans perfected it, Evenari rebuilt walls and terraces and restored cisterns. Every drop of rain from the hills was thus conducted to his plantations, and he now grows abundant produce – asparagus and artichokes, onions and olives, carobs and almonds, figs and apricots, cherries and apples, peaches and grapes. We enjoyed a delicious lunch of vegetables grown on the farm, in company with Evenari and his team of workers, sharing their enthusiasm for this thrilling revival of an agriculture which dates back over 4,000 years.

A remarkable book has been written about this work by Evenari and his colleagues, *The Negev: The Challenge of a Desert* (Harvard University Press, 1971). It is a patient and loving study of the power of life under conditions of extreme hardship, and of the fantastic triumph of re-adapting an ancient system.

General Yoffe had planned a Reserve in the vicinity of Eilat, where all the animals and shrubs mentioned in the Bible could live and multiply. The desert is gentler down there, with moist sea-breezes helping the growth of grass and trees. He has also set up a Marine Nature Reserve on Eilat's shore, rich in varied and beautiful under-water life – joy for schnorkelers and skin-divers.

A few miles from Eilat we visited King Solomon's Mines, driving first along an old caravan and pilgrim route, winding stony-rutted through the naked gorge, past scraggy necks of reddish rocks, slowly eroded by wind and scant rains, rising like shaggy manes against the brilliant blue sky.

Copper was mined at Timna, almost certainly by Solomon, after long exploitation by earlier chiefs, in a vast, desolate area of dark-red dust, with stone bastions rising in immense and shapeless humps, dwarfing the landscape. Hell might look like that – and hell it must have been for the men – mostly prisoners – who slaved in that arid desert. The modern copper mines at the edge of this mineral-rich area are efficiently run with scientific machinery. The millennial exploitation continues.

Jerusalem, in 1965, was still divided into Israeli and Jordanian areas. Since 1967, it has all been in Israeli hands. I am sure they will never agree to a renewed division, though I hope, in the interests of international sanity and goodwill, that they will make it an open city, accessible to all – of whatever faith or nationality. Its very name stirs one's heart, for it is essentially a charismatic city, cradle of three major religions, for which rivers of blood have been spilt. We were able to live a few days within its pale and absorb unforgettable impressions.

Space forbids further description. Yet there is so much in this ancient land of Israel which took our breath away with the wonder and delight of re-discovery; for the names of these biblical places and the events associated with them had been familiar from childhood days. The sources of the Jordan, the ford where John baptized Jesus, Nazareth, with the cave where He lived as a child, Caesarea, Mount Tabor, the Lake of Galilee (now called Tiberias) where He walked upon the water, Capernaum, where He preached – and fields of rich red soil where He walked, apricot and ochre-grey, with stony ridges in the distance, amethystine in the clear evening light.

Then, too, there were the fabulous places associated with the Crusaders, vainly attempting to establish a Christian kingdom in the alien Semite world – Jaffa, Acre, the Horns of Hittin's disastrous battle-ground, Mount Carmel, Ascalon ... so many evocations of past history revived before our eyes. Rich beyond words is this little country, which we promised ourselves to visit again when the desert blossomed with spring flowers.

Before leaving it, however, I must mention that important element of Israel's life, the kibbutz. We visited several kibbutzim and were impressed by their efficiency, their single-minded dedication and their acceptance of a difficult communal system. The old-established kibbutzim enjoy greater comforts; the new ones still have to fight for them, to work hard until the soil is rejuvenated and begins to yield its harvest. To be a member of such a community is a challenge, which calls for great endurance and courage, especially when the kibbutz is situated near the frontier, in danger of Arab raiding.

This is not the place to discuss this vast collective experiment, involving as it does a whole new system of shared parenthood and social responsibility. Nor can I embark on the subject of Israel itself, a crucible of many ethnic groups reassembled from all parts of the world, gradually moulded into a unified nation, not only by its own efforts but in reaction against Arab hostility. It is a colossal enterprise, but still hampered by tribal notions and biblical traditions and by the hard core of 'Old Believers', who cling to the Old Testament and Talmud, with their ancient rituals and taboos. No one, I think, can predict Israel's eventual future, but no one can deny its present energy and validity.

CHAPTER 17

Ageing, but Still Active

WHEN we got back to England I was feeling very tired – Israel had been wonderful, but had involved so much travelling, so many new facts and ideas to absorb, talks with so many people on so many different subjects, that with the tiredness came the dreaded feeling of depression and the fact of sleeplessness. It became clear that I was in for another breakdown, and finally Juliette took me to a nursing home, where I spent two most miserable and disastrous weeks. Whatever the reason, everything went wrong, so she took me home, with a nurse.

1966 was therefore a black year, and it was a long time before I felt reasonably fit again. However, a holiday in Tunisia in April 1967, in the welcome company of Max Nicholson, helped a great deal. We enjoyed swimming in a transparent blue sea and basking in the blessed sun.

After our return, Juliette brought me an ordinary school exercise note-book, and suggested I start writing my memoirs. To my surprise, I found an unsuspected spring of memories rising into my mind. The process was slow and needed much effort, but finally the first volume emerged and was published in 1970. And now the second volume is nearly done, and I know I shall miss the companionable memories it brings, memories of people and of places, of successful and frustrated efforts.

Midsummer day 1967 was my 80th birthday. We had a lovely party, and I felt honoured that the BBC should stage a TV programme for the occasion. I was specially delighted by Ernst Mayr's contribution from across the Atlantic. In answer to my thanks for what he said, he wrote me a letter which, coming from one of the world's greatest evolutionary biologists, I deeply appreciated. He wrote:

I still remember with gratitude the encouragement you gave me during the difficult period of founding the Evolution Society ... You have always unselfishly supported – or actively promoted – various movements in favour of worthy causes, whether it be conservation, taxonomy, and other neglected fields of research. And as a genuinely good biologist, you have never lost sight of *Man* as an object of biological concern. I have chosen the word *concern* deliberately, because your interests range all the way from physical anthropology to man's spiritual needs. I still consider your *Religion without Revelation* far superior to anything else in that genre.

Such letters are not only personally gratifying, but help one to feel the continuity of scientific work. Perhaps I may mention another appreciation, which has reached me more recently (December 1970), from Charles Elton, replying to a letter of mine congratulating him on the award of the Royal Society's Darwin Medal. He wrote: 'It was mainly you and your teachings and later your books that kept my interest in evolution alive.' Then, regretting that speeches were not usually made by the medallist, 'I had meant to say publicly how much I owed to you in the difficult early days of my ecological work' (in the early 1920s ecology was a new subject, not fully approved of by 'classical' zoologists, who thought more about the anatomical structure of dead animals than what they did when alive, or their relations with their environment), 'for encouragement of my research and also of the expression of my ideas.'

Later that year, we went to see Dr Humphrey Osmond, on holiday from Princeton. He was the pioneer of the study of lysergic acid and other hallucinogenic drugs, and coiner of the term *psychedelic* for their effects.

He is also a leading authority on schizophrenia and the role of chemistry (as well as environment) in its causation and possible cure. As a result of further discussions with him and correspondence with Abe Hoffer, we three published a joint paper on schizophrenia, pointing out that there must be some genetic basis for proneness to this disease, that probably one gene is mainly responsible, and that this gene must confer some counteracting biological advantage if the percentage of schizophrenics in the population is to remain more or less constant, in spite of their handicap in the business of living. Osmond also pointed out that this biological advantage does exist: schizophrenics are surprisingly resistant to shock, wounds, burns and various noxious substances, and recover much more quickly than 'normal' people from such damage. We are still far from finding a method to cure schizophrenia (which affects over 1 per cent of most human populations), but are at last beginning to attack the problem from every angle and to evaluate the role of many factors in its causation.

I must mention a little curiosity of biology; Juliette would never accept my statement, though it can be checked by simple arithmetic, that the red blood-corpuscles of a single average man, if placed end to end, would stretch three times round the equator. H. G. Wells had refused to insert it in *The Science of Life*, because, he said, no one would believe it, and then they would doubt everything in the book. Though the diameter of each corpuscle is only seven thousandths of a millimetre, there are nearly five million in each cubic millimetre of blood – five billions a litre, and each of us contains an average of four and a half litres. At my request, the eminent physiologist, A. V. Hill, agreed to verify this, and it turned out that I was actually under-estimating the distance – my red blood-corpuscles could encircle the earth over four times, almost half the distance to the moon!

Around this time I was clearing my mind as to the real meaning of humanism and its significance as a successor – or substitute – for a theistic religion. In various articles, I again pointed out that our planet's evolution has passed through three successive phases: the first, longest in duration, when its physical and chemical features were established; the second, the biological phase, when life originated and blossomed into its inconceivable variety of structure and adaptation, to produce over-all a steadily higher degree of organization, of body, perception and emergent mind; and thirdly, to borrow Teilhard de Chardin's useful term, the psycho-social phase, which appears rudimentarily in higher mammals, but only comes to full flower in man. Evolution in this phase is based on the cumulative growth of knowledge, and operates mainly by a conscious or subconscious selection of ideas and aims. In the two later phases, dead ends are frequent, but are circumvented

231

by the rise of some new and more effective organization – of animal and plant bodies, of human societies and ideas.

I ended one article as follows:

Man's most sacred duty is to realize his possibilities of knowing, feeling and willing to the fullest extent, both in individual achievement, in social development and in the further evolution of mankind ... this will be the most powerful religious motive in the next stage of our evolution.

Elsewhere, from a slightly different angle:

The human species can, if it wishes, transcend itself, not just sporadically, in individuals here and there, but in its entirety, as Humanity. We need a name for this new belief. Perhaps *Transhumanism* will serve – man remaining man, but transcending himself by realizing new possibilities of, and for, his human nature. Once there are enough people who can truly say 'I believe in Transhumanism', our species will be on the threshold of a new kind of existence, as different from ours as ours is from that of Peking man. It will at last be fulfilling its own destiny.

The growth of the Humanist movement, the establishment of humanist societies in many countries, often in universities, shows that something is in the air which fosters humanist or transhumanist beliefs – and actions.

On the other hand, the continuance of wars and strikes, the terribly slow advance of education, above all the failure of man to curb his own increase and save his environment from pollution – these make it clear that the full 'humanizing' of our evolution will be long and drawn-out.

I also intervened in an argument with C. P. Snow about what he called *The Two Cultures* now competing in the Western world: the scientific and technological as against the literary and artistic. He suggested that a 'third culture', bridging the gap between the other two, was now emerging, a culture based on the disciplines concerned with human beings – social history, sociology, medicine and architecture.

I wrote an article in the *Cornhill* agreeing that he was right, 'but insufficiently right. The third culture must be humanist and must have an evolutionary basis, seeing human living as a process of evolution.' Such an evolutionary humanism, I continued, 'will not merely bridge the gap, but will transcend the conflict in a new and integrated pattern of thought'.

I had a very encouraging letter about this from Lewis Mumford, writer and editor, sociologist and planner, educator and conservationist – one of the keenest minds in the USA, both critical and creative. He wrote to me about the founding of an *American Journal of Humanistic Psychology*, which some wished to deal with parapsychological, mystical and religious phenomena, as well as with psycho-analysis and behaviour. He wrote: 'I don't like the notion of four separate psychologies, and have argued for their adopting your *Transhumanism*.' And added:

How nice, dear Julian, to find that such an early work of yours on the grebe gave ethology its start – and therefore the extension of pure ethology to cover human behaviour in all its aspects – intellectual, aesthetic, critical and religious – as well as the various displacement activities, physical and mental, that we practise when thwarted or checked in our aims.

I followed on with an essay entitled *Psychometabolism* – another term I coined, which soon gained general acceptance. Its key paragraph was as follows:

The process of evolution as a whole tends towards the reproduction of types that can utilize more of the world's resources, and do so more efficiently. To achieve this, the processes of physiological metabolism are improved and new types of metabolic utilization appear (e.g. in the capacity of termites to utilize wood cellulose as food).

The other major tendency in biological evolution is a trend in the evolution of mind – a trend towards a higher degree of awareness ... Brains can be regarded as psycho-metabolic organs. Just as the physiological metabolic systems of organisms utilize as raw material the physico-chemical resources of the environment, so brains utilize the raw materials of experience and transform them into special systems of organized awareness, or 'idea-systems', which then play important roles affecting both individual behaviour and social evolution. Among such idea-systems are religions and philosophies, art and modes of literary and aesthetic expression, and, it must be admitted, false delusions of infallibility, false deductions like that of the flat-earthers or the belief in the imminent end of the world.

It was good to realize that my early resolve to be a generalist, instead of a specialist in one of biology's many branches, had led to such comprehensive views on the role of mind in the human or 'psycho-social' phase of evolution; and it was cheering to find that my ideas on the subject aroused general interest – leading to requests for articles and lectures and invitations to important conferences.

In March 1969, Juliette and I celebrated our Golden Wedding anniversary. As a venue appropriate for this special *Rite de Passage* of ours, we chose the Fellows' Restaurant at the Zoo and gave a party to as many of our friends as it could accommodate. It was a good party. Sir John Redcliffe-Maud gave one of his inimitable speeches and made us all laugh with his wit and audacious imitations. Lord Holford, an old friend from PEP days, bravely overcame a bad tooth-ache to second a vote of congratulations, which he did splendidly. Juliette and I moved in a euphoric dream, not quite believing that it was really ourselves who had worked our way through fifty years of married life, and were being fêted by our many wonderful friends.

We both resisted answering questions by reporters as to what we really thought of such enduring marriage. Marriage poses as many problems as it solves: indeed, the flavour and essence of long-lasting marriage cannot be put into words.

Probably, busy as I was with my many avocations, I took less account of the problems and adjustments involved; Juliette had to make the relevant adaptations and for this I give her every credit. She sometimes teases me by saying that had she known what she was in for when she accepted my proposal, she would have run for miles. But she willingly admits that, whatever the inevitable squalls we suffered, we have led a tremendously interesting life together, involving a great variety of experience with our different but complementary awareness.

Perhaps the key to a good marriage is *acceptance*, which in its turn creates a capacity both for independent growth and for joint perception. One might also say that there is no such thing as a 'perfect' marriage, for human beings are always in some degree imperfect. But I can certainly affirm that our marriage has been fruitful and sustaining. How fortunate I was to be accepted by the lovely girl from Neuchâtel whom I met at Garsington, fifty-three years ago – a girl who has retained her freshness in her maturity; a woman with many interests and a rare capacity for making friends and for enriching our joint existence!

We further celebrated the occasion by a tour down the Dalmatian coast, which in early April was already flowering and warm. These so-called package tours have much to recommend them; having had to organize so many of my earlier travels myself, I found it restful to follow a well-planned programme and be content with what was chosen. We later took similar trips to Turkey, with Leonard Elmhirst, a delightful companion, and to Corfu with our Hampstead friends, the Fred Uhlmanns – welcome breaks from life in London.

The latest celebration we have attended was in Paris, commemorating the twenty-fifth anniversary of UNESCO's founding. It was a great occasion, with the organization's five Directors-General present – myself from its earliest years, followed by the Mexican diplomat and educator, Torres-Bodet; the American, former Librarian of Congress, Luther Evans; the Italian financier-statesman Vittorino Veronese; and today, the brilliant many-faceted Frenchman René Maheu.

All five were on the platform during the formal sessions, listening with diverse feelings on the many messages and speeches customary on such occasions. Old colleagues and friends appeared and shook hands, bringing to life a host of memories. But I could no longer identify with what has become a colossal and multiple organization, while considering with sympathetic understanding the immense burden now resting on the present Director-General, René Maheu.

On the last evening he gave a superb party for UNESCO, at the unusual venue of the Musée de l'Homme. It was exciting to drink champagne and toast our various friends against the exotic background of Bushmen paintings, formidable West African maternity idols and awe-making masks from New Guinea.

I have now just received a book published by UNESCO, *In*

the Minds of Men, summarizing the organization's twenty-five years of activity, 1946–1971, which, though not specifically mentioning population-control, implies the need for it if the human race is to survive, or at any rate to have sufficient food and water, and to live in an unspoilt environment. It is a most interesting outline of UNESCO's general projects, written by fifteen participants – covering the world's major problems and the efforts which UNESCO is making and co-ordinating for their solution.

These last years have been saddened by the death of many dear friends. I have already written about Dorothy Elmhirst, her character and radiant charm, her love of beauty – in nature, in gardening, in music and the arts. Another grievous loss was Mary Spears, wife of General Sir Louis Spears. She was a wonderful hostess as well as a warm and tried friend, forgetting her own troubles to give comfort to those who needed it.

Then there was the death of our old housekeeper Alice Pirie, who had looked after us devotedly for over thirty years; Jack Haldane, after at last achieving a measure of contentment in India, where he had been doing some remarkable work; and Bertie Russell, robbed by three years of his centenary, happily married at last to his fourth wife Edith, still enjoying a fabulous memory, which enriched his conversation, still deeply concerned about violence and the horrors of war; he bequeathed most of his possessions to the Peace Foundation that he founded and fostered.

Unforgettable is the memory of Bridget Tallents, widow of Sir Stephen Tallents (who had so successfully organized the Empire Marketing Board with the aid of my cousin Gervas Huxley, and had then become Assistant Director-General of the BBC). Bridget was the welcoming hostess of their lovely old house, St John's Jerusalem, near Dartford – a relic of the Templars in England, surrounded by a moat and enclosing a wonderful garden, with great horse-chestnuts, a towering copper-beech and spreading cedar. We spent many happy days in that small island of peace and beauty (now belonging to the National Trust), secluded from ever-growing suburbia, returning home glowing with the radiance of Bridget's enduring charm, vitality and love – and with armfuls of flowers from the garden.

Juliette's aunt, 'Tante Juliette', a commanding figure, died at 93, fighting to the end. The list is long and continues to grow.

One of the outcomes of my interest in field natural history as well as in laboratory biology has been my commitment to the cause of conservation. This has involved me lately in several protests about anti-conservationist proposals and practices in Africa – a projected large hotel on the floor of the magnificent Ngorongoro Crater (which President Nyerere, pressed by several European experts, agreed was undesirable); the harnessing of the Murchison Falls to a hydro-electric project, which would not only convert the Falls from a grand spectacle to a miserable trickle, but would lead to the scaring and even killing of the Park's splendid wild life by the large labour force involved (this was a scheme which President Obote was determined to proceed with, but which we have heard recently, with great relief, has been shelved by his successor, General Amin); excessive poaching in Ethiopia and the violation of Mt Semien's high sanctuary, which H.M. the Emperor of Ethiopia undertook to protect.

I was also concerned recently in the welcome decision not to use the coral island of Aldabra as an international airport, but as a natural ecological laboratory, sponsored by the Royal Society.

The foundation of the IUCN, and of its associated body, the World Wildlife Fund, had for me a gratifying sequel. Late in 1970, at their International Congress in London, they presented me with a gold medal and also a splendid gold watch (Swiss of course) of almost miraculous properties: self-winding, waterproof to at least sixty fathoms, and even showing the day of the month. I treasure these gifts, but still more the citation, which stated the award was for

his outstanding contribution to scientific research relating to conservation; for the leading part he played as Director-General of Unesco in initiating the formation of the International Union for the Conservation of Nature and Natural Resources; and for his efforts

237

during 1960 and 1961 to arouse public concern about the threat to wild nature and the natural environment which led to the formation of the Wildlife Fund.

This crowned sixty-three years of my passionate interest in conserving wild life and natural beauty: I was very proud.

Nevertheless, it is all too clear that the future prospects of our planet are far from hopeful. By the year 2000, unless we tame our technology, drastically cut back our increase, and set up new standards of values for human living, our world will collapse in unsavoury chaos, with many species of wild animals extinct – except in zoos, where they are no longer wild, no longer in their own environment – the spiritual refreshment of unspoilt nature obliterated by the motor-car (whose numbers increase even faster than our own), and pollution everywhere.

All this has been said by many others, but it will have to be repeated, over and over again. However, conservationist pressure has already lead to the appointment in Britain of a Minister for the Environment (who made an excellent speech at the World Wildlife Congress), and now I read that in the USA pollution and conservation have become of even greater public concern than the war in Vietnam.

Here at home, the publicity by the *Ecologist* of a formidable document, 'Blue Print for Survival', supported by a long list of distinguished names, has rekindled both our apprehensions and our hopes. *Eppur si muove*: but are we moving too late?

In 1971, stimulated by our old friend G. G. Simpson's energy in visiting the Antarctic (and writing on the evolution of penguins) in his late 70s, we decided to mark my 84th year by yet another visit to East Africa. John Owen cordially invited us to revisit the Tanzanian National Parks and in Kenya we stayed with our old friends the Sorsbies in their palatial house in Nairobi's flowery suburbs.

The trip was a great success. We again used the comfortable little guest-house of the chief warden, built at the foot of a great kopje haunted by dassies (those comic little furry creatures with a fixed smile on their faces), and again during breakfast on the veranda watched zebra and antelopes grazing peacefully a mere 200 yards off. At the very tips of slender branches overhead, black-hooded vitelline weavers were busy weaving their inverted bottle-nests with long grasses. The gnus had left for greener pastures, but we had luck with most of the larger mammals. The sight of these wild creatures never fails to transport one's imagination to a few million years ago, when Africa belonged to strange creatures like hippos, rhinos and elephants, and many others whose fossils alone remain – before modern man had cast his life-destroying shadow upon the land.

We were taken by Hugh Lamprey to the River Mara in his small observation plane, and saw 106 hippos huddled together in a bend of the river, the babies standing on their mothers' backs to avoid being squashed between the two-ton bodies of this sausagey mass. Ostriches displayed vainly at the little plane, and a Kori bustard in angry display looked like an animated chrysanthemum.

We also flew to the new Reserve at Lobo, where we saw the most surprising hotel built astride a large kopje, exploiting its sheer granite flanks as background and walls, a bathing pool scooped out in its side. It is a triumph of imaginative architecture, inspired by Lloyd Wright, yet part of the African landscape.

Most interesting to me as a biologist was the enlarged Research Institute at Seronera. It was originally started by Dr Bernard Grzimek, the famous Director of Frankfurt Zoo, in memory of his son Michael, killed when his plane hit a vulture during a vast study carried out in 1958, a study which actually surveyed the colossal migration of hundreds of thousands of herbivores – gnus, zebra, and gazelles; and their followers and predators – lions, hyenas, and wild dogs.

Impelled by an obscure but powerful urge, these animals leave the central plain just before the rainy season, moving in Indian file along well-defined, ancient tracks to the southern regions of the Serengeti, where fresh grass awaits them. Their numbers defy description. They just amble along in continuous procession, marching for miles and miles, until they reach the new feeding grounds – to return later in the year, when fresh grass has grown. On the way, the female gnus give birth to their calves and zebras drop their foals. As soon as born, the youngsters stagger up to join the march, though the predators harass and pull down many of them. It is estimated that over half a million large quadrupeds roam over the vastness of the Serengeti plains. As Dr Grzimek wrote in his admirable book, *Serengeti Shall Not Die*, animal migration such as this occurred all over the world before man intervened.

The Serengeti Research Institute is in fact the world's largest ecological laboratory – and the results of the work done in that natural environment are already proving useful to those concerned with conservation in other parts of Africa and, indeed, all over the world. Its importance will grow as knowledge increases, and the complex links which connect all forms of life are disclosed.

It is undoubtedly an inspiring venture. We listened with eagerness to those dedicated young men as they told the story of their long watches and detailed observations. And as we flew over the vast plain, we glimpsed new meanings in the strange microcosm that they were investigating.

The Research team was not unlike a graduate college at Oxford or Cambridge, but sited in the midst of the greatest wild life refuge in the world. They use a small computer to work out the interrelations of different elements in the Park's life – soil, water, types and number of animals, the relation of predators and prey, vegetation, the effects of fire and climate, and so forth.

Down in the south, we visited Jane Goodall-Lawick and her husband, putting the final touches to their study of wild hunting dogs. They also took us to see the gnu migration at close range – herds uncountable like the sea.

One man, Bryan Bertram, had fitted a radio collar on a (previously tranquillized) lioness, and with the aid of his bleeper, was able to keep in touch with her, day or night. He learnt some interesting facts; for instance, that mating takes place twice a year, over a period of three days, the animals coupling every twelve minutes. We asked how they responded to this orgy of mating. 'The male went about his business in a rather obsessive manner, while the female appeared indifferent; but when it was over, she rolled on her back with an ecstatic smile on her face ...'

Dr Harvey Croze, another ecologist, was just about to fix a radio collar on an elephant. Meanwhile, he had been the first to see – and to record – an elephant's death and its 'funeral' ceremonies. This had deeply moved him and he later published an account of it in the *Sunday Times Magazine*, with a sequence of wonderful photographs.

He had been driving round his 'parish' with a photographer when he noticed a herd of elephants behaving strangely. In fact, one of them was clearly on the point of death, its skin hanging loosely on the huge frame and its head drooping. The large bull of the herd was standing by, and the other elephants were making a half-circle round this poor creature, uttering strange noises, while stroking her with their trunks. The bull then tried to prop her up, but she fell on her briskets and remained prostrate, in spite of his continued efforts to lift her with his tusks. He then picked a bunch of grass, which he inserted in her mouth – and finally, in despair, tried to mount her, in the belief that sex might revive her. She was dead by then, and the herd set up a joint ritual ululation, such as he had never heard before. They all left as dusk was falling, except one large cow who remained behind, not facing the corpse but looking at it over its shoulder, making a last farewell. As Croze said, there can be no doubt that elephants love elephants.

New light has thus been thrown on the little-known private life of these giant animals. And in general, the understanding of the Serengeti's ecological system – and of the measures taken to preserve its integrity – are providing the world with guidance in all problems relating to conservation.

John Owen, ex-Director of Tanzania's National Parks, had the wisdom to support, and the energy to raise funds to enlarge the original station created by Dr Grzimek. The Director of the Institute is Dr Hugh Lamprey, a brilliant young biologist, and his staff now numbers some twenty scientists from Africa, Europe and America. They work as a team, keen and enterprising within a wide range of projects. I was full of admiration for the whole establishment and its work.

As a result of one of our many visits to East Africa, Juliette had acquired a wonderful if rather odd memento – a real elephant skull. She lovingly placed it in a corner of our little garden, where for three years it presided, its bony structure architectural in quality, still exuding the giant creature's past vitality. We found the remains of a wren's nest (or was it a great tit's?) actually in the *foramen magnum* – the aperture giving passage to the animal's spinal cord, which, directed from the brain, once controlled its movements. The skull, like the animal itself, was constructed on a vast scale – we could reach our arm up to the elbow in the empty sockets of its tusks.

Juliette showed it to Henry Moore just after he had finished his superb memorial bronze to Fermi called 'Atom', which, by an odd coincidence, was not unlike an elephant's skull. Much as she loved this strange brooding presence in her garden, she sensed that Henry was entranced by it, just as she had been when she first saw that domed construction of interlocking bones in Africa, stamped by its complex evolution; she gave it to him – and I must say we both missed it, for I too had come to love it. However, Henry not only took it to his heart but proceeded to explore its massive outline, its tunnels and cavities, its recesses and blind eye-sockets, and to etch every aspect of its complex lineaments. He learnt the technique of drawing directly on the copper plate with the assistance of the master-etcher Jacques Frélaut.

As he wrote in the preface of the handsome catalogue produced for the exhibition of the result (thirty exciting etchings): 'One finds in it all sorts of qualities that bones generally seem to have, including some parts very thick and solid and others almost paper-thin. Nature's sense of strength and structure is one of the things you discover in studying such bones.'

Henry Moore also created several pieces of sculpture bearing the unmistakable stamp of his genius fused with an evocation of the skull's construction. The elephant skull, and through it our love of wild Africa, has indeed been immortalized.

My most recent activity was a visit to Oxford where, in the new palatial Department of Zoology, I had been asked to unveil a picture-portrait of three of my earliest students, all now Fellows of the Royal Society – Sir Alister Hardy, Professor E. B. Ford and Professor John Baker. Each has successfully developed his own speciality; for Hardy, the oceans (now retired, his interest lies in the study of telepathy and religious experience); for Ford, evolutionary genetics and mimicry; and for Baker, the earliest study of methods of chemical contraception, cell-chemistry, inter-sexuality in pigs in the New Hebrides, exploration of fine details of cell-structure by the new tool of electron microscopy, and the factors which control the breeding season in higher vertebrates – and now, in his retirement, indefatigably writing a comprehensive book on *Race*.

Absence abroad had robbed the occasion of one of my star-pupils, Sir Gavin de Beer; one-time Director of the Natural History Museum, who, in addition to his brilliant work in vertebrate anatomy, embryology and evolution, wrote on Hannibal's crossing of the Alps, on the history of mountaineering in the Mont Blanc range, on Alpine travel in general, on J. J. Rousseau etc., a true polymath. Alas, he died a few months later.

Elton, too modestly, had refused to be included in the portrait, but in my speech I deliberately included him and his contribution to ecology, indeed making it a recognized branch of biology (p. 230). Many other old friends and colleagues were there, including Sir Peter Medawar, Professor Tinbergen, Hans Kruuk (returned from research on hyenas in the Serengeti to work with Tinbergen), and of course the head of the Department, Professor John Pringle – a Cambridge man who had done a great deal for Oxford Zoology. To my great interest, he is setting up a new alternative Honours course on Man – not his societies, which are the concern of sociology (and I suppose economics), nor his machines, his ideas or his culture, his art and his history but, to paraphrase his own words, 'man himself, the thinking, reasoning creature that has emerged from the long process of evolution into biological dominion, with power over the whole of nature. What is he, and how has he come to be what he is? Our aim will be not only to tell what is known – but what could be known, if truly scientific investigation were applied to man himself.'

The occasion – and Pringle's plans – crowned my career. I was proud of the work of my pupils (and of the grateful letters they later wrote to me), and delighted that Oxford Zoology was going to include Man in its studies. So much of my own work had been on man – as evolutionary climax, as conservationist (but at the same time polluter and destroyer of nature), as overbreeding species doomed to catastrophe unless his population is drastically limited.[1]

It put the seal on my work as a truly general biologist, interested not only in animals' anatomy, but in their general behaviour and ecology, and also in man as a special product of evolution, bewildered at finding that he holds the world's destiny in his clumsy hands.

1. Furthermore, my old pupils and others in the Oxford Zoology Department are writing an introduction to the third edition (after twenty-one years!) of my *Evolution: The Modern Synthesis*.

Conclusion

DURING my 84 years, I have lived through a social transformation in Britain, from Edwardian class-ridden days to the society of today, far from classless, more a competitive bourgeoisie, yet now in the throes of attempting to create an improved social order.

The young are in revolt against the type of society in which they have to live, against the war-prone world, against authority, against the strains of our overcrowded life – and also against traditional morality, which is going overboard in favour of 'permissiveness' with its different rules and limitations. At present a deep sense of insecurity prevails all over our planet, leading to hatred and violence, but not as yet towards the new world order and type of society that is needed. Social revolution is *now*, is *today*. What it will bring forth is still a source of deep concern.

Incredible technical progress has been made in my life-time – from high bicycles to supersonic aircraft, from shot-guns to atomic rockets, from traditional doctoring to asepsis and organ replacement, to antibiotics and vitamins, extending the average life-span some twenty years, with an alarming excess of old people, including old people like myself.

The accelerated explosion of scientifically based technology has now reached a perilous level. We watch with a mixture of exaltation and fear; on the one hand modern man rising victoriously into new knowledge and understanding, and on the other the disastrous consequences of his discoveries and of his increasing meddling with nature, with the population explosion looming darkly over the world's future.

The only encouraging fact is that most thinking people, and many governments, now realize the gravity of the problems, including excessive population growth, and are even beginning to act against its worst symptoms. Together with many others, I have campaigned for controlling these dangerous trends, and am still fighting whenever opportunity offers. However, as the Duke of Edinburgh said when summing up at the World Wildlife Conference in November 1970, *everyone* of us must join together in carrying on this fight to save the world, and ourselves, from irrevocable disaster.

I have been an optimist all my life, trusting in reason, man's natural intelligence and his conscience. I cannot but believe that so many clear warnings will be heeded, and that in perhaps fifty years, man will look back on these decades of crisis and rejoice in the reconciliation of our problems in some overall progress towards safeguarding our planet's future.

There is much talk of the social responsibilty of scientists for many of these problems. But to be fair, one must agree that the responsibility rests as much on the technologists and others who apply the scientists' discoveries to industry and war, to agriculture and social life, often with disastrous results.

This awareness of the fragility of our world, and of the many threats to its future, has been a matter of concern to me throughout my life, as is apparent from my narrative. If I stress it again in these concluding lines, it is because the importance of it far outweighs what happens to individuals like myself. This record of my life is that of a witness, one among many, who has travelled widely and enjoyed the munificent diversity of life, but, more importantly, realized that it must be dominated by one overruling principle, that we are all jointly and severally responsible for the future of our earthly home, and for the survival of a worthwhile society.

Konrad Lorenz, in his book on aggression, wrote, 'the long-sought missing link between animals and the really humane being is ourselves.' Ourselves, whom we boastfully name *Homo sapiens,* the Knowing one.

We have indeed amassed a vast store of knowledge. The question remains, what shall we do with it? It seems clear that only if we cease merely adding to that store for selfish purposes, and use it to plan for a better future shall we graduate from *Homo sapiens* to *Homo humanus,* the hopeful and hard-working trustee for our own, and our planet's, evolutionary future.

Index